LOW-FAT
MICROWAVE
COOKING

250
QUICK AND HEALTHY RECIPES
YOU'LL ENJOY EVERY DAY

BY SHARON CLAESSENS

RODALE PRESS, EMMAUS, PENNSYLVANIA

To the Meemer family and all of their very special friends.

Edited by Jean Rogers
Book design by Debbie Sfetsios
Cover design by Debbie Sfetsios
Cover photography by Angelo Caggiano
Illustrations by Barbara Fritz
Copyedited by Laura Stevens
Indexed by Andrea Chesman

If you have any questions or comments concerning this book, please write:
Rodale Press
Book Readers' Service
33 East Minor Street
Emmaus, PA 18098

Library of Congress Cataloging-in-Publication Data

Claessens, Sharon.
    Low-fat microwave cooking : 250 quick and healthy recipes you'll
enjoy every day / by Sharon Claessens.
        p.   cm.
    Includes index.
    ISBN 0–87596–112–6   hardcover
    1. Microwave cookery.   2. Low-fat diet—Recipes.   I. Title.
TX832.C53   1992
641.5′638—dc20   91–47060
                                                            CIP

Distributed in the book trade by St. Martin's Press

2   4   6   8   10   9   7   5   3   1   hardcover

CONTENTS

CHAPTER 1

THE WAVE OF THE FUTURE

1

CHAPTER 2

BREAKFASTS & DAY STARTERS

16

CHAPTER 3

APPETIZERS & PARTY FARE

36

CHAPTER 4

MEATY MAIN DISHES

52

CHAPTER 5

PERFECTLY DELICIOUS POULTRY

79

CHAPTER 6

TREASURES FROM THE DEEP

110

CHAPTER 7

MARVELOUS VEGETARIAN MEALS

141

CHAPTER 8

SOUPS, STEWS & STOCKS

178

CHAPTER 9

VEGETABLES & COMPANY

209

CHAPTER 10

THE MICROWAVE BAKERY

237

CHAPTER 11

FOR THE SWEET TOOTH

255

INDEX

274

ACKNOWLEDGMENTS

I have shared many meals with friends and loved ones as a result of working on this book. For honest feedback, valuable suggestions, and even taking recipes home to try them in their own microwaves, I want to thank: Anne Huey, who cooked up and taste-tested more than a fair share of dishes, offering unfailing encouragement and helping me to achieve clarity in my rough drafts; my son, Adam, 11, who slowly (and even, on occasion, enthusiastically) expanded his gustatory horizons and helped me keep younger tastes in mind; tasters and supporters Annie Marans, Rose Craig, Sandra Wiens, Irmina Pulc, Peggy and Charlie Lucke, Mary and Kevin Hughes, Bonnie and Larry Markle, Dean and Ila Shah, Art Tingue, Bonnie Cameron, Susan Skelly, Ed Gerber, Michael Moore, Bernadette Cunningham, Carol and Stan Rinkunas, Andrea and Jerry Gritman, Melissa and Rick Lee, Bill Wycoff and Diane Koerber-Wycoff, Allan and Nancy Kramer-Moyer, Peter Skelly, Brian Salisbury, Lenore Urban and Thom Bernitsky, Linda and Rob Stefanowicz, Charles Babian, Lorraine Latsch, Rosemary Lundell, Barb Stevens, Pat Oren, Maryann Haytmanek, Nancy and George Wrobel, Terry Scott; Dusty Sacks and Sally Behler, who shared homegrown herbs and garden produce; and Dawn Sinclair, who was there absolutely whenever I needed her with an uncanny ability to decipher my rough drafts.

The excellent staff at Rodale Press took my ideas, recipes, and text and transformed them into the book you are holding: JoAnn Brader and Nancy Zelko of the Rodale Food Center double-checked recipes for accuracy and taste (which helps guarantee your success with these dishes); Debbie Sfetsios and Barb Fritz made the book visually appealing with their considerable design and illustration skills; Debora Tkac and Jean Rogers edited and helped give valuable direction to the project; and Laura Stevens added her talents to the book as copy editor.

Special thanks to CiCi Williamson, a certified home economist and microwave expert whose syndicated column "MicroScope" appears in more than 150 newspapers nationwide, for reviewing the manuscript upon its completion.

And mention must be made of two people who forever influenced my love of good food: my late father, Lee Sassaman, whose sense of adventure in the kitchen rubbed off on me at an early age, and my mother, Jane Matheson Murray, whose talent with desserts is, as my son says, "awesome!"

THE WAVE OF THE FUTURE

*M*agic in the kitchen! That just about sums up your microwave. This handy appliance lets you take every shortcut in the book and still dish out delicious, healthy meals every day of the week. With a microwave at your fingertips, the concept of fast food takes on a whole new meaning.

Below are just a few of the microwave's main virtues. (Further on in this chapter—and throughout the book—I'll let you in on all the other healthy secrets and shortcuts the microwave has to offer.) Using your microwave, you can:

❧ *Slash cooking times by up to 75 percent.*

◕ Reduce fat in dishes anywhere from 50 percent all the way up to an amazing 100 percent.

◕ Preserve valuable nutrients that would be lost by some other cooking methods.

◕ Simplify cleanup tremendously—often you can mix, cook, and serve a dish in one casserole.

Other benefits of microwave usage: You'll keep the kitchen cool in hot weather, and you can even save money in the bargain. Utility experts estimate that a microwave uses 30 to 70 percent less power than conventional cooking methods.

The one thing you have to remember about microwaving is that it's different from any other cooking method you've ever used. The microwave is more than just a turbocharged oven or a fancy electric frying pan. Foods are actually heated in a whole new way. Unconventional types of cookware can be used. Different cooking techniques apply than the ones you're used to. Judging doneness requires a fresh perspective.

While it may all seem daunting at first, I assure you it's not. I'll cover all the basics in this chapter so you can prepare supernutritious meals with ease and confidence. One thing I *won't* do is pretend that the microwave is the only appliance you need. Like your oven, a food processor, or a chef's knife, the microwave is a kitchen tool that has its own special uses and strengths. I'll show you how to put it to work doing the things it does best.

HIGH-POWERED HEALTH

If all you know about the microwave is that it can reheat pizza in a flash, consider this: A microwave can let you quick-cook healthy foods that are ordinarily too time-consuming for everyday preparation. Here are a few examples.

◕ Butternut squash—so rich in cancer-fighting beta-carotene—takes about an hour in a conventional oven. You can slash that time to 12 minutes or less with a microwave.

◕ A pound of fresh beets can be ready to eat in 20 minutes rather than the hour required for stove-top cooking.

◕ So-called quick breads need a good hour in an oven. With the microwave, they live up to their name, baking in 10 to 15 minutes.

◕ Whole-grain muffins can literally be done in seconds.

◕ Ultra-lean meat loaf takes no more time than the mashed potatoes that accompany it.

◕ Chinese stir-fries become simple indeed. You can slice some of the vegetables and get them cooking—no need for constant stirring—as you ready the remaining ingredients.

Baked potatoes for a family in 10 to 15 minutes. Lean pot roast in less than an hour. Low-sodium homemade soups in little more than the time it takes to reheat canned soup. The time-saving possibilities are endless, and they're all the more appealing because they let you follow the type of diet doctors recommend for optimum health.

Let's look at some of the guidelines for a healthy diet and see how microwave cookery can help you meet them. Two major government reports—*The Surgeon General's Report on Nutrition and Health* and the National Academy of Sciences' *Diet and Health*—detail the association between diet and disease and suggest basic ways to minimize your risk of several chronic illnesses. And the U.S. Department of Agriculture (USDA) has drawn up a list of important dietary guidelines for healthy living. They all agree that you should live by these four fundamental principles: Avoid too much dietary fat, eat foods with adequate fiber, avoid too much sodium, and maintain a desirable weight. To learn how your microwave can help, just read on.

AVOID TOO MUCH DIETARY FAT

The average American diet is loaded with fat. In fact, about 40 percent of its total calories typically come from fat. Meals from fast-food establishments contribute their unfair share, with individual dishes often running as high as 55 percent of calories from fat. Both figures are well above the 30 percent or less recommended by the American Heart Association.

Worse, much of the fat we eat is highly saturated, which means it helps raise blood cholesterol—often to dangerous levels. And high fat intake has been directly implicated in heart disease, obesity, and certain types of cancer.

Here's how your microwave can help you cut fat to the bone:

- You can prepare nutritious microwave meals in minutes, so you won't need to rely on fatty fast foods when time is short.
- Microwaving is a moist cooking method, so it doesn't dry out food like conventional cooking can. That means you don't need to add butter, margarine, or fatty

CONVERTING YOUR FAVORITE RECIPES

If you have some family-favorite dishes you'd like to try in the microwave, you'll have a better chance of success by following these tips:

- Choose a recipe that cooks by moist heat or steaming, such as poached fish, spaghetti sauce, or cooked vegetables.
- Reduce any liquid in the recipe by about one-third. (Less liquid evaporates with microwaving than with other cooking methods.) So if the recipe calls for 1 cup of liquid, use 2/3 cup.
- Shorten the cooking time. Figure on one-quarter to one-third of the original time. If the dish was supposed to

cook for 30 minutes on the stove, do it for 7½ to 10 minutes in the microwave. This is just an approximation, so you'll need to keep an eye on things.
- Reduce fat—oil, margarine, and butter—by half or more.
- Eliminate salt.
- For most foods, choose a dish that's similar in size to what you would use with a conventional cooking method. A round dish or one with rounded corners is usually a good bet.
- Mixtures with a lot of liquid that will boil and bubble—such as soups, sauces, rice, and puddings—require a deep dish to prevent boil-overs. Stir occasionally to promote even heating.

sauces to vegetables, fish, or other foods to moisten them up and make them more appealing.

◐ For the same reason, you don't need to add butter or oil to pans—foods just don't stick.

◐ Microwaved meat contains less fat and fewer calories than meat cooked by electric broiling, charbroiling, roasting, convection cooking, or frying. That's because fat heats more rapidly than lean meat in a microwave. For best results, you should trim excess fat from outer edges of meat as it can burn before the meat is cooked through.

◐ Deep-frying is unsuitable for the microwave. In fact, it's downright dangerous—and unhealthy—so you won't even want to try it.

◐ The microwave perfectly "sautés" onions and other vegetables without a drop of fat.

To further minimize your susceptibility to illness, doctors say to:

EAT FOODS WITH ADEQUATE FIBER

Your grandma probably called it roughage and warned you that you needed it to stay "regular." But fiber does more than aid digestion and regulate elimination. It's been shown to be protective against heart disease, cancer, diabetes, and obesity.

Certain types of fiber help reduce cholesterol levels. Researchers have shown that soluble fiber—the kind found in oat bran, for instance—helps to decrease harmful low-density lipoprotein (LDL) cholesterol without also decreasing beneficial high-density lipoprotein (HDL) cholesterol. That's good news for your heart. Insoluble fiber—so prominent in wheat bran—helps

keep your digestive system in good working order.

The microwave can help you get more fiber into your diet in these ways:

◐ Traditionally long-cooking fiber-filled vegetables—such as artichokes, winter squash, spaghetti squash, potatoes, and sweet potatoes—take only minutes in the microwave, making them a really convenient part of a healthy diet.

◐ Hearty whole-grain breads can be done in minutes.

◐ High-fiber breakfast cereals like oatmeal are a snap in the microwave, so you can cook them up fresh every morning. (Often, you can make them right in your cereal bowl, thereby cutting cleanup time.)

Here's another important dietary guideline recommended by the USDA:

AVOID TOO MUCH SODIUM

According to doctors, high sodium intake is the culprit behind many people's high blood pressure. And elevated blood pressure can lead to heart disease and stroke. Even if you don't salt your food at the stove or table, you may be consuming more than is prudent. That's because much of the sodium in our diet is hidden, used by food packagers and processors to enhance flavor in convenience foods. Just 1 cup of canned soup, for instance, can hold 1,000 milligrams of sodium. That's about as much as some doctors recommend for an entire day.

Fortunately, your microwave can help you shake the salt habit. Here are some ways:

◐ You can make your own low-sodium versions of salty convenience foods, such as soup and stock, in no time.

- Salting foods before microwaving causes them to dehydrate, so you won't even want to do it.
- Quickly cooking vegetables in a tiny bit of water safeguards their natural flavor, color, and texture. They simply won't need salt!
- Fresh herbs also retain more flavor than they do with many stove-top methods because the dishes they're in cook so quickly.
- You can use tasty marinades rather than salt to bring out the flavor of chicken, beef, lamb, pork, or seafood. (And you can speed up the marinating process by microwaving the food on the lowest power setting for 1 to 2 minutes before cooking.)

More advice from doctors:

MAINTAIN A DESIRABLE WEIGHT

If you are overweight, slimming down is probably one of the best things you can do for your overall health. Obesity is associated with high blood pressure, increased cholesterol, heart disease, strokes, and certain types of cancer. By changing your diet in sensible ways, you can help avoid some of these serious problems. Here's how your microwave can help you tip the scales in your favor:

- Fresh fruits and vegetables, lean meats, poultry, and seafood are almost tailor-made for the microwave. With such great-tasting ingredients, you can enjoy sensible, nutritious, low-calorie meals without feeling deprived.
- Meals are on the table so quickly that you won't even have time to nibble before they're ready.

- Ounce for ounce, fat has twice the calories of carbohydrates and protein. But thanks to the fat-free cooking techniques that microwaving permits, you can cut calories where they count most.
- You can easily cook or reheat single servings, so you won't be tempted to overeat—and you won't have those little leftover bits and pieces that you tend to eat rather than throw away.
- Studies show that eating low-fat soup on a regular basis can help you lose weight— and you can quickly prepare healthy soups in the microwave.

HOW THE MICROWAVE WORKS

Now that we've looked at the health benefits of microwaving, let's get down to the basics of using this terrific appliance. But first a note for those of you who habitually file away owner's manuals without reading them: Make sure you read and understand your microwave manual. It will familiarize you with the individual features of your microwave and give you important care and usage tips. It may very well spare you expensive service calls later on.

Most conventional cooking is accomplished by placing food in a hot environment: in an oven, on a stove top, under a broiler, or on a grill. Heat is conducted from the external source to the surface of the food, and it slowly penetrates to the food's interior.

Microwave cooking works in another way, so it really is important to understand how it works before taking the plunge. Microwave ovens contain a magnetron tube, which converts electricity into *microwaves* rather than heat. Microwaves are high-frequency electromagnetic waves, similar to radio waves.

These microwaves are distributed throughout the oven cavity. As they come into contact with food, they cause molecules within the food to vibrate. The molecules rub against each other and create heat. Contrary to popular opinion, microwaves do not cook "from the inside out." Microwaves are quite short and go little more than 1 inch deep into most foods. The center of any thicker food cooks when the heat travels inward.

Although microwaves do not directly heat cookware, heat building up in food can be *transferred* to its dish. So containers can become very hot. Always use pot holders when removing dishes from the microwave.

SMART CHOICES

You can buy a small microwave for as little as $100. Although a bargain in cost, a compact 400- to 500-watt microwave oven cooks much more slowly than a larger model. And it's not suitable for certain types of food, such as pork, egg mixtures, and large roasts.

A WONDERFUL KITCHEN TOOL

As marvelous as the microwave is, it isn't the only appliance in your kitchen. Trying to turn it into a jack-of-all-trades is inefficient and will leave you frustrated.

The recipes in this book rely on the microwave for its ability to let you take healthy shortcuts and for its ability to cook the kinds of dishes a microwave does best. So you may find yourself making applesauce in the microwave and then using the applesauce in a coffee cake that you bake in your regular oven. Or you might make a microwave sauce for stove-top rice or pasta.

If you choose to make an entire meal in the microwave, take advantage of standing times. You might, for instance, microwave a roast or a chicken. During the time it needs to stand to finish cooking, you can microwave your vegetable side dishes or heat up your first-course soup.

Most foods can stand—tightly covered—for the same amount of time they were cooked, up to 30 minutes. When planning which foods to do first, keep in mind that dense foods and those with a high moisture content—meats, rice, and potatoes, for example—retain heat well. So you can do them first.

Less-dense foods, such as most vegetables, fruits, and bread, can be put into the oven last, since they cool more quickly. They also tend to require a shorter cooking time.

If a food does cool too much while you're preparing another dish, remember that it is easy to reheat foods in the microwave without losing flavor or quality. Use care, however, to avoid overcooking your dishes. Reheat at a lower power setting: Try low (10% power) or medium (50% power). At reduced power, the microwave cycles on and off, giving heat time to equalize throughout the food.

If you're serious about getting real *use* from a microwave, a midsize oven is a better bet. It won't be that much more expensive, it will be plenty versatile, and it won't overwhelm a crowded kitchen. Look for a model with 650 to 700 watts of power.

As for interior size, a capacity of 1.5 cubic feet is adequate for most purposes. But exact dimensions vary widely from model to model, so make sure the oven cavity will hold the size cookware you use most often. For instance, I made sure mine would hold a 7 × 11-inch baking dish. Measure some of your larger pans (and don't forget to include the handles in the measurement), then take a tape measure with you to the store. In the long run, you'll find that generous floor space is more useful than extra height.

I also recommend that you get a microwave with a built-in turntable (preferably one you can remove or turn off when necessary). That will do away with some—but not all—of the stirring, rotating, and rearranging that's necessary for even cooking.

All of the recipes in this book were developed and tested in a 650-watt microwave with a turntable. In order to make sure they work in microwaves without a turntable, I've included directions for rotating dishes. When I say to give dishes a quarter turn, that means to rotate the dish 90 degrees; a half turn means 180 degrees. If you do have a turntable, you can skip these steps.

You'll find that the recipes in this book often give a range of cooking times (say, 5 to 7 minutes). If you have a 650- to 700-watt oven, test foods after the shorter time. If your oven has less power, you'll probably need the longer cooking time. Always err on the side of caution. It's better to undercook food in the microwave than to overcook it. After all, you can always pop it

back into the oven for a few more seconds or minutes. What you can't do with many foods is salvage them if they've been over-microwaved.

WHAT WATTS?

If you already own a microwave, check your owner's manual for the wattage. It may also be listed on the back of your oven near the Underwriters Laboratories seal. But be aware that even ovens with the same wattage can vary in cooking speed. You'll need to get a feel for your own microwave. If dishes are usually done in less than the recommended time, keep this in mind when trying new recipes and cut back slightly on the cooking time.

If you can't otherwise determine the wattage of your microwave, try the following test:

1. In a bowl, make a mixture of half ice and half water. Let stand a minute, then pour 1 cup of the water (no ice) into a glass measuring cup.

2. Place the cup in the center of the microwave. Heat on high for 5 minutes, or until the water begins to boil.

❑ If the water boils in less than 3½ minutes, consider your microwave to be "high power."

❑ If the water takes longer to boil, your microwave is "low power."

POWER PLAYS

Some microwaves offer only a *high* (100% power) setting; others may have ten different power levels. In order to accommodate most ovens, I've designed nearly all of the recipes in this book to be microwaved on a high setting. Just a few recipes require a medium (50% power) setting. And using the microwave to raise yeast dough takes a low (10% power) setting.

When the power is set on high, the oven is making microwaves 100 percent of the time it is turned on. At medium (50% power), the oven is making microwaves for only half of the time it is on. That allows for slower cooking, in the same way that reducing the heat slows cooking on a stove or in a conventional oven. The higher the power, the faster the food cooks. Selecting an oven with various power settings affords you more flexibility.

TIMING IS EVERYTHING

Timing is critical to successful microwave cooking. The process goes so fast that small variations in a number of factors can affect cooking time. Here are some of the factors you need to consider.

Starting temperature of food. The colder the ingredients, the longer the cooking time they'll require. In creating recipes, I've assumed that foods usually stored in the refrigerator—such as meats, fish, poultry, milk, eggs, and most vegetables—will be at refrigerator temperature. Canned and dry goods are assumed to be at room temperature.

Amount of food. The microwave produces the same amount of energy whether you're cooking one potato or four. When there's a larger amount of food, the energy must be shared, and cooking time needs to be increased.

Density of food. Porous foods, such as bread, heat more quickly than dense foods of the same size.

Fat and sugar content of food. Fat and sugar attract microwaves. So fatty ground beef will cook faster than an equal amount of extra-lean ground beef. Foods with a high sugar content heat more quickly than those that are not sweet.

Size and shape of food. Small, uniform pieces and round shapes cook more quickly and evenly than assorted sizes and irregularly shaped foods.

Wattage. Small variables in cooking times can be due to several factors. Power surges and changes in voltage during peak electrical usage periods can have an effect. Simultaneously operating other appliances that are plugged into the same outlet can also reduce available power. For this reason, the microwave should always be plugged into its own grounded circuit.

Placement of food. Each microwave has its own unique cooking pattern, which is affected by how the microwaves are distributed throughout the oven cavity. To find out what yours looks like, line the bottom evenly with a single layer of sliced white bread. Microwave the slices on high for 5 to 7 minutes. Notice where the browned areas are. They indicate hot spots where energy concentrates. Foods placed in those areas will cook faster than those situated elsewhere.

Covering food. Covered foods cook more quickly and evenly than uncovered ones. This is an important concept, so I go into more detail in "The Cover Story" on page 10.

STANDING AROUND

Standing time is a crucial element in the microwave process. With conventional cooking methods, food starts to cool after it's removed from its heat source. But with a microwave, food continues to cook after you turn off the power. That's because heat continues to be created *within* the food due to the activity of the food molecules. Removing the food from the microwave will not stop the cooking process.

This is a difficult concept for many people. Most of us are, after all, used to judging doneness in certain ways. We know the rice is ready because all the liquid has been absorbed and the grains are tender. We know the meat is done when it's browned on the outside and a thermometer registers a certain internal temperature. We look for carrots, potatoes, winter squash, and other vegetables to be tender all the way through, whether they've been baked, broiled, steamed, or sautéed.

You won't be able to use all of these visual and textural cues when microwaving. So to avoid overcooking many dishes, you'll need to stop microwaving them just a little ahead of when your instinct tells you to. Whole potatoes, for instance, should have a small uncooked area in the very center when you remove them from the microwave. After 5 minutes of standing time, they'll be perfectly done.

You'll need to remove meat from the microwave before it's quite reached the standard internal temperature. Cover it with foil, a lid, or anything else that will efficiently hold in the heat. Then let it stand until the internal temperature rises to the appropriate level. That way, the outer edges won't end up overcooked before the center is done.

With poultry, standing time is extra important. Because poultry harbors potentially serious bacteria, heat must be distributed evenly throughout the meat. The USDA recommends cooking poultry to an internal temperature of 160° for safety purposes. (For actual doneness, cook white meat to a temperature of 170°; do dark meat and whole birds to 180°.) But cool spots in your microwave may leave dangerous *Salmonella* bacteria on the skin untouched. That's one reason rotating both foods and their containers is so important. Covering the poultry and letting it stand after microwaving also allows heat to be distributed so that it can kill any remaining bacteria.

STAY WARM

Microwaved food tends to cool off more quickly than conventionally cooked food. That's because only the food gets hot during cooking. Any warmth you feel in the dish came from the food inside it. Here are some ways to ensure that your food stays appetizingly warm at the table:

- As you cook or reheat foods, keep them covered to help hold in warmth.
- At the table, place dishes in pretty towels or quilted casserole holders to help retain heat, or set them on a warming tray.

THE PERFECT COOKWARE

Having a microwave doesn't mean you need to buy all new cookware. Check your cabinets for the following, which are all microwave-safe:

- Heat-resistant glass, oven-tempered glass, and glass-ceramic cookware are ideal. Glass containers have two distinct advantages: You can see what's cooking and how it's coming along, and glass containers can go safely from freezer to microwave to table. This saves on cleanup and storage space.
- Ceramic dishes, such as pottery, porcelain, fine china, and stoneware are usually good bets. But do not choose dishes with metallic glazes or metallic trim, which can cause arcing or sparks.
- Clay pots and clay cookers produce excellent results, especially when microwaving poultry.
- Paper plates, towels, and napkins may be used for short-term cooking and reheating. See "Don't Try This at Home" on page 11 for more on this subject.

◗ Wood or straw products can be used for quick reheating. But don't use straw baskets with metal staples, joints, or handles.

If you are unsure whether a container is safe for the microwave, try the following test:

1. Fill a glass measure with 1 cup of tap water. Place it and the dish you wish to test in the microwave, with neither touching the other. (The water will keep the oven from being damaged if the container is not microwave-safe, so don't eliminate this step.)

2. Microwave on high for 1 minute.

◗ If the dish remains cool, it is safe for microwaving.

◗ If it is hot or even slightly warm, do not use it in the microwave.

When purchasing microwave cookware, base your selections on the size of your family and whether the dish will fit into your oven cavity. If you have a built-in turntable, be sure the dishes you choose can rotate without hitting oven walls. Rectangular dishes fit best when they have rounded corners.

BARE ESSENTIALS

The following basic containers should hold you in good stead. I don't believe in buying a lot of fancy equipment, so they'll certainly be sufficient for all of the recipes in this book. If you find yourself doing certain dishes over and over again that need a specialized pan, by all means get it. Just don't feel that you *must* buy every microwave gadget there is.

Make sure you do have:

◗ Round, deep dishes of various sizes for soups, sauces, and other liquids that need to be stirred.

◗ A ring mold or Bundt pan for foods that cannot be stirred, such as breads.

◗ A few shallow, square or rectangular dishes with rounded corners and lids.

◗ Glass measuring cups for heating liquids quickly.

◗ Single- or double-serving-size dishes for reheating leftovers.

You may also want to keep in mind that oven cooking bags are suitable for the microwave. Just be sure to use the plastic ties that come with them; don't substitute twist-ties that have metal in them.

Here are some more tips to help you select the proper dish for the cooking task at hand:

◗ Using round, oval, or rounded-off dishes helps prevent overcooking of food in the corners, especially if it's something like brownies or lasagna that can't be stirred.

◗ For even cooking, select dishes just large enough to contain the food being cooked.

◗ If, however, there's a lot of liquid in the dish—as when making rice, pudding, and soup—use oversize bowls to avoid boil-overs.

THE COVER STORY

Here's a general rule: If you would cover a particular food when cooking it by conventional means, cover it in the microwave. Main-dish casseroles, fresh and frozen vegetables, poultry, meat, and seafood are often covered.

A cover promotes steam, leaving foods moist, tender, and evenly and safely cooked. It also helps shorten the cooking time by sealing in heat. There are quite a few materials that can be used as covers. Some seal in a lot of heat and steam; others let most of the steam escape. The cover you choose will depend upon what food you're cooking. Here are the most common choices.

Microwave-safe lids. This is the kind of cover that usually comes with a casserole. If a lid is made of glass or clear plastic, you can view the food without lifting it. If the cover is opaque, take care in removing it when you check the food. Because the lid effectively seals in moisture, steam will have built up in the container. Always lift the side farthest from your face so excess steam can escape.

Plates and saucers. Dinner plates are good for covering soufflé dishes and other round containers. Saucers work well for cups and small bowls. Be sure the dishware does not have metal trim and is microwave-safe.

Wax paper. Wax paper provides a loose seal that prevents spattering. Use it with foods that do not require a lot of trapped steam to make them tender. It's also good on food that would get too wet from extra moisture, such as a leftover omelet or a dish of sauced pasta.

Parchment. Like wax paper, parchment holds in just a little moisture. It makes a good tent for foods like chicken and seafood. It's also sturdier than wax paper, so you can use the same piece to reheat several individual plates at the same meal. Parchment's only drawback is that it's more expensive than wax paper.

Paper towels. Choose towels marked as safe for microwave use. Paper towels absorb spatters but do not retain heat or keep in steam. They can be used as a covering for food that contains enough moisture to be reheated without drying out, such as muffins. They also prevent bread from turning soggy because the towels absorb excess moisture, so they're good to use when reheating sandwiches.

Plastic wrap. Plastic holds in both heat and steam. There's been concern that chemicals in some wraps may migrate into food, and studies are under way to assess the situation. If you use plastic, follow some basic guidelines to ensure safety. Do not make the seal airtight—leave room for some steam to escape by folding back a corner or piercing the plastic in several places. Also, do not allow the wrap to touch food— particularly fatty foods, which reach high temperatures. When removing the wrap, be sure to lift the side of the covering that is farthest from your face first—there will be enough steam in the container to cause burns.

Many foods don't need a cover as they cook. In my recipes, foods are always *uncovered* unless the directions say otherwise. Don't be concerned if moisture forms on your oven walls or door. It is normal for foods to give off steam while cooking. Just wipe the excess away when the cooking is complete.

DON'T TRY THIS AT HOME

Don't assume that because the microwave can accommodate unusual materials like paper plates and napkins that just *any* container or material is suitable. Protect yourself and your food by noting the following cautions.

Avoid metal containers. The exception to this rule is containers that are specifically designed for microwave use. Always check your owner's manual before using any kind of metal in your oven. Most metal containers reflect microwaves away from food so it doesn't cook evenly. Only very shallow containers would even be suitable. Metal may cause arcing that could damage your microwave. If you do use metal, make sure it's at least 1 inch away from any of the interior walls.

FOR KIDS' SAKE

As a parent, you may feel more confident letting your child use a microwave, rather than other kitchen appliances. Because the microwave doesn't heat up the way a gas or electric stove does, you may feel that it's a lot safer. And to a large extent, that's true. Yet microwaving does pose its own dangers for little ones.

"Children should not use the microwave unsupervised until they have the motor skills to handle foods in the oven. And they should be able to read and follow directions," says Joyce Kenneally, director of microwave cooking at the Good Housekeeping Institute. "It's important for parents to be well informed and to teach young children the rules."

To minimize the risk of a microwave mishap, heed these rules:

- Keep the microwave *out of reach* until children are old enough to use it without supervision.
- When you do let young children use the microwave under your supervision, limit them to small tasks, such as pushing a button or closing the door.
- When children are old enough to use the microwave by themselves, place it on a counter or a cart within easy reach. That will simplify the task of placing food in the oven. More important, it will allow a child to remove hot food from the microwave safely.
- Having the microwave within easy reach also lessens the chance that children will accidentally push the wrong buttons.
- Set aside a few microwave-safe dishes, with covers, for your child to use. Choose cookware with easy-to-grip handles and covers.
- Take the time to teach children how to cook their favorite meals and snacks. Show them how to pierce foods that have a membrane or skin, such as hot dogs and potatoes. Have them poke the food several times with a fork before cooking to avoid steam buildup that can cause such foods to burst.
- Remind kids never to cook an egg in its shell—it may explode while cooking or even after it's taken out of the oven.
- Tell them to stir or turn foods *slowly,* using the proper utensils, to avoid splashing themselves with hot liquids.
- Have children use pot holders. Teach them that although the inside of the oven remains cool, the dishes can be hot and the food inside even hotter.
- Show them how to uncover dishes in a safe way—*away* from their face—so steam can escape. And show them how to open popcorn bags safely so they don't get steam burns.
- Warn them that foods may heat unevenly. Something that seems cool on the surface may be very hot inside. That's a particular danger with filled foods such as jelly-filled doughnuts.

And do not place it on a metal shelf if your microwave is equipped with one.

Beware of hidden metal. Small thin pieces of wire, such as those inside twist-ties, can be problematic. If you're using an oven cooking bag, for instance, be sure to use the safe ties that come with it. In a pinch, substitute string.

Take care with foil. If you use aluminum foil to shield parts of food as they cook or thaw, use only small pieces. Be sure the foil molds tightly to the food and take care that it doesn't come in contact with the oven walls or a metal shelf. Leave at least half of the food exposed to microwave energy.

Be cautious with plastic containers. They vary in their suitability to the microwave. Butter and margarine tubs, melamine, foam, and yogurt or cottage cheese containers, for instance, are not recommended. Even the sturdier plastics may melt if they contain foods that become very hot, such as those high in fat or sugar. To play it safe, I just don't cook or reheat foods in plastic.

Do not use recycled paper towels. Towels made from recycled paper might contain metal fragments that could spark a fire.

Never use brown grocery bags or newspapers. Like the recycled paper towels, they contain materials and metals that could ignite.

Do not reuse convenience-food trays and containers. Most of the containers that frozen foods and other prepackaged items come in are designed for one-time use. Many are made only for the specific food that they contain. However, hard plastic plates and containers can safely be reused.

SAFE AND SOUND

Properly used, the microwave is extremely safe, according to the Food and Drug Administration (FDA). The FDA requires that microwave ovens made after 1971 meet radiation safety standards. It also requires two independent interlock systems to stop microwave production the moment the door latch is released. The whirring noise some ovens make after the door is opened comes from a fan and has nothing to do with microwave production.

Still, a microwave is no toy, and there are some safety considerations that you should heed:

- *Always* follow the owner's manual for operating procedures and safety precautions.
- Never turn on an empty oven. Running a microwave with nothing in it may damage the magnetron tube.
- Don't use the microwave if anything is caught in the door, if the door doesn't close firmly, or if the door is in any way damaged.
- Some older models have a soft mesh door gasket; check it periodically for deterioration, which would require servicing.
- Never use a microwave that has obviously been damaged. And don't use one that has had a fire or even serious overheating. These things may cause a warped or misaligned door. Get it checked by a qualified service center.
- If there are signs of rusting inside the microwave, have the oven repaired. Or fix the spots yourself with touch-up paint made especially for this purpose.

HANDLE WITH CARE

To ensure that foods are handled properly and cooked thoroughly enough to destroy any disease-causing organisms, observe the following rules.

- When you use the microwave to defrost food—especially meat and poultry—plan to cook the food as soon as it's thawed. Don't set it aside and cook it later. Some areas of larger food items may begin to cook during the defrost cycle, raising the temperature to a point at which bacteria can flourish.
- Several times during defrosting, turn and rearrange the food so that it thaws evenly. Rotate the dish a few times during the process. Separate items when possible, and remove them as soon as they're thawed.
- Never partially cook food, then put it away. If you plan to combine microwaving with conventional roasting, grilling, or boiling, complete the cooking immediately.
- Make sure that meat is pretty well thawed before microwaving it. Ice crystals that remain in frozen spots will not be heated well by microwaves. They can leave cold spots that won't be cooked thoroughly.
- Remove food from its packaging before thawing or cooking. Foam-insulated trays and store wraps are not stable at high temperatures; they can melt or warp from the food's heat.
- Debone large pieces of meat. Bone can shield the meat around it and prevent it from cooking thoroughly.
- Move food around several times during cooking to ensure that all parts of it become hot. Stir soups, stews, and casseroles when you can. For items that cannot be stirred, rotate the entire dish while cooking.
- Use a temperature probe or meat thermometer to verify that food has reached a safe temperature. Check the temperature in several places, avoiding fat and bone. Temperatures should reach 160° for red meat, 180° for whole chickens, 170° for chicken white meat, 180° for chicken dark meat, and 160° for pork.
- Since microwaves do not cook some foods evenly without a fair amount of stirring and turning, it's easy to undercook irregularly shaped meat and poultry. Cover the food with foil, a lid, or plastic, and allow it to stand for 5 to 15 minutes after cooking to let heat equalize throughout.
- If preparing stuffing for poultry, cook it separately to minimize opportunities for bacterial growth. The USDA does not recommend microwaving a stuffed whole turkey.
- Always pierce foods that have a skin or membrane over them before microwaving. This prevents steam that builds up inside the food from causing the food to explode. Potatoes, sweet potatoes, eggplant, sausages, tomatoes, egg yolks, and peaches are a few examples of foods that need piercing.
- When warming leftovers and other pre-cooked foods, cover with wax paper, a glass lid, or a microwave heating dome to promote even cooking. Heat the food to 165°. The food should steam throughout, and the center of the dish bottom should be very hot to the touch.
- Don't use the microwave for home-canning. Properly canned food must be conventionally heated or pressure-canned to a specified temperature throughout or you risk botulism.
- Don't use the microwave for deep-frying. It's dangerous.

CLEANING UP

Food spattered on the inside of your microwave absorbs energy just as surely as the food you actually *mean* to cook. That can increase cooking time. Too much buildup can even interfere with the proper closing of the oven's door. So it really is important to keep your microwave clean.

The quickest and easiest way, of course, is to wipe the interior with a damp cloth or sponge just after the spatters have occurred. The spots will still be moist and easy to remove. If they're a little stubborn, use a bit of mild dishwashing detergent in the water.

Once spatters have dried, you need to take a tougher approach. But *don't* turn to scouring powder, steel wool, or other abrasives unless their labels say they're safe for the microwave. Instead, boil a cup of water in the microwave for a few minutes. That will allow steam to form in the oven. Wait a few minutes for the steam to soften the baked-on particles, then wipe the interior clean.

If odors cling to your microwave, freshen it by wiping it out with a solution of baking soda and water. Or microwave a mixture of 1 cup of water and 1 teaspoon of lemon juice or vanilla until boiling; let stand for 5 to 10 minutes and then wipe out the oven interior with a soft cloth or sponge.

Never use products containing ammonia, because the odor might linger and be transferred to food. And never use commercial oven cleaners not designed specifically for a microwave.

BREAKFASTS & DAY STARTERS

Your mother was right: Breakfast is the most important meal of the day. Researchers have confirmed that calories consumed early in the day have a better chance of being burned off than those eaten later—a hot tip for anyone trying to lose weight or, more important, maintain a weight loss.

But you and I know that breakfast is the meal most likely to get short shrift. For many people, a "balanced" breakfast means a doughnut in one hand and a cup of coffee in the other. That's not good on a lot of counts. But your microwave can help you tip that balance in the direction of top-

notch nutrition—no matter how big a hurry you're in. For example, you can:

- ❍ Cook up fiber-rich whole-grain cereals with a minimum amount of fuss.
- ❍ Make tender, fluffy, reduced-cholesterol eggs with no added fat.
- ❍ Have healthy, hassle-free, low-fat waffles, pancakes, or French toast any day of the week.

HOT AND HEARTY CEREALS

Let's start with hot cereals, champions of the breakfast table. Whole-grain cereals are an excellent source of B vitamins, essential for healthy skin, muscles, blood, and nerves. They're loaded with fiber—both the insoluble form that regulates bowel function and the soluble form that can help control cholesterol and might even prevent certain types of cancer. And a morning's worth of demanding activities can easily be built on the protein these cereals contain.

Their only drawback? They tend to take a while to cook, and they often need stirring or other attention to keep them from sticking to the pan or boiling over. That's where your microwave comes in handy. Although it's true that you don't always save time, depending on the grain involved, cereals made in the microwave don't need constant stirring as they would on the stove—freeing you up to do morning chores or get dressed for work while your breakfast cooks itself. When you're ready, so is your cereal. And the cereal won't boil over as long as you use a large enough bowl.

I've included lots of my favorite cereal recipes in this chapter. I hope they'll become your favorites, too. (For details on cooking grains for quick breakfasts, including exact measurements and cooking times, see "Cereals at a Glance" on page 21.)

Leftover cooked grains, such as rice or barley, can form the base of an instant breakfast. Just add a little milk or juice and heat them right in your cereal bowl. It takes but a few seconds, and you won't even have a saucepan to wash. Serve with sliced fruit for an extra helping of fiber.

HEART-SMART EGGS

Naturally, eggs are high in cholesterol, so I wouldn't recommended them as daily fare. But there are ways to cut back on the cholesterol when you're in the mood for eggs, such as extending whole eggs with egg whites. And if you're among those who use cholesterol-free egg substitute, it works just fine in the microwave.

Frittatas, scrambled eggs, and other egg dishes can be prepared easily in the microwave, and you'll find several recipes for them in the pages that follow. Microwaved eggs won't stick to the pan as they often do with conventional heat, so you can reduce or totally eliminate fat from many of your recipes. And I've discovered a trick that works well in many recipes and ensures that eggs don't turn out rubbery: Beat the egg whites until stiff before folding in the yolks.

As for having homemade pancakes, waffles, and French toast on busy mornings, there's no sorcery involved. Just do up a batch on the stove at your leisure (I've included several recipes, including an all-purpose Pancake Mix on page 28 that really simplifies preparation). Freeze pancakes in individual packets and reheat them in the microwave.

Other elements of a good breakfast include low-fat dairy products and fresh fruit (higher in fiber than juice). Cantaloupe, tangerines, kiwifruit, and strawberries, for example, are all delicious at breakfast, and they're high in vitamin C for stronger immunity and potassium to help regulate blood pressure. You can easily take a pear, banana, or apple with you to eat in the car or on the bus if you just don't have time for them at home.

Ground turkey—far lower in fat than standard breakfast meats such as ham, bacon, and sausage—is excellent for patties that you can microwave. If bacon makes an occasional appearance on your table, be aware that fewer cancer-causing nitrosamines form when it's microwaved rather than cooked on the stove or under the broiler. It's still not what you'd call health food, but it's at least a tad safer.

With your microwave handy, you've no excuse for skipping a good breakfast! Here are some recipes that'll give a leading edge to your day.

MOROCCAN PILAF PORRIDGE

An unusual twist to an exotic Moroccan dish—a cereal bursting with Middle Eastern flavor. Eat this just as it comes from the microwave, or stir in your choice of skim milk, cider, or apple juice.

⅓ cup couscous
½ cup cider or apple juice
1 tablespoon ground almonds
1 tablespoon finely chopped walnuts

1 tablespoon raisins
1 teaspoon finely chopped dates
Pinch of grated lemon rind

Pinch of ground cardamom
Pinch of ground cinnamon

In a large cereal bowl, combine the couscous, cider or apple juice, almonds, walnuts, raisins, dates, lemon rind, cardamom, and cinnamon. Microwave on high for 2 minutes, or until the couscous is tender.

MAKES 1 SERVING.

BASIC GRANOLA

This tasty granola does not need oil or sweeteners for great taste. And it doesn't require frequent stirring as oven-baked granola does. Serve with skim milk and fresh fruit.

½ cup apple juice

¼ cup raisins

2 cups old-fashioned rolled oats

½ cup soy flakes

¼ cup barley flakes

¼ cup nonfat dry milk

¼ cup wheat germ

¼ cup bran or rice bran

¼ cup finely chopped walnuts or almonds

½ teaspoon ground cinnamon

In a 2-cup glass measure, combine the apple juice and raisins. Microwave on high for 2 minutes. Remove from the microwave, cover with foil, and set aside.

In a large bowl, combine the oats, soy flakes, barley flakes, dry milk, wheat germ, bran or rice bran, walnuts or almonds, and cinnamon.

Drain the liquid from the raisins and pour it over the dry ingredients (reserve the raisins). Toss until the granola is well moistened.

Place a piece of parchment on the floor of the microwave or on the turntable. Spread half of the granola mixture in a thin layer on the paper. Microwave on high for 2 minutes. Stir in half of the raisins and microwave on high for 20 seconds.

Transfer to a platter or baking sheet lined with paper towels (to absorb excess moisture), and allow to cool.

Repeat with the remaining granola and raisins.

Store in a tightly closed container in the refrigerator or freezer.

MAKES ABOUT 4 CUPS.

Note: Do not use wax paper in place of parchment. It will stick to the floor of the microwave.

BULGUR HOT CEREAL
WITH WALNUTS

½ cup apple juice or water

¼ cup bulgur

1 tablespoon raisins

1 tablespoon coarsely chopped walnuts

1 teaspoon molasses

Skim milk

Pinch of ground cinnamon (optional)

In a small deep bowl, combine the apple juice or water, bulgur, raisins, walnuts, and molasses. Microwave on high for 3 minutes, or until the bulgur is just tender.

Remove from the microwave. Cover with foil and let stand for 1 to 2 minutes to finish the cooking process. Serve with the milk and a dusting of cinnamon (if using).

MAKES 1 SERVING.

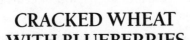

CRACKED WHEAT
WITH BLUEBERRIES

⅔ cup water

¼ cup cracked wheat

⅓ cup skim milk or apple juice

⅓ cup blueberries

1 teaspoon maple syrup

¼ teaspoon grated lemon rind

In a large cereal bowl, combine the water and cracked wheat. Microwave on high for 7 minutes, or until the grain is tender.

Remove from the microwave and stir in the milk or apple juice, blueberries, maple syrup, and lemon rind.

MAKES 1 SERVING.

CEREALS AT A GLANCE

Use this handy chart to prepare breakfast cereal in no time flat. In all cases, the quantities given yield one serving. That makes it easy for each family member to have his or her favorite cereal and to prepare it as needed.

For all the cereals, combine the grain and liquid in a 4-cup glass measure. Stir in the optional ingredients. I generally use no more than 1 teaspoon of sweetener, a pinch of spice, and 2 tablespoons of chopped nuts or dried fruit. If using diced fresh apples, I increase the quantity to ¼ cup.

GRAIN	AMOUNT (cup)	LIQUID	OPTIONAL INGREDIENTS	COOKING TIME (minutes)	STANDING TIME (minutes)
BULGUR	⅓	¾ cup apple juice, milk, or water	Nuts, molasses	3	1–2
COUSCOUS	⅓	1 cup apple juice or water	Almonds, currants, dates, cinnamon	2	None
MILLET, HULLED	¼	½ cup apple juice and ½ cup water	Raisins, apples	7	3
OATS, QUICK	⅓	¾ cup water	Raisins, maple syrup, cinnamon	2–2½	None
QUINOA	¼	⅔ cup apple juice or water	Apples, maple syrup	7	1–2
RICE, COOKED	⅔	⅓ cup skim milk or apple juice	Raisins, nuts, cinnamon	2½	None
WHEAT, CRACKED	¼	⅔ cup water	Lemon rind	7	1–2

RICE-PUDDING PORRIDGE

Having cooked rice on hand means you can enjoy a fast and delicious breakfast treat!

²/₃ cup cooked rice
¹/₃ cup skim milk

1 teaspoon raisins
½ teaspoon maple syrup

Pinch of ground cinnamon

In a large cereal bowl, combine the rice, milk, raisins, maple syrup, and cinnamon. Microwave on high for 2½ minutes.

MAKES 1 SERVING.

Variations: For Walnut Rice-Pudding Porridge, *add 1 teaspoon chopped walnuts to the cereal before microwaving. For* Apricot Rice-Pudding Porridge, *substitute water for the milk. Replace the raisins with 2 tablespoons minced fresh apricots and eliminate the cinnamon.*

MAPLE OATMEAL

¾ cup water
¹/₃ cup quick-cooking rolled oats

1 tablespoon raisins
1 teaspoon maple syrup

¼ teaspoon ground cinnamon (optional)
Skim milk

In a large cereal bowl, combine the water, oats, raisins, maple syrup, and cinnamon (if using). Microwave on high for 2 minutes. Stir and serve with the milk.

MAKES 1 SERVING.

Variations: For Date and Walnut Oatmeal, *replace the raisins with 2 dates (chopped) and 1 to 2 teaspoons chopped or ground walnuts.*

For Cider Oatmeal, *substitute cider or apple juice for the water.*

For Fresh Fruited Oatmeal, *eliminate the raisins. Add ¼ apple or pear (cubed) before cooking. Or add banana slices after cooking.*

APPLE-RAISIN MILLET CEREAL

Millet is a tiny grain that makes an excellent change-of-pace breakfast. One advantage of cooking it in the microwave is that it doesn't need any stirring at all, so you don't have to stand over it. You can easily reheat any leftover cereal. Just stir in a small amount of apple juice or water and microwave it until heated through—about 30 seconds.

½ cup apple juice
½ cup water

¼ cup millet
2 tablespoons raisins

½ tart apple, cubed
Pinch of ground cinnamon

In a 4-cup glass measure, combine the apple juice, water, millet, and raisins. Microwave on high for 7 minutes, or until most of the water has been absorbed and the millet is tender.

Remove from the microwave. Cover with foil and let stand for 3 minutes to finish the cooking process.

Stir, then spoon into a cereal bowl. Add the apples and dust with the cinnamon.

MAKES 1 SERVING.

BREAKFAST POLENTA

1 cup skim milk
1 cup water

½ cup yellow cornmeal
1 tablespoon maple syrup

Skim milk
Fresh berries

In a 2-quart casserole, combine the 1 cup milk, water, and cornmeal. Cover with a lid. Microwave on high for 4 minutes. Whisk and microwave on high, covered, for 4 to 5 minutes, or until the cornmeal is cooked. Whisk in the maple syrup. Serve with the milk and berries.

MAKES 2 SERVINGS.

MIXED-GRAIN PORRIDGE

The combination of grains in this porridge provides vitamins, minerals, and fiber—plus a bonus: a nutty, hearty flavor. Serve it with your choice of sliced or cooked fruit.

½ cup cracked wheat
3¼ cups water

¼ cup millet
¼ cup couscous

¼ cup bulgur
¼ cup oat bran

In a large bowl, combine the cracked wheat and 1¼ cups of the water. Microwave on high for 5 minutes.

Add the millet, couscous, bulgur, oat bran, and remaining 2 cups water. Microwave on high for 8 minutes. Cover with foil and let stand for 5 minutes.

MAKES 6 SERVINGS.

Note: To really save time at breakfast, you can prepare this cereal ahead and reheat individual servings. Combine ⅔ cup of the porridge with ¼ cup water, skim milk, or apple juice in a large cereal bowl. Microwave on high for 1 ½ minutes, or until heated through. For variety, combine ⅓ cup of the porridge with ¼ cup cooked brown rice and your choice of liquid. If desired, sprinkle either version with some raisins, nuts, or chopped dates and a little cinnamon.

INCA BREAKFAST BOWL

Deliciously nutty in flavor, quinoa is a grainlike cereal that the ancient Incas just adored. You'll love it, too. Although its spelling is exotic, it's simply pronounced "KEEN-wah." It's extremely versatile—as well as rich in fiber, minerals, and B vitamins. As a breakfast cereal, it offers a change from the usual morning fare.

¼ cup quinoa	½ apple, chopped	1 teaspoon maple syrup
½ cup apple juice or water	Pinch of ground cinnamon	Skim milk

Place the quinoa in a fine strainer and rinse well. Transfer to a large cereal bowl. Add the apple juice or water. Microwave on high for 4 minutes.

Top with the apples and a dusting of cinnamon. Cover the bowl with a small plate and microwave on high for 3 minutes. Stir in the maple syrup. Serve hot with the milk.

MAKES 1 SERVING.

Variation: For Raisin Quinoa, replace the apples with 1 tablespoon raisins; microwave on high for 2 minutes.

FRENCH TOAST WITH FRUIT SAUCE

I like to use a nice hearty homemade bread and cut the slices about 1" thick. Keep in mind that slightly stale bread absorbs the batter better—so this is a good way to use up day-old bread. In winter, you can easily substitute frozen mixed fruit for the fresh.

FRENCH TOAST
1 egg or ¼ cup fat-free egg substitute
1 egg white
2 tablespoons skim milk
¼ teaspoon vanilla
¼ teaspoon ground cinnamon

Pinch of grated nutmeg
2 thick (or 4 regular) slices whole-grain bread

FRUIT SAUCE
1 large tart apple or firm pear, thinly sliced
2 tablespoons maple syrup

1 nectarine or peach, thinly sliced
½ cup halved strawberries
¼ cup red raspberries
½ teaspoon grated orange rind

To make the French toast: In a shallow bowl large enough to hold the bread in a single layer, beat together the egg, egg white, milk, vanilla, cinnamon, and nutmeg until well mixed. Add the bread and turn to coat both sides. Let soak while you prepare the sauce.

To make the fruit sauce: In a medium bowl, combine the apples or pears and maple syrup. Microwave on high for 1 minute. Stir in the nectarines or peaches, strawberries, raspberries, and orange rind. Microwave on high for 1 minute.

To serve: Heat a large frying pan over medium heat. Lightly coat with no-stick spray. Add the bread in a single layer and reduce the heat to medium-low. Cook until the bottom is browned, about 3 or 4 minutes. Flip the pieces and cook for a few more minutes to brown.

Serve the French toast topped with the sauce.

MAKES 2 SERVINGS.

Variations: Serve the French toast with other sauces, such as Strawberry-Apple Sauce (page 29). For a really quick sauce, sweeten plain applesauce with maple syrup and microwave on high for about 1 minute.

PUFFED PEACH PANCAKE

4 egg whites
2 egg yolks or ¼ cup fat-free egg substitute
3 tablespoons skim milk

2 tablespoons whole wheat pastry flour
Grated rind from 1 lemon
1 teaspoon honey

1 peach, thinly sliced
1 tablespoon ground almonds
Pinch of grated nutmeg

In a large bowl, beat the egg whites with an electric mixer until stiff peaks form. Set aside.

In a medium bowl, beat together the egg yolks, milk, flour, lemon rind, and honey until smooth.

Lightly stir half of the yolk mixture into the whites. Then fold this mixture into the remaining yolks.

Coat an 8″ × 8″ baking dish with no-stick spray. Spoon the batter into the dish. Top it with the peaches, almonds, and nutmeg. Microwave on high for 4 minutes, or until set.

Cut into quarters and serve warm.

MAKES 4 SERVINGS.

Variations: For Puffed Nectarine Pancake, *substitute 1 nectarine for the peach.*

For Puffed Apricot Pancake, *substitute 2 apricots for the peach.*

EASY PANCAKES AND WAFFLES

It's not really practical to make pancakes or waffles in a microwave, but there are ways you can enjoy these treats often without a lot of fuss. One way is to freeze any leftovers for later enjoyment. (This also works nicely for French toast.) Then you can reheat them in your microwave in seconds.

Allow the pancakes or waffles to cool completely. Then stack them, placing squares of wax paper between the pieces for easier separation later. Wrap the stack well and freeze. To reheat, simply remove as many pieces as needed. Microwave single pancakes and waffles on a plate on high for 30 to 45 seconds, depending on the thickness. Flip the piece over and microwave it on high for 10 to 20 seconds, or until heated through. Serve with maple syrup or fruit sauce (try one of the "Quick Fruit Toppings" on the opposite page).

Here's one of my favorite pancake recipes. To simplify things on busy mornings, I mix up a large quantity of the dry ingredients and keep it on hand. The basic mix is enough for 30 pancakes. At breakfast time, just beat in the few additional ingredients listed under "Perfect Pancakes" to make a half dozen hot and hearty flapjacks.

PANCAKE MIX

3 cups whole wheat pastry flour

2 cups quick-cooking rolled oats

½ cup bran or oat bran

1 tablespoon baking powder

1 teaspoon ground cinnamon

In a large bowl, combine the flour, oats, bran or oat bran, baking powder, and cinnamon. Transfer to a plastic bag or a container with a tight-fitting lid. Store in the refrigerator or a cool, dry place.

MAKES ABOUT 5 CUPS; ENOUGH FOR 30 PANCAKES.

PERFECT PANCAKES

1 cup Pancake Mix (opposite page)

²⁄₃ cup skim milk

1 egg or ¼ cup fat-free egg substitute

1 teaspoon maple syrup

½ teaspoon canola oil

In a large bowl, combine the pancake mix, milk, egg, maple syrup, and oil until thoroughly mixed.

Lightly coat a griddle or large frying pan with no-stick spray. Set over medium heat until hot (water sprinkled on the pan will dance and sputter). Using a ladle, pour in ¼ cup of the batter for each pancake. Cook until bubbles are visible on the top surface and the bottom of each is browned. Flip and cook for a few more minutes to brown the underside.

MAKES 6 (4″ TO 5″) PANCAKES.

Variations: For Fruit or Nut Pancakes, *sprinkle fresh fruit pieces, berries, raisins, or chopped nuts on the pancakes soon after placing the batter in the pan (before bubbles are visible on the surface).*

For Buckwheat Pancakes, *use ¾ cup Pancake Mix and ¼ cup buckwheat flour in place of 1 cup Pancake Mix.*

QUICK FRUIT TOPPINGS

Strawberry-Apple Sauce: In a 4-cup glass measure, combine 2½ cups cubed tart apples and ¼ cup cider or apple juice. Microwave on high for 4 minutes. Transfer to a blender or food processor. Add ½ cup sliced strawberries. Process until smooth. Serve hot or chilled.

Blueberry Sauce: In a blender, puree 2 cups blueberries and ⅓ cup maple syrup. Transfer to a 4-cup glass measure and microwave on high for 2 minutes, or until cooked through.

Honey-Apple Sauce: Core and cube 2 tart apples. Place in a blender with ⅓ cup apple juice or cider, 2 tablespoons honey, and a pinch of cinnamon. Transfer to a 4-cup glass measure and microwave on high for 3 minutes, or until cooked through.

TURKEY SAUSAGE
WITH HOME-STYLE POTATOES

The meat 'n' potatoes lovers in your household will go for this low-fat version of sausage and home fries. If you have any leftover sausage, refrigerate or freeze it, then reheat it in the microwave when needed. Thawed patties should take about 1 minute.

POTATOES
1 medium onion, chopped
2 teaspoons soy sauce
2 potatoes, diced
SAUSAGE
1 cup ground turkey
1 egg white
⅓ cup fresh whole-grain
   breadcrumbs

½ teaspoon dried sage
½ teaspoon ground coriander
¼ teaspoon fennel seeds
¼ teaspoon paprika
¼ teaspoon ground black
   pepper

⅛ teaspoon dried marjoram
⅛ teaspoon dried thyme
⅛ teaspoon summer savory
   Pinch of grated nutmeg
   Pinch of ground red pepper

To make the potatoes: In a 6-cup glass measure, combine the onions and soy sauce. Microwave on high for 3 minutes. Add the potatoes and toss to combine. Cover with wax paper and microwave on high for 4 minutes. Stir, cover again, and microwave on high for 4 minutes. Let stand, covered, until ready to serve.

To make the sausage: In a medium bowl, combine the turkey, egg white, breadcrumbs, sage, coriander, fennel, paprika, black pepper, marjoram, thyme, savory, nutmeg, and red pepper. Mix well. Form into four patties.

Place the patties on a baking sheet and broil about 4″ from the heat for about 4 minutes, or until lightly browned on top. Flip and broil several more minutes to brown. Serve hot with the potatoes.

MAKES 4 SERVINGS.

Note: The sausage patties are also good with frittatas, such as Western Frittata (page 34), or with poached eggs and whole-grain toast.

APPLE-CIDER COFFEE CAKE

Serve this moist and delicious coffee cake when you want to add a festive note to breakfast or brunch or teatime.

½ small tart apple, diced
¼ cup cider
2 cups whole wheat pastry flour
1½ teaspoons baking soda
½ teaspoon ground cinnamon

⅛ teaspoon ground cloves
¾ cup skim milk
⅓ cup maple syrup or honey
1 egg or ¼ cup fat-free egg substitute

1 egg white
1 teaspoon lemon juice
1 tablespoon wheat germ
1 tablespoon chopped walnuts

In a 4-cup glass measure, combine the apples and cider. Microwave on high for 2 minutes. Transfer to a blender or food processor and process until smooth.

In a large bowl, combine the flour, baking soda, cinnamon, and cloves.

In a small bowl, whisk together the milk, maple syrup or honey, egg, egg white, and lemon juice. Add the applesauce.

Pour the liquid ingredients over the dry ones. Mix until well combined.

Coat an 8″ × 8″ baking dish with no-stick spray. Add the batter and smooth the top with a rubber spatula. Sprinkle with the wheat germ and walnuts.

Bake at 325° for 40 to 45 minutes, or until a toothpick inserted in the center of the coffee cake comes out clean. Serve warm or cold.

MAKES 8 TO 10 SERVINGS.

DILLED PITA-POCKET EGGS

1 egg or ¼ cup fat-free egg substitute

1 egg white

1 teaspoon minced fresh dill

½ whole wheat pita

Coat a ramekin or custard cup with no-stick spray. Add the egg and egg white. Beat with a fork to combine. Add the dill.

Microwave on high for 1 minute, or until slightly puffed.

Microwave the pita on high for 20 seconds.

Break up the eggs with a fork. Spoon into the pita.

MAKES 1 SERVING.

VEGETABLE OMELET

¼ cup thinly sliced onions

¼ cup thinly sliced zucchini

3 cherry tomatoes, halved

2 mushrooms, thinly sliced

1 teaspoon minced fresh parsley or dill

1 egg or ¼ cup fat-free egg substitute

1 egg white

1 tablespoon skim milk

Parsley or dill sprigs (garnish)

In a 4-cup glass measure, combine the onions, zucchini, tomatoes, mushrooms, and parsley or dill. Microwave on high for 4 minutes, or until the vegetables are crisp-tender.

In a small bowl, whisk together the egg, egg white, and milk until well combined.

Coat an omelet pan or medium frying pan with no-stick spray. Heat the pan on the stove top on medium heat until hot enough for water dropped on the surface to dance.

Add the egg mixture and cook, lifting the edges of the omelet toward the center of the pan with a table knife. Swirl the pan to distribute the uncooked portion of eggs toward the outside edges of the pan.

When the eggs are set, remove the pan from the heat. Place the cooked vegetables in a line down the center of the omelet. Fold the eggs over the vegetables and slide the omelet onto a plate. Garnish with the parsley or dill.

MAKES 1 SERVING.

EGGS IN THE MICROWAVE: HANDLE WITH CARE

Few foods are as sensitive to heat as eggs, which require some special attention in the microwave.

One thing that's definitely *not* recommended is microwaving an egg in its shell. Internal pressure can build up very quickly, causing the egg to burst, even after it has been removed from the microwave.

Even an egg without its shell needs special treatment. Raw yolks can also build up steam that could lead to bursting. So you should always pierce them with a toothpick or cake tester before cooking. Don't worry that the pierced yolks will run; they'll hold their shape.

Egg yolks contain fat, so they cook faster than whites. For overall even cooking, cover the eggs with wax paper. And unless you're making scrambled eggs, don't cook eggs on a high setting.

Set your timer for the shortest cooking time given in the recipe. Check for doneness. If more time is needed, add it in small increments—no more than 15 to 30 seconds at a time. An undercooked egg can easily be returned to the microwave for extra cooking, but an overcooked one is ruined.

The microwave makes very tender scrambled eggs. For breakfast that you can eat on your way to work, you can even scramble eggs in a paper cup. Use one that's suitable for hot beverages (and, of course, microwavable). Place ½ teaspoon margarine or butter in the cup. Microwave on high for 20 to 30 seconds, until melted. Break 2 large eggs into the cup. Add 2 teaspoons water and a pinch of ground pepper. Beat with a fork just until blended. Microwave on high for 45 to 60 seconds, or until the eggs look firm around the edges. (The center will still be loose.) Stir the set portions of the egg from the outside edges to the center of the cup. Microwave on high for 1 to 1½ minutes longer, stirring once, until the mixture is soft, creamy, and just past the runny stage. Cover and let stand for 1 minute, or until set. Stir, and take the eggs with you!

WESTERN FRITTATA

A rakish takeoff on the western omelet, this breakfast frittata can be served with herbed muffins or whole wheat toast and half a grapefruit for a memorable breakfast.

1 small onion, chopped
¼ teaspoon olive oil (optional)
1 potato, diced
1 tablespoon diced sweet red peppers

1 tablespoon diced green peppers
1 teaspoon minced fresh parsley
3 egg whites

3 egg yolks or ⅓ cup fat-free egg substitute
1 tablespoon skim milk
Red pepper rings (garnish)
Parsley sprigs (garnish)

Place the onions in an 8″ × 8″ baking dish. Mix with the oil (if using). Microwave on high for 1 minute.

Add the potatoes, red peppers, and green peppers. Microwave on high for 3 minutes. Stir in the parsley.

In a small bowl, beat the egg whites until stiff. Fold in the egg yolks and milk. Add to the vegetables and stir to combine.

Microwave on high for 3 minutes, or until the eggs are cooked through. Serve garnished with the peppers and parsley.

MAKES 2 SERVINGS.

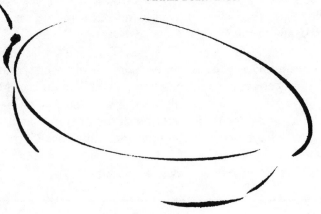

WARREN STREET CHEESE SOUFFLÉ OMELET

A food-loving Louisiana friend of mine prefers a savory egg dish—like this—to pancakes in the morning. Serve with high-fiber muffins and your favorite fresh fruit.

4 egg whites
2 egg yolks or ½ cup fat-free egg substitute

½ cup shredded reduced-fat Cheddar cheese
2 tablespoons skim milk

1 tablespoon unbleached flour
Basil sprigs (garnish)

In a medium bowl, beat the egg whites with an electric mixer until stiff peaks form. Set aside.

Place the egg yolks, Cheddar, milk, and flour in a large bowl. Use the mixer to combine well.

Fold the egg whites into the yolk mixture.

Coat an 8″ × 8″ baking dish with no-stick spray. Add the egg mixture. Microwave on high for 5 minutes, or until the eggs look set. Serve garnished with the basil.

MAKES 4 SERVINGS.

APPETIZERS & PARTY FARE

～～～～～

When you're entertaining, the last thing you want is to be stuck in the kitchen, away from your guests. Your microwave can have you mingling in no time—proud of the tasty, creative, and low-fat appetizers you're ready to serve. With your microwave lending a hand at party time, you can:

- ❥ *Gain total control over the quality of the food you serve. (You don't need to settle for fatty, salty, or expensive snacks just because they're convenient to buy.)*
- ❥ *Prepare a large part of your menu ahead and reheat foods as needed.*

◑ Whip up instant appetizers from scratch for impromptu gatherings.

Parties are traditionally a time to splurge—on calories, on gourmet-shop hors d'oeuvres, or on salty chips and fatty dips you might not ordinarily serve. With a little help from your microwave, you can avoid all those standard party pitfalls.

One of the microwave's main advantages, of course, is that foods cook so quickly you can prepare lots of different dishes in no time. Another is that most foods—including lean poultry, meat, and seafood—need little or no fat to keep them moist or from sticking to their pans. That automatically saves you calories you'd unthinkingly add to recipes.

In addition, your microwave lets you take fresh foods and bring out their best flavors—with a minimum of fuss. One of my favorite appetizers is baby garden vegetables microwaved until just crisp-tender and then stuffed with low-fat yogurt cheese (see "Baby Vegetables: Ripe for Stuffing" on page 39). They're simple, quick, and inexpensive. And I can make wonderful shrimp and scallop dishes—such as Honey-Gingered Shrimp (page 40) and Scallop Coins with Dill Sauce (page 40)—in minutes. They're real crowd pleasers!

NOBODY DOES IT BETTER

Fancy hors d'oeuvres that would cost plenty in a gourmet shop are a snap to make at home. Using the microwave, you can prepare all sorts of stuffed mushroom caps, for instance. (Try Turkey-Stuffed Mushroom Caps on page 46 and Marrakech Stuffed Mushrooms on page 44.) Prepare them—and other finger foods—ahead of time, place on microwave-safe serving plates, and store in the refrigerator. When your guests arrive, just reheat the foods as you need them.

And why settle for salty, greasy tortilla chips from the market when you can whip up better ones yourself? You can even make fresh-tasting salsa (see Super Salsa on page 59) and all sorts of enticing low-fat dips. I've always been fond of Eggplant Caviar (page 38), for example, but I love it even more now that I can prepare it in a mere fraction of the time it used to take. The same goes for Baba Ghanoush (page 46), a savory Middle Eastern dip.

Simply put, the microwave can let you entertain in princely fashion without spending an inordinate amount of time—or money. So whether it's a large-scale bash or a more intimate dinner party that you're planning, make sure your microwave is first on your invitation list.

HOT CHICKEN WINGS

2½ pounds chicken wings

½ cup tomato sauce

3 tablespoons soy sauce

1 tablespoon honey

2 teaspoons minced fresh ginger or 1 teaspoon ground ginger

2 teaspoons minced garlic

1 teaspoon minced jalapeño peppers (wear plastic gloves when handling)

¼ teaspoon ground red pepper

¼ teaspoon ground black pepper

Cut the wings at the joints and reserve the tips for stock or another use. You should have about 2 pounds of remaining wings.

In a large bowl, combine the tomato sauce, soy sauce, honey, ginger, garlic, jalapeños, red pepper, and black pepper. Add the wings and toss well to combine. Cover, refrigerate, and allow the wings to marinate for several hours or overnight.

Drain off and discard all but ¼ to ½ cup of the marinade. Spread the chicken wings in a single layer in a 7″ × 11″ baking dish. Cover with wax paper and microwave on high for 10 minutes. Stir. Microwave, uncovered, on high for 12 minutes.

MAKES 10 SERVINGS.

EGGPLANT CAVIAR

Serve at room temperature with melba toast.

1 ripe tomato

1 eggplant (about 1 pound)

1 tablespoon grated onions

1 tablespoon minced scallions

1 clove garlic, minced

2 tablespoons lemon juice

1 tablespoon olive oil

Pinch of ground black pepper

Tomato wedges (garnish)

Minced fresh parsley (garnish)

Pierce the tomato in several places with a knife. Set on a plate or paper towel. Microwave on high for 1 minute. Remove and set aside.

Place the eggplant on a plate and cut a 4" to 6" slit lengthwise along the top. Leave the stem attached. Microwave on high for 10 minutes, or until the eggplant is quite soft and has collapsed.

Let the eggplant cool for 2 minutes, then scoop the pulp from the skin and place it in a bowl. Use a knife and fork to break up long strands of the flesh. Stir in the onions, scallions, and garlic.

Peel and core the microwaved tomato. Cut it in half crosswise and squeeze out the seeds and excess juice. Chop finely (you should have about ½ cup).

Add the tomatoes, lemon juice, oil, and pepper to the eggplant. Let the mixture cool. Serve on a platter garnished with the tomato wedges and parsley.

MAKES ABOUT 1½ CUPS.

BABY VEGETABLES: RIPE FOR STUFFING

Baby vegetables add visual impact to appetizers or party fare. Choose vegetables that are well-formed miniatures of their mature selves, such as summer squash, zucchini, eggplant, carrots, beets, and potatoes.

Your microwave can help you maintain the unparalleled fresh flavor of just-picked vegetables. Arrange the tiny vegetables around the outer rim of a 9" glass pie plate or microwave-safe serving dish. Pierce the skins several times with a sharp knife or a fork.

Depending upon the number and size of the vegetables you're preparing, microwave them on high from 3 to 15 minutes. You want them to be crisp-tender so they retain their garden-fresh goodness.

To stuff the baby vegetables, simply hollow them out slightly and spoon in a small portion of flavored yogurt cheese (see "Yogurt-Cheese Spreads" on page 51). Serve the vegetables hot, slightly chilled, or at room temperature.

HONEY-GINGERED SHRIMP

2 tablespoons lemon juice

2 tablespoons honey

1 tablespoon soy sauce

1 teaspoon minced fresh ginger

¼ teaspoon finely grated lemon rind

12 large shrimp, peeled and deveined

Belgian endive leaves

Lemon slices (garnish)

In a 1½-quart casserole, combine the lemon juice, honey, soy sauce, ginger, and lemon rind. Add the shrimp and toss well to coat with the seasonings. Move the shrimp to the edges of the dish.

Cover with wax paper. Microwave on high for 2 to 3 minutes. Let stand for 1 minute; the shrimp should be opaque throughout. Serve hot or chilled on a bed of Belgian endive, garnished with the lemons.

MAKES 4 SERVINGS.

SCALLOP COINS WITH DILL SAUCE

If you have extra sauce, use it with your choice of raw or lightly steamed vegetables.

12 large sea scallops (about 8 ounces)

½ lime

¼ cup peeled, seeded, and coarsely chopped cucumber

2–4 tablespoons minced fresh dill

¼ cup nonfat yogurt

2 tablespoons part-skim ricotta or low-fat cottage cheese

1 tablespoon low-fat mayonnaise

½ clove garlic, minced

Pinch of ground black pepper

Radicchio leaves

Dill sprigs or cucumber slices (garnish)

Halve each scallop crosswise to form two "coins." Arrange the scallops on a 9″ pie plate without overlapping them. Squeeze the lime half over all.

Microwave on high for 1½ to 2 minutes. Let stand for 1 minute, then drain and chill.

To prepare the sauce, process the cucumbers, dill, yogurt, ricotta or cottage cheese, mayonnaise, garlic, and pepper in a blender until smooth.

Arrange the radicchio on a platter. Place the scallops on the leaves and spoon a ribbon of sauce over them. Garnish with the dill or cucumbers.

MAKES 4 SERVINGS.

LOW-FAT TORTILLA CHIPS

24 soft corn tortillas

1 teaspoon canola oil

Lightly brush the top side of each soft corn tortilla with the oil.

Arrange four of the tortillas, oiled-side up, on a paper towel and place them in the microwave.

Microwave on high for 2 minutes. Remove the paper towel. Return the tortillas to the microwave, placing them directly on the floor of the oven. Microwave on high for 2 minutes, or until the tortillas are crisp but not brown. Allow to cool, then break into chips.

Repeat with four tortillas at a time until all have been crisped.

MAKES 10 TO 12 SERVINGS.

Note: You can make these chips even lower in fat by replacing the oil with no-stick spray (try olive oil–flavored) or by crisping the tortillas without any oil or spray.

ANNE'S SUPER-BOWL SHRIMP

Make this in quantity for the Super Bowl!

16 large shrimp, peeled and deveined

½ lemon

⅔ cup ketchup

2 teaspoons prepared horseradish

2 teaspoons lemon juice

2 small cloves garlic, minced

Place the shrimp in a single layer around the outside edge of a shallow casserole with the tail ends facing toward the center. Squeeze the lemon half over the shrimp. Microwave on high for 2 to 3 minutes, then cover and let stand for 1 to 2 minutes. The shrimp should just be cooked through. Let cool.

In a small cup, combine the ketchup, horseradish, lemon juice, and garlic. Serve as a dipping sauce for the shrimp.

MAKES 4 SERVINGS.

GARLIC EGGPLANT AND PEPPERS

This Mediterranean-inspired dish makes a simple and delicious first course that can be served hot or at room temperature.

1 eggplant (about 1 pound)

1 clove garlic, minced

1 tablespoon minced fresh parsley

1 tablespoon olive oil

1 tablespoon lemon juice

1 sweet red pepper, cut into thin rings

Parsley sprigs (garnish)

Place the eggplant on a plate and cut a 4" to 6" slit lengthwise along the top. Leave the stem attached.

Microwave on high for 10 minutes, or until the eggplant is quite soft and has collapsed. Set aside to cool.

In a small cup, combine the garlic, parsley, oil, and lemon juice.

Cut the eggplant into eighths lengthwise and remove the stem. Place the wedges, skin-side down, on individual serving plates. Cut ½″-deep slashes in each wedge. Spread each wedge with some of the garlic mixture.

Divide the peppers among the plates. Serve garnished with the parsley.

MAKES 8 SERVINGS.

PARMESAN PITA TRIANGLES

Flavorful cheese spread on whole wheat pita bread provides a quick but tasty snack for informal parties. Serve with plenty of raw vegetables.

3 whole wheat pitas (about 4½″ in diameter)

1 tablespoon margarine or butter

1 clove garlic, minced

2 tablespoons grated Parmesan cheese

¼ teaspoon dried oregano

Cut the pitas into quarters, then separate the tops and bottoms to make 24 triangles.

Combine the margarine or butter and garlic in a 1-cup glass measure. Microwave on high for 1 minute. Stir in the Parmesan and oregano.

Spread a small amount of the cheese mixture on the top side of each pita triangle. Arrange the triangles on three paper plates. Microwave one plateful at a time on high for 1 minute. Serve immediately.

MAKES 8 SERVINGS.

MARRAKECH STUFFED MUSHROOMS

Couscous, a traditional ingredient in Moroccan cuisine, lends a Middle Eastern flavor to stuffed mushrooms and is a nice departure from the usual breadcrumb stuffing. At first glance you may think there's not enough liquid in the filling to cook the couscous, but moisture exuded from the mushrooms does the job just fine.

8 large mushrooms	1 clove garlic, minced	¼ teaspoon turmeric
¼ cup couscous	2 teaspoons olive oil	¼ teaspoon paprika
1 tablespoon lemon juice	1 teaspoon soy sauce	Parsley sprigs (garnish)
1 tablespoon chopped fresh parsley	¼ teaspoon ground coriander	

Brush any dirt off the mushrooms and trim tough ends from the stems. Carefully remove the remaining mushroom stems and reserve them.

Place the mushroom caps stem-side down in a 9″ pie plate. Cover with wax paper. Microwave on high for 2 minutes. Rotate the dish a half turn. Microwave on high for 2 minutes. Turn the caps over and drain the liquid from the dish.

Finely chop the stems and place in a medium bowl. Add the couscous, lemon juice, parsley, garlic, oil, soy sauce, coriander, turmeric, and paprika. Divide the mixture among the mushroom caps, filling them generously.

Cover the mushrooms with wax paper. Microwave on high for 4½ to 5 minutes, or until the mushrooms are tender. Let stand for 1 to 2 minutes. Garnish with the parsley.

MAKES 4 SERVINGS.

BASIL GAZPACHO WITH SHRIMP

*A cross between a soup and a salad, this
gazpacho gets an elegant lift from a garlic-flavored
shrimp garnish.*

2 teaspoons olive oil

1 clove garlic, minced

4 medium shrimp, peeled and deveined

Pinch of paprika

½ cup sliced mushrooms

2 large tomatoes

1½ cups tomato juice or vegetable-juice cocktail

¾ cup finely chopped green or sweet red peppers

½ cup finely chopped scallions

½ cup peeled, seeded, and diced cucumber

¼ cup finely chopped celery

2 tablespoons red wine vinegar

1 tablespoon minced fresh basil

1 teaspoon minced fresh parsley

Basil sprigs (garnish)

Combine the oil and garlic in a small dish. Microwave on high for 30 seconds, or until the garlic is tender. Stir in the shrimp. Sprinkle with the paprika. Cover with a lid or wax paper and microwave on high for 1 minute, or until the shrimp are cooked through. Using a fork or tongs, remove the shrimp from the dish and set them aside to cool.

Add the mushrooms to the dish and stir to coat with the oil and garlic. Cover and microwave on high for 2 minutes, or until the mushrooms are cooked through. Transfer to a large bowl.

Pierce the tomatoes in several places with a knife. Set on a plate and microwave on high for 2 minutes. Remove the cores. Cut the tomatoes in half crosswise and squeeze gently to remove the seeds and excess liquid. Peel and finely chop the tomatoes. Add to the bowl with the mushrooms.

Stir in the juice, peppers, scallions, cucumbers, celery, vinegar, basil, and parsley.

Divide the gazpacho among four soup bowls. Coarsely chop the shrimp and sprinkle over the soup. Chill well. Serve garnished with the basil.

MAKES 4 SERVINGS.

BABA GHANOUSH

1 eggplant (about 1 pound)
¼ cup tahini (sesame-seed paste)
¼ cup lemon juice

2 tablespoons olive oil
1 tablespoon grated onions

1 tablespoon minced garlic
¼ cup minced fresh parsley
Pitas, cut in quarters

Place the eggplant on a plate and cut a 4″ to 6″ slit lengthwise along the top. Leave the stem attached. Microwave on high for 10 minutes, or until the eggplant is quite soft and has collapsed.

Let the eggplant cool for 2 minutes, then scoop the pulp from the skin and place it in a bowl. Use a knife and fork to break up long strands of the flesh. Stir in the tahini, lemon juice, oil, onions, and garlic.

Spread on a large plate and sprinkle with the parsley. Serve at room temperature, with the pitas.

MAKES 10 TO 12 SERVINGS.

TURKEY-STUFFED MUSHROOM CAPS

8 large mushrooms
½ cup ground turkey breast
½ cup fresh breadcrumbs
1 clove garlic, minced
1 teaspoon soy sauce

½ teaspoon dried sage
¼ teaspoon ground coriander
¼ teaspoon dried marjoram
¼ teaspoon paprika

¼ teaspoon ground black pepper
⅛ teaspoon grated nutmeg
Pinch of ground red pepper

Brush any dirt off the mushrooms and trim tough ends from the stems. Carefully remove the remaining mushroom stems. Reserve the caps.

Finely chop the stems and place in a medium bowl. Add the turkey, breadcrumbs, garlic, soy sauce, sage, coriander, marjoram, paprika, black pepper, nutmeg, and red pepper. Mix well.

Stuff the mushroom caps generously with the turkey mixture. Place in a shallow casserole and cover with a lid or wax paper. Microwave on high for 3 minutes. Rotate the dish a half turn and microwave on high for 2 to 3 minutes, or until the turkey is cooked through.

MAKES 4 TO 8 SERVINGS.

MUSHROOM PÂTÉ

This creamy low-fat pâté is perfect spread on whole-grain crackers or melba toast.

¼ cup chopped scallions

1 tablespoon olive oil or butter

1½ tablespoons unbleached flour

½ pound mushrooms, finely chopped

2 tablespoons nonfat yogurt

2 tablespoons minced fresh parsley

¼ teaspoon sherry extract

¼ teaspoon ground black pepper

⅛ teaspoon grated nutmeg

⅓ cup finely chopped walnuts or pecans

1 tablespoon minced fresh chives

In a 1-quart casserole, combine the scallions and oil or butter. Microwave on high for 2 minutes, or until the scallions are tender. Stir in the flour and mix well.

Stir in the mushrooms, yogurt, parsley, sherry extract, pepper, and nutmeg. Mix well. Microwave on high for 2 to 3 minutes. Stir and microwave on high for 2 to 3 minutes, or until the mushrooms are soft.

Transfer half of the mixture to a food processor or blender. Process until smooth. Stir back into the remaining mushrooms. Fold in the nuts.

Pack the pâté into a crock or serving dish. Sprinkle with the chives. Chill before serving.

MAKES 1 CUP.

TACO DIP

½ pound lean ground beef or ground turkey

1 large tomato

1 jalapeño pepper, halved and seeded (wear plastic gloves when handling)

2 scallions, chopped

1 cup cooked pinto or kidney beans, mashed

¼ cup finely chopped green peppers

3 tablespoons grated onions

2 cloves garlic, minced

1½ teaspoons chili powder

½ teaspoon ground cumin

¼ cup finely shredded lettuce

¼ cup shredded reduced-fat Cheddar cheese

Low-Fat Tortilla Chips (page 41) or corn chips

Crumble the beef or turkey into a 1½-quart casserole. Microwave on high for 2 to 3 minutes, or until very little pink remains. Stir and drain off the fat.

While the meat is cooking, core, seed, and coarsely chop the tomato. Combine in a blender with the jalapeños and scallions. Blend until smooth. Add to the meat mixture.

Stir in the beans, green peppers, onions, garlic, chili powder, and cumin.

Just before serving, cover with a lid or wax paper and microwave on high for 5 minutes, or until hot and bubbly. Sprinkle with the lettuce and Cheddar. Serve with the tortilla chips or corn chips.

MAKES 8 TO 10 SERVINGS.

BABY POTATOES STUFFED WITH HERBED CHEESE

Attractive as a first course or on a party buffet. For variety, you may stuff other baby vegetables (see "Baby Vegetables: Ripe for Stuffing" on page 39) or lightly cooked snow peas.

| 8 small new potatoes (½–¾ pound) | ¼ cup Herbed Yogurt Cheese (page 51) | Basil or tarragon sprigs (garnish) |

Scrub the potatoes, prick them with a fork, and arrange them around the outside rim of a 9″ glass pie plate. Microwave on high for 5 minutes. Turn each potato over and microwave on high for 3 minutes, or until the potatoes are tender but still keep their shape.

With a sharp knife, partially hollow out each potato by cutting a cone-shaped section from the top. (The hole should be just large enough to hold a small spoonful of the yogurt cheese.) Reserve the tops for another use, if desired.

Fill each potato with a dollop of the yogurt cheese. Serve hot or at room temperature, garnished with the basil or tarragon.

MAKES 4 SERVINGS.

Variations: You may replace the Herbed Yogurt Cheese with Chive Yogurt Cheese or Pimento-Cheese Spread (see "Yogurt-Cheese Spreads" on page 51).

FETA-SPINACH SQUARES

2 tablespoons margarine or butter

1 clove garlic, minced

4 cups packed fresh spinach leaves, chopped*

½ cup unbleached flour

½ teaspoon baking powder

2 eggs or ½ cup fat-free egg substitute

½ cup skim milk

½ cup crumbled feta cheese

1 tablespoon minced fresh dill

Dill sprigs (garnish)

Cherry tomatoes, halved (garnish)

Place the margarine or butter in an 8″ × 8″ baking dish and microwave on high for 2 minutes. Add the garlic and stir to combine. Stir in the spinach, cover with a lid, and microwave on high for 3 to 4 minutes, or until the spinach is wilted.

In a medium bowl, combine the flour and baking powder. Stir in the eggs, milk, feta, and minced dill. Stir in the cooked spinach, then return the mixture to the baking dish.

Microwave on high for 3 minutes. Rotate the dish a half turn. Microwave on high for 4 minutes, or until a knife inserted in the center comes out clean.

Cut into squares and serve garnished with the dill sprigs and tomatoes.

MAKES 8 TO 10 SERVINGS.

* Since spinach is grown in sandy soils, thorough washing is essential to remove grit. To do so, immerse the leaves in a sinkful of water and agitate gently. The dirt will sink, so you can just lift out the leaves. Shake or pat the leaves dry.

YOGURT-CHEESE SPREADS

Fat-free yogurt cheese is a healthy alternative to sour cream and cream cheese. It's got the same rich and creamy texture as the high-fat products but only a fraction of their fat and calories. Although you don't prepare it in a microwave, I consider it so indispensable for dips, spreads, and other party favorites that I'm including directions here.

To make yogurt cheese, set a colander over a bowl and line it with three or four layers of cheesecloth. Pour 2 to 4 cups of nonfat (or low-fat) yogurt into the cheesecloth and gather up the ends to form a bag. Tie the cheesecloth shut with string. Wrap the string around the colander handles so the bag is suspended and the liquid from the yogurt can drip into the bowl.

Place the whole works in the refrigerator and allow the yogurt to drain for about 5 hours. If it drains longer, the cheese will become too dry. Unwrap the yogurt cheese and use it plain or flavored (see the following suggestions). Yogurt cheese is great on melba toast, atop baked potatoes, stuffed into lightly cooked snow peas or baby vegetables (see "Baby Vegetables: Ripe for Stuffing" on page 39), and as a dip for raw vegetables.

Here are some of my favorite yogurt-cheese spreads:

- *Herbed Yogurt Cheese:* Combine ½ cup yogurt cheese, 2 teaspoons minced fresh parsley, ½ teaspoon minced fresh tarragon, ½ teaspoon minced fresh basil, ½ teaspoon minced garlic, and a pinch of ground black pepper.
- *Pimento-Cheese Spread:* Combine ½ cup yogurt cheese, 1 tablespoon minced pimentos, and ¼ teaspoon paprika.
- *Chive Yogurt Cheese:* Combine ½ cup yogurt cheese, 2 teaspoons minced chives, ½ teaspoon minced garlic (optional), and a pinch of ground black pepper.
- *Minted Yogurt Cheese:* Combine ½ cup yogurt cheese and 1 tablespoon minced fresh mint. To serve with fruit, stir in 1 teaspoon maple syrup.

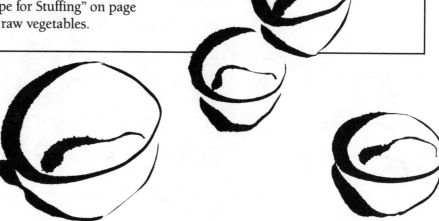

Meaty
Main Dishes

If you like meat but are worried there's no place for it in a healthy diet because of its fat content, I have good news. Your microwave can help you cook meat lean as well as fast. Here are a few examples:

- *Microwaving renders more fat from meat than other cooking methods, so you can drain away the excess.*

- *Meat and vegetable stir-fries require much less oil—and less overall attention from you— than they would in a wok.*

- *Pot roast doesn't need to be seared in hot fat before cooking, and it turns out moist and succulent in less than an hour.*

One of the microwave's healthiest talents is the way it deals with fat marbled throughout meat. Simply put, microwaves are attracted to fat, heating it up more quickly than the surrounding meat so it can melt away. Ground meat, in particular, turns out beautifully in the microwave. Just drain off the accumulated fat and proceed with your recipe.

And here's interesting news: You might just retire your wok when you learn how easy it is to "stir-fry" in the microwave. Microwaving keeps meat juicy and vegetables firm and tasty—in best Chinese tradition—but uses only a fraction of the oil you'd need for stove-top preparation. And unlike the procedure needed for stove-top stir-fries, you needn't have all your ingredients chopped ahead of time. I usually slice the quick-cooking vegetables and other items while the long-cooking ones are in the microwave.

You can even use your microwave to augment your grill. Microwaving meats (and poultry) before barbecuing them not only cuts fat but also lessens the time these foods need on the grill, which may reduce the risk of possible carcinogenic compounds linked with prolonged high-heat grilling. By precooking meats in the microwave, you'll never again have to face food that's burned on the outside but raw in the middle.

Of course, in microwave cookery, as with traditional methods, it pays to start out with the leanest meats you can buy. And always trim away all visible fat before cooking. Lean beef cuts include the round, sirloin, chuck, and loin cuts. For the leanest lamb, choose leg, arm, and loin pieces. As for pork, the loin and leg are good choices. Pork tenderloin has only slightly more fat and cholesterol than skinned chicken breast, long a favorite of health-conscious eaters.

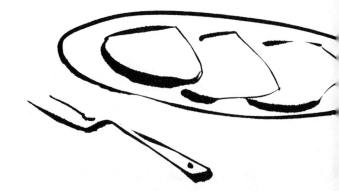

1 PART MEAT, 1 PART VEGETABLES

Although meat seems fibrous, it contains no fiber—so necessary for proper digestion. That's one reason I add lots of vegetables, brown rice, and other fiber-rich ingredients to my recipes. And using generous quantities of these foods helps fill you up so you can get by with less meat—and still satisfy your taste for meat. Vegetables also add delicious low-fat flavor to pot roasts, meat loaves, spaghetti sauces, and other traditional favorites.

Some microwave cookbooks call for using microwave browning dishes when cooking meat. But you won't find that to be the case in this cookbook. Those browning dishes require extra fat to prevent food from sticking and to facilitate browning. To me, it's just as easy to quickly brown meat—in the few cases where it's actually necessary—under a broiler or in a no-stick frying pan.

I hope you'll like the down-home recipes in this chapter. While I've included a few more exotic dishes to expand your repertoire, the basics—like spaghetti and meatballs, chili, stuffed cabbage, beef stroganoff, pot roast, and meat loaf—highlight how easy it is to eat well without spending your life in the kitchen.

TANGY PORK CHOPS WITH ROSY TOMATO RICE

A delicious combination of vegetables highlights pork chops.

2 green peppers, each cut into 8 strips

1 large onion, cut into 8 wedges

1 teaspoon minced jalapeño peppers (wear plastic gloves when handling)

2 cloves garlic, minced

½ teaspoon olive oil

2 cups peeled, seeded, and chopped tomatoes

¾ teaspoon dried oregano

1⅓ cups chicken stock

1¼ cups quick-cooking brown rice

4 pork loin chops, 1″ thick, trimmed of all visible fat

In a 7″ × 11″ shallow baking dish, stir together the green peppers, onions, jalapeños, garlic, and oil. Microwave on high for 3 minutes. Stir and microwave on high for 2 minutes.

Reserve ¼ cup of the tomatoes. Add the remaining 1¾ cups of tomatoes and the oregano to the vegetables in the baking dish. Microwave on high for 3 minutes. Stir well.

In a blender, puree the reserved tomatoes with ½ cup of the stock. Place in a 2-quart saucepan. Add the remaining stock. Bring to a boil over medium heat. Add the rice. Reduce the heat to low, cover the pan, and simmer the rice for 10 minutes. Set aside and keep warm.

Place the chops in the baking dish on top of the vegetables (make sure the bones are facing toward the center of the dish). Microwave on high for 5 minutes.

Flip each pork chop, keeping the bones facing the center of the dish. As you turn the chops, stir the vegetables. Give the dish a quarter or half turn. Cook for 5 to 7 minutes, or until the meat reaches an internal temperature of 150° and there is no hint of pink. Cover the dish with foil and let stand for 2 to 3 minutes.

Serve the pork chops with the rice and vegetables.

MAKES 4 SERVINGS.

SHEPHERD'S PIE

A combination of vegetables with a meat "crust" makes this pie unique. You'll find lots of fiber, vitamins, and minerals in the vegetables, all of which are a savory complement to the meat.

2 cups cubed potatoes

¾ cup skim milk

1 pound extra-lean ground beef or lamb

1 egg, lightly beaten, or ¼ cup fat-free egg substitute

½ cup dry whole-grain breadcrumbs

2 tablespoons grated onions

⅛ teaspoon ground black pepper

⅛ teaspoon grated nutmeg

½ cup chopped broccoli florets

½ cup thinly sliced carrots

½ cup chopped cauliflower florets

¼ cup chopped onions

2 tablespoons chopped scallions

2 tablespoons tomato sauce

½ cup shredded reduced-fat Cheddar or longhorn cheese

Place the potatoes in a 2-quart saucepan with cold water to cover. Bring to a boil and cook until tender, about 10 to 12 minutes. Drain. Add ¼ cup of the milk and mash well. Set aside.

In a large bowl, mix the beef or lamb, egg, breadcrumbs, grated onions, pepper, nutmeg, and remaining ½ cup milk until well blended. Press the mixture over the bottom and up the sides of a 9″ pie plate. Cover loosely with wax paper.

Microwave on high for 5 to 7 minutes, or until the meat is no longer pink. Carefully drain off any accumulated fat.

In a deep 1-quart casserole, combine the broccoli, carrots, cauliflower, chopped onions, scallions, and tomato sauce. Cover with a lid. Microwave on high for 4 to 5 minutes, or until crisp-tender.

To assemble the pie, spread the mashed potatoes over the meat. Top with the vegetables and sprinkle with the Cheddar or longhorn. Microwave on high for 2 to 3 minutes, or until the cheese is melted and the pie is hot throughout. Cut into wedges to serve.

MAKES 6 SERVINGS.

PARTY MEAT LOAF
WITH PARSLEY MASHED POTATOES

In the time it takes to prepare mashed potatoes on the stove, you can have a microwaved meat loaf.

1 package (10 ounces) frozen chopped spinach

1 pound extra-lean ground chuck or top round

1¼ cups fresh whole wheat breadcrumbs

1 small onion, finely chopped

1 egg, lightly beaten, or ¼ cup fat-free egg substitute

2 tablespoons finely chopped sweet red peppers

4 teaspoons soy sauce

1 teaspoon minced fresh basil or ¼ teaspoon dried basil

2 tablespoons minced fresh parsley

¼ cup tomato sauce

3 cups cubed potatoes

½ celery stalk

⅓ cup skim milk

Place the spinach in a 9″ pie plate. Microwave on high for 2 minutes. Rotate the dish a half turn. Microwave on high for 2 to 4 minutes, or until defrosted. Transfer the spinach to a sieve and drain well, pressing with the back of a spoon to remove all excess moisture.

Place the spinach in a large bowl. Add the beef, breadcrumbs, onions, egg, peppers, soy sauce, basil, and 1 tablespoon of the parsley. Mix well. Place in a 7″ round casserole or soufflé dish. Top with the tomato sauce.

Microwave on high for 6 to 7 minutes. Rotate the dish partway. Repeat twice more for a total cooking time of 18 to 20 minutes, or until the meat loaf reaches 160° in the center. Carefully drain off any accumulated fat. Let stand for 5 minutes.

While the meat loaf is cooking, place the potatoes and celery (do not slice) in a 2-quart saucepan with cold water to cover. Bring to a boil and cook until tender, about 12 to 14 minutes. Drain. Discard the celery. Add the milk and mash well. Stir in the remaining 1 tablespoon of parsley. Cover the pan and place over very low heat for up to 5 minutes before serving.

MAKES 6 SERVINGS.

MEXICAN-STYLE TACOS WITH SALAD TOPPINGS

Piled high with fresh, raw vegetables, these tasty tacos place an emphasis on healthy eating.

8 ounces extra-lean ground beef
¼ cup chopped onions
¼ cup chopped green peppers
1 clove garlic, minced
1 small tomato, peeled, seeded, and finely chopped
1 tablespoon tomato paste

½ teaspoon chili powder
¼ teaspoon ground cumin
   Pinch of ground red pepper
8 taco shells
2 cups shredded lettuce
1 cup peeled, seeded, and chopped tomatoes

½ cup shredded zucchini (optional)
½ cup shredded reduced-fat Cheddar cheese
¼ cup alfalfa sprouts
1 cup Super Salsa (page 59)
½ cup nonfat yogurt

Crumble the beef into a 2-quart casserole. Scatter the onions and peppers over the meat. Cover with a lid. Microwave on high for 4 to 5 minutes, or until the beef is no longer pink. Carefully drain off any accumulated fat.

Stir in the garlic, tomatoes, tomato paste, chili powder, cumin, and red pepper. Microwave on high for 3 minutes.

While the meat is cooking, warm the taco shells for a few minutes in a conventional oven at 250°.

To serve, divide the meat mixture among the taco shells. Top with lettuce, tomatoes, zucchini (if using), Cheddar, and sprouts. Drizzle with the salsa and yogurt.

MAKES 4 SERVINGS.

STACKED ENCHILADAS

Serve with steamed vegetables or a tossed salad.

5 ounces extra-lean ground beef

¼ cup finely chopped onions

½ teaspoon chili powder

¼ teaspoon ground cumin

1 clove garlic, minced

1 cup cooked pinto or kidney beans

1½ cups Super Salsa (opposite page)

4 soft corn tortillas

½ cup thinly sliced scallions

1 cup shredded lettuce

¼ cup shredded reduced-fat Cheddar cheese

Crumble the beef into a 2-quart casserole. Lightly toss with the onions, chili powder, cumin, and garlic. Microwave on high for 3 to 4 minutes, or until the meat is no longer pink. Carefully drain off any accumulated fat.

In a medium bowl, mash the beans with ¼ cup of the salsa. Microwave on high for 2 to 3 minutes, or until heated through.

Spoon ¼ cup of the salsa into the bottom of a 9″ glass pie plate.

Spread one tortilla with one-third of the bean mixture and place in the center of the plate. Top with ¼ cup of the salsa. Sprinkle with one-third of the meat mixture, one-third of the scallions, ⅓ cup shredded lettuce, and 1 tablespoon Cheddar.

Repeat to make two more layers. Top with the remaining tortilla. Press down slightly on the whole stack. Top with the remaining salsa and Cheddar.

Microwave on high for 4 to 5 minutes, or until the cheese is melted and the sauce is bubbly. Cut into quarters to serve.

MAKES 4 SERVINGS.

SALSA IN A FLASH

Voted "Best Salsa" by my friends! It's easy to make as a dip for parties, and of course, it complements tortillas, enchiladas, other Tex-Mex dishes, meats, fish, poultry, and vegetables. It's especially good with Low-Fat Tortilla Chips (see page 41).

SUPER SALSA

1 cup chopped onions
2 jalapeño peppers, seeded and minced (wear plastic gloves when handling)
1 clove garlic, minced
2 teaspoons olive oil
3½ cups canned whole tomatoes, drained and chopped

1 cup tomato sauce
¼ cup canned mild green chili peppers, rinsed and diced
1 teaspoon minced fresh coriander

1 teaspoon ground cumin
¼ teaspoon dried oregano
⅛ teaspoon ground black pepper

In a 2-quart casserole, combine the onions, jalapeños, garlic, and oil. Microwave on high for 3 minutes, or until the onions are crisp-tender.

Stir in the tomatoes, tomato sauce, chili peppers, coriander, cumin, oregano, and black pepper. Microwave on high for 5 minutes. Stir, then microwave on high for 5 to 7 minutes, or until hot. Chill before serving.

MAKES ABOUT 3 CUPS.

GRILLING TIPS

Put an end to burned-on-the-outside, raw-on-the-inside grilled meats. By precooking meats in the microwave, you can speed up total grilling time *and* ensure that those foods are thoroughly cooked but not charred. Also, you minimize exposure of the food to any possible carcinogenic compounds associated with prolonged grilling.

For best results—and to prevent the growth of food-borne bacteria—do the microwaving just before grilling so the meat stays hot and benefits from continuous cooking. (It's not safe to partially cook meat and finish cooking it later.)

To do, arrange meats in a microwave-safe pan with the thickest parts facing the outside of the dish. Cover the dish with wax paper. Microwave roasts, spareribs, chicken, Cornish hens, or turkey on high for 5 minutes per pound (rearrange the pieces halfway through the total time).

Pour off any accumulated fat and juices before grilling. Discarding these meat juices gets rid of compounds that could conceivably develop into carcinogens when exposed to high heat. Since the foods will be nearly done at this point, you need to grill them only long enough to brown them. Let me again stress that you should grill the food *immediately* after microwaving it to avoid bacterial growth.

Small or thin pieces of meat, such as steaks, shish kebabs, and hamburger patties, cook so quickly on the grill that they don't really need a stint in the microwave first. But there is a way to involve the microwave: Grill extra pieces of meat (undercooking them slightly), then wrap and freeze for up to 6 months. For just-grilled flavor in an instant, unwrap the pieces and place them on a plate. Microwave them on medium (50% power) until heated through. Do one hamburger for 1½ to 3 minutes. Give two burgers 2½ to 4 minutes.

A few words about marinades: Marinades impart wonderful flavor to low-fat meats. And they can help tenderize tough cuts. Because marinades have been in contact with raw meat, you need to follow a few safety precautions. Don't baste meat with the marinade during the final few minutes of cooking. Don't reuse marinade. And if you want to turn the marinade into a sauce for your meat, transfer it to a clean saucepan and bring it to a full boil to kill any bacteria. An alternative is to prepare extra marinade that you keep separate from the meat and use as sauce.

BARBECUED RIBS

4 pounds beef short ribs or pork baby back ribs

¼ cup water

Barbecue Sauce (opposite page)

In a 7″ × 11″ baking dish, arrange the ribs in a single layer. Add the water and cover with wax paper. Microwave on high for 2½ minutes. Rotate the dish a half turn and rearrange the ribs. Microwave on high for 2½ minutes.

Rotate the dish again. Microwave on medium (50% power) for 7 minutes. Turn the ribs over and microwave on medium (50% power) for 8 minutes. Drain well.

Transfer the ribs to a hot grill. Baste with the barbecue sauce. Grill, basting occasionally, for 20 to 25 minutes, or until tender.

MAKES 4 SERVINGS.

BARBECUE SAUCE

1 medium onion, finely chopped
2 cloves garlic, minced
½ teaspoon olive oil
¼ cup ketchup
3 tablespoons lemon juice

2 tablespoons honey
1 tablespoon red wine vinegar
2 teaspoons soy sauce
1 teaspoon ground coriander
½ teaspoon ground ginger

½ teaspoon ground cumin
½ teaspoon paprika
¼ teaspoon ground red pepper
¼ teaspoon ground black pepper

In a medium bowl, combine the onions, garlic, and oil. Microwave on high for 3 minutes. Stir in the ketchup, lemon juice, honey, vinegar, soy sauce, coriander, ginger, cumin, paprika, red pepper, and black pepper. Microwave on high for 3 minutes.

MAKES ¾ CUP.

SUNDAY-BEST PORK STIR-FRY

Easy enough for weekday dinners.

8 ounces pork tenderloin, trimmed of all visible fat
1 tablespoon lemon juice
1 tablespoon soy sauce
½ teaspoon sherry extract
½ teaspoon honey
⅛ teaspoon ground ginger

3 scallions, julienned
2 cups chicken stock
1¼ cups quick-cooking brown rice
1 small onion, thinly sliced
½ teaspoon sesame oil

2 medium carrots, julienned
1 yellow squash (about 8 ounces), julienned
2 cups thinly sliced mushrooms
2 cups snow peas
2 teaspoons cornstarch

Freeze the pork until firm enough to slice easily, about 30 minutes. Cut across the grain into thin slices, about 2″ long.

In a large bowl, combine the lemon juice, soy sauce, sherry extract, honey, and ginger. Add the pork and scallions. Stir well to combine. Set aside to marinate.

In a 2-quart saucepan over medium heat, bring 1½ cups of the stock to a boil. Stir in the rice, reduce the heat to low, cover the pan, and simmer for 10 minutes. Keep warm.

While the rice is cooking, place the onions and oil in a deep 2-quart casserole. Microwave on high for 2 minutes.

Add the pork mixture. Microwave on high for 4 minutes. Stir. Microwave on high for 3 to 4 minutes, or until the pork is cooked through.

Add the carrots, squash, mushrooms, and snow peas. Microwave on high for 2 to 3 minutes. Stir well. Microwave on high for 3 to 4 minutes, or until the vegetables are crisp-tender.

In a 1-quart saucepan, combine the cornstarch and the remaining ½ cup stock. Stir over medium heat until the mixture comes to a boil and thickens. Add to the casserole and stir well. Cover and let stand for 4 to 5 minutes.

Serve over the rice.

MAKES 4 SERVINGS.

SWEET-AND-SOUR PORK WITH VEGETABLES

Sweet-and-sour sauce is a natural with pork and vegetables. Served over brown rice, it's an attractive low-fat, high-fiber one-dish meal.

1 onion, thinly sliced	1¾ cups chicken stock	¼ cup rice wine vinegar
1 teaspoon minced garlic	1¼ cups quick-cooking brown rice	¼ cup tomato sauce
1 teaspoon grated fresh ginger or ¼ teaspoon ground ginger	2 carrots, sliced diagonally	2 tablespoons honey
1 teaspoon canola oil	4 scallions, sliced diagonally	1 tablespoon cornstarch
12 ounces pork loin, trimmed of all visible fat and cut into 1″ cubes	1 cup pineapple chunks	2 teaspoons soy sauce
		½ teaspoon grated lemon rind

In a deep 2-quart casserole, combine the onions, garlic, ginger, and oil. Microwave on high for 2 minutes.

Move the onions to the center of the dish and place the pork around the edges. Cover with wax paper and microwave on high for 5 minutes. Stir and microwave on high for 5 minutes, or until the pork is cooked through.

While the pork is cooking, bring 1½ cups of the stock to a boil in a 2-quart saucepan. Stir in the rice, reduce the heat to low, cover the pan, and simmer for 10 minutes. Keep warm.

Add the carrots, scallions, and pineapple to the pork. Microwave on high for 3 to 4 minutes. Stir well. Microwave on high for 4 minutes, or until the vegetables are crisp-tender.

While the vegetables are cooking, combine the vinegar, tomato sauce, honey, cornstarch, soy sauce, lemon rind, and remaining ¼ cup stock in a 1-quart saucepan. Stir over medium heat until thickened. Pour over the pork mixture.

Serve over the rice.

MAKES 4 SERVINGS.

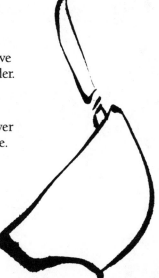

MY FAVORITE STUFFED PEPPERS

Microwaving your stuffed peppers saves you some prep time: You don't need to blanch the peppers first for a tender finished product. Take your choice of green, yellow, or red peppers.

4 large peppers

12 ounces extra-lean ground beef

½ cup finely chopped onions

½ cup shredded carrots

½ teaspoon dried marjoram

½ clove garlic, minced

1½ cups cooked brown or white rice

½ cup shredded reduced-fat Cheddar cheese

1 cup tomato sauce

Cut the tops off the peppers. Discard the stems, seeds, and inner white membranes. Finely dice the pepper tops and place in a 1½-quart shallow casserole. Reserve the rest of the peppers.

Crumble the beef into the casserole. Add the onions, carrots, marjoram, and garlic. Mix well. Cover with wax paper and microwave on high for 4 to 6 minutes, stirring once, until the meat is no longer pink. Carefully pour off any accumulated fat.

Stir in the rice, ¼ cup of the Cheddar, and ½ cup of the tomato sauce. Spoon the meat mixture into the reserved peppers.

Spoon ¼ cup of the tomato sauce into the bottom of the casserole. Stand peppers upright in the dish. Cover with wax paper. Microwave on high for 12 to 15 minutes, or until the peppers are crisp-tender and the filling is hot.

Spoon the remaining ¼ cup of tomato sauce over the tops, then sprinkle with the remaining ¼ cup of Cheddar.

Microwave on high for 2 to 3 minutes, or until the sauce is hot and the cheese is melted. Let stand for 5 minutes before serving.

MAKES 4 SERVINGS.

POT ROAST WITH VEGETABLES

You can microwave a pot roast in a fraction of the time it would take atop the stove. This recipe makes enough to serve four with plenty of leftovers for sandwiches. Microwaving the meat uncovered gives it a delicious oven-roasted flavor.

1 chuck roast (2 pounds), trimmed of all visible fat

4 cloves garlic, minced

1 onion, quartered

8 carrots, halved crosswise

8 small potatoes, halved

½ bay leaf

1 cup tomato juice or tomato sauce

½ cup chicken stock

Rub all sides of the roast with the garlic. Place in a 2½-quart casserole. Surround with the onions, carrots, potatoes, and bay leaf. Pour in the tomato juice or tomato sauce and chicken stock.

Microwave on high for 15 minutes. Rotate the dish a half turn and microwave on high for 20 minutes. Turn the meat over and rearrange the vegetables. Microwave on high for 15 minutes. Rotate the dish and microwave on high for 10 minutes.

Remove the meat and vegetables to a platter. Remove and discard the bay leaf. Pour the juices into a gravy boat and skim off any fat from the surface. Slice the meat thinly across the grain. Serve with the vegetables and juices.

MAKES 4 TO 8 SERVINGS.

ORIENTAL BEEF

8 ounces sirloin tip steak

1 small red onion, thinly sliced

1 cup sliced mushrooms

1 teaspoon minced jalapeño peppers (wear plastic gloves when handling)

1 green pepper, cubed

1 yellow or sweet red pepper, cubed

1 large broccoli stalk

4 scallions, sliced diagonally

½ cup peas

1½ cups water

1¼ cups quick-cooking brown rice

1½ tablespoons soy sauce

1 clove garlic, minced

¾ cup stock

1 tablespoon cornstarch

½ teaspoon grated fresh ginger or ¼ teaspoon ground ginger

Pinch of ground red pepper

Freeze the beef until firm enough to slice easily, about 30 minutes. Cut across the grain into thin strips, about 1½" to 2" long. Set aside.

In a 2½-quart casserole, combine the onions, mushrooms, and jalapeños. Microwave on high for 3 minutes. Add the green peppers and yellow or red peppers. Microwave on high for 3 minutes.

Cut the florets from the broccoli stalk and separate them into bite-size pieces. Peel the stem and slice thinly. Add both to the casserole and microwave on high for 2 minutes.

Add the scallions and peas. Microwave on high for 2 minutes. Drain off any excess liquid. Cover with foil and set aside.

While the vegetables are cooking, bring the water to a boil in a 2-quart saucepan. Stir in the rice, reduce the heat to low, cover the pan, and simmer for 10 minutes. Keep warm.

Place the meat on a plate. Sprinkle with the soy sauce and garlic; toss to combine. Microwave on high for 3 minutes. Stir the meat gently. Microwave on high for 2 minutes. Rotate the dish and microwave on high for 1 to 2 minutes, or until the meat is tender. Add to the vegetables.

While the meat is cooking, combine the stock, cornstarch, ginger, and ground pepper in a 1-quart saucepan. Stir over medium heat until thickened. Pour over the beef and vegetables. Microwave on high for 2 to 3 minutes.

Serve over the rice.

MAKES 4 SERVINGS.

LEAN AND LIGHT LASAGNA

You don't even have to precook the lasagna noodles to make this casserole.

8 ounces extra-lean ground beef

2½ cups tomato sauce

1 clove garlic, minced

¼ teaspoon dried basil

¼ teaspoon dried marjoram

¼ teaspoon dried oregano

1 small zucchini (about 6 ounces), thinly sliced

4 lasagna noodles

1 cup part-skim ricotta cheese

½ cup low-fat cottage cheese

1 egg or ¼ cup fat-free egg substitute

Pinch of grated nutmeg

½ cup shredded part-skim mozzarella cheese

1 tablespoon minced fresh parsley

Crumble the beef into a 7″ × 11″ baking dish. Microwave on high for 4 to 5 minutes, or until the meat is no longer pink. Carefully drain off any accumulated fat.

Transfer the meat to a 4-cup glass measure or large bowl. Stir in the tomato sauce, garlic, basil, marjoram, and oregano. Microwave on high for 2 to 3 minutes, or until bubbly.

Pour 1 cup of the sauce into the bottom of the baking dish and spread it evenly. Arrange half of the zucchini slices, slightly overlapped, over the sauce. Top with two uncooked lasagna noodles.

In a small bowl, stir together the ricotta cheese, cottage cheese, egg, and nutmeg. Spoon over the noodles and gently spread in an even layer. Sprinkle with half of the mozzarella. Top with ¾ cup of the sauce.

Top with the remaining zucchini, noodles, and sauce. Sprinkle with the remaining mozzarella.

Cover with wax paper and microwave on high for 5 minutes. Rotate the dish a half turn. Microwave on medium (50% power) for 20 to 26 minutes, rotating the dish a total of three times during this period, until the noodles are tender and the sauce is bubbling. Let stand, covered, for 8 to 10 minutes. Sprinkle with the parsley.

MAKES 6 TO 8 SERVINGS.

LAMB CURRY WITH YELLOW RICE

The spices give a delicately exotic flavor to this lamb curry.

1 large onion, chopped
3 cloves garlic, minced
1 tablespoon grated fresh ginger
1 teaspoon canola oil
½ teaspoon ground coriander
½ teaspoon ground cardamom
½ teaspoon ground cumin
¼ teaspoon ground cinnamon

¼ teaspoon chili powder
¼ teaspoon ground black pepper
½ teaspoon turmeric
1 pound lean leg of lamb, trimmed of all visible fat and cut into 1″ cubes
1½ cups chicken stock
1 tart green apple, diced

1½ cups water
2 tablespoons grated onions
1 tablespoon grated coconut (optional)
1¼ cups quick-cooking brown rice
½ cup raisins
Chutney (optional)

In a deep 2½-quart casserole, combine the chopped onions, garlic, ginger, and oil. Microwave on high for 4 minutes.

Add the coriander, cardamom, cumin, cinnamon, chili powder, and pepper. Stir in ¼ teaspoon of the turmeric. Mix well. Stir in the lamb, stock, and apples. Microwave on high for 15 minutes, stirring the meat and rotating the casserole twice during this time.

While the lamb is cooking, bring the water, grated onions, coconut (if using), and remaining ¼ teaspoon turmeric to a boil in a 2-quart saucepan. Stir in the rice, reduce the heat to low, cover the pan, and simmer for 10 minutes. Keep warm.

Stir the raisins into the lamb mixture. Microwave on high for 5 minutes. Stir well and microwave on high for 5 minutes.

Serve over the rice. Accompany with the chutney (if using).

MAKES 4 SERVINGS.

LAMB PATTIES IN PITA

Packed with fresh vegetables, these lamb-stuffed pitas are a Middle Eastern change of pace from regular ground-meat fare.

1 slice whole wheat bread, cubed

1 pound ground lamb

½ cup finely chopped onions

1 tablespoon minced fresh parsley

¾ teaspoon ground coriander

½ teaspoon ground black pepper

½ teaspoon ground allspice

1 clove garlic, minced

1 large tomato, seeded and chopped

1 scallion, thinly sliced

2 teaspoons red wine vinegar

1 teaspoon olive oil

¾ cup nonfat yogurt

2 tablespoons minced fresh coriander

4 large whole wheat pitas

In a food processor or blender, process the bread cubes in short bursts to make soft crumbs. Transfer to a large bowl.

Add the lamb, onions, parsley, ½ teaspoon of the ground coriander, and the pepper, allspice, and garlic. Mix well. Form into 16 meatballs; flatten each slightly to ¾" thick.

Arrange the patties in a 9" glass pie plate. Cover with wax paper and microwave on high for 3 minutes. Turn and rearrange the patties, moving the least cooked ones to the outside. Cover and microwave on high for 3 to 4 minutes, or until the patties are no longer pink.

In a small bowl, combine the tomatoes, scallions, vinegar, oil, and remaining ¼ teaspoon ground coriander.

In another small bowl, combine the yogurt and fresh coriander.

To serve, halve the pitas and open the pockets. Place four lamb patties in each pocket. Top each serving with tomatoes and yogurt.

MAKES 4 SERVINGS.

INDIAN CURRIED CASSEROLE WITH PINE NUTS

Served over rice, spicy lamb makes an exotic but uncomplicated meal. For variety, replace the lamb with lean ground pork, beef, or turkey.

1½ cups chicken stock

1¼ cups quick-cooking brown rice

1 pound ground lamb

1 cup finely chopped onions

1 teaspoon minced garlic

1 tablespoon grated fresh ginger or 1 teaspoon ground ginger

1 tablespoon curry powder

¼ teaspoon ground cinnamon

¼ teaspoon ground coriander

¼ teaspoon ground cumin

⅛ teaspoon turmeric

1 cup canned Italian tomatoes, drained and chopped

1 teaspoon molasses

⅛ teaspoon ground black pepper

1 cup frozen peas, thawed

¼ cup pine nuts

In a 2-quart saucepan, bring the stock to a boil. Stir in the rice, reduce the heat to low, cover the pan, and simmer for 10 minutes. Keep warm.

In an 8″ × 8″ baking dish, combine the lamb, onions, and garlic. Cover loosely with wax paper. Microwave on high for 3 minutes. Stir to break up the meat. Microwave on high for 2 to 3 minutes, or until very little pink remains. Carefully pour off any accumulated fat.

Stir in the ginger, curry powder, cinnamon, coriander, cumin, and turmeric. Microwave on high for 1 minute.

Add the tomatoes, molasses, and pepper. Microwave on high for 4 minutes. Stir in the peas and pine nuts. Microwave on high for 2 minutes.

Serve over the rice.

MAKES 4 SERVINGS.

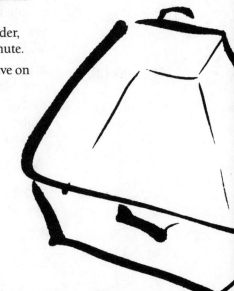

LEW'S SKINNY CHILI

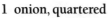

*My friend Lew enjoys treating his family to this
spicy chili.*

1 onion, quartered

2 cloves garlic

2 jalapeño peppers, halved and
seeded (wear plastic gloves
when handling)

2 cups canned Italian tomatoes,
drained

1 tablespoon chili powder

1 teaspoon ground cumin

1 teaspoon paprika

½ teaspoon dried oregano

1½ cups tomato juice

1¼ cups quick-cooking brown
rice

1 tablespoon soy sauce

1 pound beef chuck cubes,
trimmed of all visible fat and
diced

¼ cup chopped pimentos

2 tablespoons minced fresh
coriander (optional)

½ cup shredded reduced-fat
Cheddar cheese

In a food processor, combine the onions, garlic,
and jalapeños. Coarsely chop with on/off turns. Add the
tomatoes and process briefly to combine.

Transfer to a deep 2½-quart casserole. Stir in the chili
powder, cumin, paprika, and oregano. Microwave on high
for 10 minutes, stirring the vegetables and rotating the
dish twice during this time.

While the vegetables are cooking, bring the tomato juice to
a boil in a 2-quart saucepan. Stir in the rice and soy sauce.
Reduce the heat to low, cover the pan, and simmer for
10 minutes, stirring twice. Keep warm.

Add the beef to the casserole. Microwave on high for
10 minutes. Stir in the pimentos and microwave on high
for 5 minutes. Cover the casserole and let stand for
10 minutes.

Stir in the coriander (if using). Serve over the rice. Top each
serving with one-fourth of the Cheddar.

MAKES 4 SERVINGS.

LIGHT BEEF
AND MUSHROOMS STROGANOFF

*Substituting yogurt for most of the traditional
sour cream cuts down substantially on fat
without sacrificing flavor.*

1½ pounds beef top round or
sirloin, trimmed of all visible fat

1 small onion, thinly sliced

1 cup quartered mushrooms

2 tablespoons tomato juice
or beef stock

1 clove garlic, minced

½ teaspoon sherry extract
(optional)

¼ teaspoon dried marjoram

8 ounces (4 cups) broad
noodles

¼ cup reduced-fat sour cream

½ teaspoon Dijon mustard

¼ teaspoon ground black
pepper

½ cup nonfat yogurt

½ teaspoon cornstarch

2 tablespoons minced fresh
parsley

Freeze the beef until firm enough to slice easily,
about 30 minutes. Cut across the grain into thin slices,
about 2" long. Place in an 8" × 8" baking dish.

Add the onions, mushrooms, tomato juice or stock, garlic,
sherry extract (if using), and marjoram. Cover with a lid
and microwave on high for 5 minutes. Stir. Microwave on
medium (50% power) for 7 to 10 minutes. Stir the meat
and rotate the dish. Microwave on medium (50% power)
for 8 to 10 minutes, or until the meat is tender.

While the meat is cooking, bring a large pot of water to a
boil on the stove. Add the noodles and simmer for 10 to
12 minutes, or until just tender. Drain, place in a bowl, and
keep warm.

Stir the sour cream, mustard, and pepper into the meat
mixture. Microwave on high for 4 minutes.

In a cup, combine the yogurt and cornstarch. Stir into the
beef. Microwave on medium (50% power) for 2 minutes.

Toss the noodles with half of the parsley. Place on a platter.
Top with the meat mixture. Sprinkle with the remaining
parsley.

MAKES 4 SERVINGS.

SPINACH LASAGNA ROLL-UPS

An easy, attractive dish to serve to company.

1 package (10 ounces) frozen chopped spinach

6 lasagna noodles

8 ounces extra-lean ground beef

1 onion, chopped

1 cup low-fat cottage cheese

1 egg yolk or ¼ cup fat-free egg substitute

1 teaspoon dried basil

½ teaspoon dried marjoram

½ teaspoon dried oregano

1 clove garlic, minced

1½ cups tomato sauce

3 tablespoons grated Parmesan cheese

Place the spinach in a 9″ pie plate. Microwave on high for 2 minutes. Rotate the dish a half turn. Microwave on high for 2 to 4 minutes, or until defrosted. Transfer the spinach to a sieve and drain well, pressing with the back of a spoon to remove all excess moisture. Place in a large bowl and set aside.

Cook the noodles in a large pot of boiling water until just tender, about 8 to 9 minutes. Drain and place in a single layer on a plate. Set aside.

Crumble the beef into an 8″ × 8″ baking dish. Stir in the onions. Microwave on high for 2 to 3 minutes. Stir to break up the pieces and push the less done portions to the outside of the dish. Microwave on high for 1 to 2 minutes, or until the beef is no longer pink. Carefully drain off any accumulated fat. Transfer the beef to the bowl with the spinach. Wipe out the baking dish with a paper towel.

Add the cottage cheese, egg yolk, basil, marjoram, oregano, and garlic to the beef. Mix well.

Divide the meat mixture among the lasagna noodles, spreading it to cover the top of each noodle. Roll each up jelly-roll style.

Pour ¼ cup of the tomato sauce in the bottom of the baking dish and spread evenly. Arrange the noodles, seam-side down, in the dish. Pour the remaining 1¼ cups of the sauce over the noodles.

Microwave on high for 10 to 12 minutes, or until heated through. Sprinkle with the Parmesan.

MAKES 6 SERVINGS.

PORK SATAY WITH YELLOW RICE AND PEANUT SAUCE

Satay is an Indonesian favorite that combines grilled meat with a savory peanut sauce. You may use beef, chicken, lamb, or as I do here, pork.

RICE
- 1 small onion, diced
- 1 teaspoon canola oil
- ¼ teaspoon turmeric
- 1⅓ cups short-grain brown rice*
- 2¼ cups chicken stock

PORK
- 2 pounds pork tenderloin, trimmed of all visible fat and cut into 1″ ribbons
- 3 tablespoons soy sauce
- 2 tablespoons lemon juice
- 1 tablespoon maple syrup
- 1 teaspoon caraway seeds, crushed
- 1 teaspoon ground coriander
- 1 teaspoon ground ginger
- 1 clove garlic, minced

PEANUT SAUCE
- ½ cup diced sweet red peppers
- ¼ cup minced onions
- 2 jalapeño peppers, seeded and minced (wear plastic gloves when handling)
- 2 tablespoons grated fresh ginger
- 3 cloves garlic, minced
- 1 cup chicken stock
- ¾ cup chunky peanut butter
- ½ cup thinly sliced scallion greens
- 1 tablespoon lemon juice

To make the rice: In a 2-quart saucepan over medium heat, sauté the onions in the oil until translucent, about 5 minutes. Stir in the turmeric, add the rice, and combine well. Add the stock. Bring to a boil over medium heat. Reduce the heat to low, cover the pan, and cook for 45 minutes, or until the rice is tender and all of the liquid has been absorbed. Set aside and keep warm.

To make the pork: In a large bowl, combine the pork, soy sauce, lemon juice, maple syrup, caraway, coriander, ginger, and garlic. Cover and refrigerate for 30 minutes.

While the meat is marinating, soak four 8″-long bamboo skewers in water.

Thread the meat onto the skewers; reserve the marinade. Place the skewers, in spoke fashion, on a 9″ or 10″ pie plate, and baste the meat with the marinade. Cover with wax

paper and microwave on high for 3 to 4 minutes. Flip the skewers and rearrange them to put the less cooked meat toward the outside. Baste with the marinade. Cover and microwave on high for 2 to 3 minutes, or until the meat is no longer pink. Cover tightly and set aside.

To make the peanut sauce: While the meat is marinating, combine the red peppers, onions, jalapeños, ginger, and garlic in a 1½-quart casserole. Microwave for 4 minutes. Stir in the stock, peanut butter, scallions, and lemon juice. Microwave on high for 4 minutes. Cover with foil and keep warm. If necessary, reheat briefly before serving. Transfer to a gravy boat or serving bowl.

To serve, place the rice on a platter. Top with the skewers. Drizzle with some of the sauce. Serve the rest of the sauce at the table.

MAKES 6 SERVINGS.

*If you should decide to substitute white rice for the brown, cooking time will be reduced to about 20 minutes. Depending on the brand of rice used, you may need to add a little more liquid.

HOMEMADE TV DINNERS

Do yourself a favor when cooking for one or two people. Prepare an entire recipe—perhaps for four. Freeze the leftovers in single-serving portions. Use shallow, microwave-safe casseroles. Cover them loosely and place in the freezer until the food has frozen.

For most efficient storage, remove the food from its container by running warm water over the bottom of the dish to loosen the frozen block. Wrap the food well in freezer paper or a heavy-duty plastic bag.

When you're ready to serve, remove the wrapping and pop the block back into its casserole or set it on a plate. Thaw and reheat according to your microwave's directions until the food is piping hot.

SPAGHETTI SQUASH
WITH PEPPERS AND MEAT SAUCE

1 tomato, quartered and seeded, or 2 Italian tomatoes, halved

1 small carrot, coarsely chopped

1 small onion, coarsely chopped

1 clove garlic

½ cup cubed green peppers

½ cup cubed sweet red peppers

1 cup tomato sauce

1 teaspoon minced fresh parsley

½ teaspoon dried basil

½ teaspoon dried oregano

¼ teaspoon dried marjoram

¼ teaspoon ground black pepper

1 spaghetti squash (2 to 3 pounds), halved lengthwise, stemmed, and seeded

8 ounces extra-lean ground beef

In a blender or food processor, process the tomatoes, carrots, onions, and garlic with on/off turns until finely chopped. Transfer to an 8″ × 8″ baking dish. Add the green peppers and red peppers. Microwave on high for 3 minutes. Stir.

Add the tomato sauce, parsley, basil, oregano, marjoram, and black pepper. Microwave on high for 5 minutes. Cover and keep warm.

Place the squash on a plate, cut-side down, and microwave on high for 8 to 10 minutes, or until tender. Cover and keep warm.

Crumble the meat into a 9″ glass pie plate. Cover with a lid or a large plate and microwave on high for 3 minutes. Stir to break up clumps. Cover and microwave on high for 3 minutes, or until the meat is no longer pink. Carefully drain off any accumulated fat. Stir the meat into the sauce.

While the meat is cooking, use a fork to separate the flesh of the squash into spaghetti-like strands. Place the squash on a platter. Top with the meat sauce. If needed, reheat briefly before serving.

MAKES 2 TO 4 SERVINGS.

SPAGHETTI AND MEATBALLS

8 ounces extra-lean ground beef

8 ounces extra-lean ground pork

1 egg, lightly beaten, or ¼ cup fat-free egg substitute

¼ cup dry whole-grain breadcrumbs

2 tablespoons grated onions

1 large carrot, cut into 1″ pieces

4 Italian tomatoes, halved, or 2 tomatoes, quartered and seeded

1 small onion, quartered

1 clove garlic

2 cups tomato sauce

1 tablespoon minced fresh parsley

1 teaspoon dried basil

½ teaspoon dried marjoram

¼ teaspoon dried oregano

¼ teaspoon ground black pepper

1 pound spaghetti

In a large bowl, combine the beef, pork, egg, breadcrumbs, and grated onions. Form into 12 large meatballs. Set aside.

In a blender or food processor, process the carrots, tomatoes, onions, and garlic with on/off turns until finely chopped. Transfer to a deep 2-quart casserole. Microwave on high for 3 minutes. Stir, then microwave on high for 2 minutes.

Add the tomato sauce, parsley, basil, marjoram, oregano, and pepper. Cover with a lid and microwave on high for 6 minutes. Set aside and keep warm.

Place the meatballs in a 9″ or 10″ glass pie plate, cover with wax paper, and microwave on high for 4 minutes. Turn over the meatballs and rearrange to bring the pieces from the center of the dish to the outside. Cover and microwave on high for 4 minutes. Add to the sauce.

While the meatballs are cooking, cook the spaghetti in a large pot of boiling water until just tender, about 10 minutes. Drain and transfer to a platter. Top with the sauce and meatballs.

MAKES 4 SERVINGS.

CABBAGE ROLLS
WITH POPPY-SEED NOODLES

8 large cabbage leaves

1 tablespoon water

1 pound extra-lean ground beef

1 cup cooked brown or white rice

¼ cup chopped onions

1 egg or ¼ cup fat-free egg substitute

2 cups tomato sauce

2 teaspoons molasses

½ teaspoon dried basil

½ teaspoon dried oregano

8 ounces (4 cups) broad noodles

1 tablespoon poppy seeds

1 teaspoon margarine or butter

Use a sharp knife to remove the hard center rib from each cabbage leaf. Place the leaves in a 7″ × 11″ baking dish. Sprinkle with the water. Cover with wax paper and microwave on high for 2 to 3 minutes, or until the leaves are pliable.

In a large bowl, combine the beef, rice, onions, and egg. Shape the mixture into eight small loaves.

Overlap the cut edges of each cabbage leaf and place one loaf at the base of each leaf. Fold in the sides and roll up to enclose the filling. Place the rolls, seam-side down, around the outer edges of the baking dish, keeping the center open.

In a small bowl, combine the tomato sauce, molasses, basil, and oregano. Pour over the rolls and cover with wax paper. Microwave on high for 8 minutes. Baste the rolls with the sauce and microwave on high for 7 to 9 minutes.

While the rolls are cooking, cook the noodles in a large pot of boiling water for 8 to 10 minutes, or until just tender. Drain and place on a platter. Toss with the poppy seeds and margarine or butter.

Top with the cabbage rolls and sauce.

MAKES 4 SERVINGS.

PERFECTLY DELICIOUS POULTRY

*P*oultry is so tender and tasty when made in the microwave that you might never want to cook it any other way.

Using your microwave, you can:

- *Cook chicken and turkey cutlets in minutes. (They remain wonderfully juicy and tender, even when done on high power without added fat.)*
- *Serve whole chickens, Cornish hens, and bone-in turkey breasts in a fraction of the usual time.*
- *Prepare one-dish meals that need virtually no cleanup.*

❑ Take full advantage of low-fat ground turkey.

Chicken and turkey breasts are popular among weight watchers and heart-smart eaters alike—with good reason: They're low in calories and fat. Their one big drawback is a tendency to become tough and dry if they're not handled with care. That's because they just don't have enough fat marbled through their tissues to keep them juicy when roasted or sautéed without additional fat. And simply poaching them all the time gets a little boring.

Thank goodness for the microwave. Never has cooking these meats been faster or easier—with such predictably delicious results. The moist heat of the microwave safeguards their natural juices. And the really fast cooking time lets you prepare them whenever the mood strikes.

Whole chickens, Cornish hens, and turkey breasts cook incredibly faster in the microwave than in your standard oven. That makes them fair game for weeknight dinners, not just special occasions. Likewise, bone-in chicken pieces cook much more quickly than in the oven, giving you great flexibility in your menu plans.

WHAT ABOUT SALMONELLA?

You may have some concern about whether microwaving effectively kills salmonella, harmful bacteria that is often present on poultry and can cause food poisoning. Experts from the U.S. Department of Agriculture (USDA) assure that it does, as long as the food is cooked to a temperature of 160° *throughout.*

There are several ways to ensure that. First, always start with pieces that are the same size, whether they're chunks of boneless breast or larger pieces of bone-in meat. Split bone-in chicken breasts in half and tuck in the wings to make triangles. Separate the drumsticks from the thighs. Whenever the recipe permits, cook similar pieces together rather than mixing different cuts. Always arrange the pieces so the meaty portions are toward the outside of the dish and the thin sections (such as wings and bony portions of drumsticks) are in the center.

In addition, stir cut-up pieces as they cook, and periodically rotate the dish (or use a carousel) so all areas are evenly exposed to the microwaves. Cover the dish or use an oven cooking bag to ensure even distribution of the heat. If you cook the poultry without a lid, be aware that bacteria may survive on the surface, so always cover it tightly after cooking (foil works well), and let it stand for 5 to 15 minutes. This distributes heat evenly on the surface.

To check that the poultry (or other meat) has reached the proper temperature, use an instant-read thermometer. Be sure to test the thickest part of the meat, making sure the probe doesn't rest on bone. If doing a whole chicken, insert the thermometer in the center of the inside thigh muscle, clear of bone.

WHERE'S THE FAT?

Here's an interesting development: Recent studies have put to rest the myth that cooking poultry with the skin on yields fattier meat. Researchers at the University of Minnesota found that there is no difference in fat or calories between chicken *meat* cooked with the skin on and that cooked without it. In other words, the fat from the skin does not migrate into the flesh. And the skin actually helps the meat to retain its natural juices. Be aware, though, that the cooked skin itself contains a substantial amount of fat, so you really shouldn't eat it.

You may notice that many of my recipes specify removing the skin from whole birds or cut-up pieces. That's just personal preference. I find it easier to take the skin off while the poultry is still raw. Besides, the moist heat of the microwave is less apt to dry out skinless meat the way the arid heat of a conventional oven can. Also, removing the skin before cooking chicken with vegetables or grains helps ensure that fat from the skin won't be absorbed by those other ingredients. For an added bit of color, try sprinkling a mixture of flour and paprika over the skinless meat during the final 5 to 10 minutes of cooking. Or use one of the basting sauces below.

If you're improvising a recipe, here's an easy way to estimate cooking time: Weigh your poultry on a kitchen scale or check the weight on the package (subtract about ¼ pound from a whole chicken if you're going to discard the neck, liver, and gizzard). Multiply the weight of bone-in poultry by 6 to 7 minutes per pound. Multiply boneless chicken by 4 to 5 minutes per pound. Cover during microwaving, and allow adequate standing time after microwaving for the meat to finish cooking—anywhere from 5 minutes (for a boneless breast) to 15 (for a whole chicken).

In the recipes that follow, I make a point of pairing chicken and other poultry with a wide variety of low-fat ingredients—such as vegetables, fruits, and grains. They lend not only flavor but also vitamins, minerals, and valuable fiber. And I rely on herbs a lot to jazz up these low-fat, low-sodium dishes.

BASIC BASTING

You can enhance the color—and flavor—of skinless poultry by basting it both before and during microwaving. Here are some of my favorite fat-free glazes:

- *Soy-Honey Glaze:* In a small bowl, combine 2 tablespoons soy sauce, 1 tablespoon honey, 1 tablespoon rice wine vinegar, 1 tablespoon apple juice, and ¼ teaspoon dry mustard. Stir until the honey is dissolved. Brush on poultry before and during microwaving.

- *Teriyaki Glaze:* In a small bowl, combine 2 tablespoons molasses, 1 tablespoon teriyaki sauce, and ½ teaspoon ground pepper. Rub into poultry before cooking and brush on the remainder during microwaving.

- *Honey-Mustard Glaze:* In a small bowl, combine 2 tablespoons honey and ¼ teaspoon dry mustard. Brush on hot poultry just before serving.

- *Jelly Glaze:* Place ¼ cup orange marmalade, currant jelly, or apple jelly in a 1-cup glass measure. Microwave on high for 30 to 60 seconds, or until melted. Brush on poultry after half the cooking time has elapsed.

HERB-STUFFED CHICKEN BREASTS WITH SWEET-AND-SOUR SAUCE

4 boneless, skinless chicken breast halves

1 tablespoon finely chopped scallions

1 tablespoon minced fresh parsley

¼ teaspoon ground coriander

⅛ teaspoon ground black pepper

1 can (8 ounces) unsweetened pineapple chunks, with juice

¼ cup chicken stock

2 tablespoons orange marmalade

2 tablespoons tomato paste

2 teaspoons soy sauce

2 teaspoons rice wine vinegar

1 tablespoon cornstarch

1½ cups water

1¼ cups quick-cooking brown rice

½ cup mandarin orange slices, drained

½ cup seedless green grapes, halved

Place each chicken piece between two pieces of wax paper and pound to ¼″ thick with a rubber mallet or meat pounder.

In a small bowl, combine the scallions, parsley, coriander, and pepper. Spread a generous teaspoonful of the mixture over each chicken piece. Fold in the sides and roll up to enclose the filling. Place seam-side down in an 8″ × 8″ baking dish and set aside.

Pour the juice from the pineapple into a 1-quart saucepan. Stir in the stock, marmalade, tomato paste, soy sauce, and vinegar. Add the cornstarch and stir well to dissolve. Cook over medium heat for 3 to 4 minutes, stirring frequently, until the mixture comes to a boil and thickens.

Meanwhile, bring the water to a boil in a 2-quart saucepan over medium heat. Stir in the rice and when the water returns to a boil, reduce the heat to low, cover the pan, and simmer for 10 minutes. Set aside.

Pour the pineapple sauce over the chicken and add the pineapple chunks. Cover with wax paper. Microwave on high for 4 to 5 minutes. Rotate the dish a half turn and microwave on high for 4 to 5 minutes, or until the chicken is no longer opaque. Add the oranges and grapes and baste with the sauce. Microwave on high for 1 minute.

Serve the chicken over the rice with sauce over all.

MAKES 4 SERVINGS.

SLIM YOUR FAVORITE STUFFINGS

Nothing complements poultry better than a hearty homemade stuffing. Unfortunately, most recipes are loaded with fat. Your microwave can help you slash the fat and still serve your family's favorite fillings.

Most stuffing recipes call for onions or other vegetables to be sautéed in butter (often as much as ½ cup). You can eliminate all that fat—not to mention unwanted calories and cholesterol—simply by microwaving the vegetables.

A few general rules: Stuff only poultry that you plan to roast in a conventional oven. Let the stuffing cool completely before placing it inside poultry. And always stuff poultry just before you roast it so bacteria don't have time to multiply. Pack the cavity lightly, allowing space for the stuffing to expand. Place any leftover stuffing in a casserole dish, moisten it with a little extra stock, and cover the dish with foil. Bake it separately.

- *Basic Poultry Stuffing:* Combine 2 cups chopped onions and 2 cups chopped celery in a 2½-quart casserole. Cover with wax paper. Microwave on high for 6 to 8 minutes, or until the vegetables are firm-tender. Stir in 4 cups day-old bread cubes, 2 tablespoons minced fresh parsley, 1 teaspoon dried basil, ½ teaspoon dried sage, ¼ teaspoon paprika, and ⅛ teaspoon grated

nutmeg. Add just enough skim milk (up to ⅓ cup, depending upon the dryness of the bread) to moisten the mixture slightly. Makes about 5 cups (enough for an 18-pound turkey).

- *Sausage Stuffing:* Spread 1 cup (about 8 ounces) low-fat turkey sausage on a plate. Microwave on high for 2 minutes. Break apart lumps and stir well. Microwave on high for 2 to 3 minutes, or until the sausage is thoroughly cooked. Drain off any accumulated fat (you might even want to pat the meat dry with paper towels) before adding to the Basic Poultry Stuffing.

- *Apple and Raisin Stuffing:* Place ½ cup raisins and 1 cup water in a 4-cup glass measure. Microwave on high for 3 minutes, or until the water boils. Let stand for 5 minutes; drain. Add 1 cup diced tart apples and mix well. Microwave on high for 1 minute to slightly soften the apples. Add to the Basic Poultry Stuffing.

- *Onion-Mushroom Stuffing:* Microwave 1 cup sliced mushrooms in a 4-cup glass measure on high for 2 minutes, or until slightly tender. Drain and stir into the Basic Poultry Stuffing.

- *Walnut Stuffing:* Add ½ cup chopped walnuts to the Basic Poultry Stuffing.

SPICY CASHEW CHICKEN

I like this type of stir-fry because I don't have to chop all the vegetables beforehand. I can continue slicing some while others are cooking. You can use leftover cooked spaghetti if you have it on hand.

4 ounces spaghetti
1 onion, thinly sliced
1 carrot, thinly sliced on the diagonal
½ teaspoon sesame oil
¼ teaspoon hot pepper flakes
3 large mushrooms, thinly sliced
1 celery stalk, thinly sliced on the diagonal

1 broccoli stalk
½ sweet red pepper, diced
¼ cup cashews
¼ cup frozen peas
2 boneless, skinless chicken breast halves, cut into thin strips
1 tablespoon fresh lemon juice

1 cup chicken stock
1½ tablespoons soy sauce
1 tablespoon cornstarch
1 clove garlic, minced
1 teaspoon minced fresh coriander (optional)

Snap the spaghetti strands in half. Cook in a large pot of boiling water until just tender, about 10 minutes. Drain, rinse with cold water, and set aside.

In a 3-quart casserole, combine the onions, carrots, oil, and pepper flakes. Microwave on high for 3 minutes.

Add the mushrooms and celery. Microwave on high for 3 minutes.

Peel the broccoli stem and slice it thinly. Cut off the florets and separate them into bite-size pieces. Add the broccoli and peppers to the casserole and microwave on high for 3 minutes. Stir in the cashews and peas. Microwave on high for 1 minute. Cover the dish with foil and set it aside.

In a medium bowl, toss the chicken with the lemon juice. Arrange the chicken in a single layer on a large plate. Cover with wax paper and microwave on high for 3 minutes. Rearrange the chicken so that any uncooked strips are toward the outside of the plate. Cover and microwave on high for 2 minutes, or until the chicken is no longer pink.

In a 1-quart saucepan, combine the stock, soy sauce, cornstarch, and garlic, making sure the cornstarch is thoroughly dissolved. Cook, stirring frequently, over medium heat until the sauce comes to a boil and thickens.

Stir the sauce, spaghetti, coriander (if using), and chicken into the vegetables. Microwave on high for 2 minutes to blend the flavors.

MAKES 4 SERVINGS.

WRAPPED CHICKEN AND VEGETABLES

1 summer squash, julienned
1 carrot, julienned
1 potato, julienned
4 scallions, julienned

Pinch of ground black pepper
4 boneless, skinless chicken breast halves
½ teaspoon paprika

4 teaspoons minced fresh parsley
4 sprigs fresh basil, tarragon, or dill

Tear off four (10" × 14") sheets of parchment. Fold each in half and trim the edges to form a half-moon shape. Open the paper and coat the top side with no-stick spray. Divide the squash, carrots, potatoes, and scallions among the papers, placing them near the crease. Season the vegetables lightly with the pepper.

For each packet, place a chicken piece on top of the vegetables, dust with ⅛ teaspoon paprika, and sprinkle with 1 teaspoon parsley. Top with an herb sprig.

Fold the papers in half and crimp the edges to seal each packet tightly. Arrange the packets in a circle on a plate. Microwave on high for 12 minutes.

MAKES 4 SERVINGS.

STIR-FRIED CHICKEN AND SNOW PEAS

Quick cooking in the microwave lets snow peas retain their vibrant color and taste—as well as their vitamins.

1½ cups water

1¼ cups quick-cooking brown rice

4 boneless, skinless chicken breast halves, cut into bite-size pieces

2 tablespoons lemon juice

1 onion, thinly sliced

1 carrot, thinly sliced on the diagonal

1 clove garlic, minced

½ teaspoon sesame oil

1 celery stalk, thinly sliced on the diagonal

1 cup small cauliflower florets

2 cups snow peas

1 cup chicken stock

1½ teaspoons soy sauce

1 tablespoon cornstarch

In a 2-quart saucepan, bring the water to a boil. Stir in the rice, reduce the heat to low, cover the pan, and simmer for 10 minutes. Keep warm.

In a 3-quart casserole, toss together the chicken and lemon juice. Spread the chicken in as even a layer as possible. Cover and microwave on high for 4 minutes. Rearrange the chicken so any uncooked strips are toward the outside of the dish. Cover and microwave on high for 3 minutes, or until the chicken is no longer pink. Use a slotted spoon to transfer the chicken to a small bowl. Cover and set aside.

To any liquid remaining in the casserole, add the onions, carrots, garlic, and oil; microwave on high for 3 minutes. Add the celery and cauliflower; microwave on high for 3 minutes. Add the snow peas; microwave on high for 4 minutes.

While the vegetables are cooking, combine the stock, soy sauce, and cornstarch in a 1-quart saucepan, making sure the cornstarch is dissolved. Stir over medium heat until the sauce comes to a boil and thickens.

Pour the sauce over the vegetables. Add the chicken. Microwave on high for 3 minutes. Serve over the rice.

MAKES 4 SERVINGS.

CHICKEN BREASTS
WITH HERBED ANGEL HAIR PASTA

A romantic dinner for two: chicken lusciously prepared in parchment and served with aromatic pasta. (Candlelight is optional.) I like to prepare this dish when garden-ripe tomatoes are at their best.

4 large tomato slices
2 tablespoons minced fresh basil
1 clove garlic, minced

2 boneless, skinless chicken breast halves
4 ounces fresh angel hair pasta
1 teaspoon margarine or butter

1 teaspoon minced fresh parsley
Pinch of ground black pepper

Tear off two (10" × 14") sheets of parchment. Fold each in half and trim the edges to form a half-moon shape. Open the paper and coat the top side with no-stick spray. Place two tomato slices, slightly overlapped, near the crease on each piece of paper.

In a small bowl, combine 4 teaspoons of the basil with the garlic. Divide the mixture among the tomato slices. Place one chicken breast half on top of the tomatoes on each wrapper. Fold the papers in half and crimp the edges to seal each packet tightly. Place the packets on a plate. Microwave on high for 6 minutes. Let stand for 2 minutes.

Cook the pasta in a large pot of boiling water until just tender, about 3 minutes for fresh angel hair. Drain and toss with the margarine or butter, parsley, pepper, and the remaining 2 teaspoons basil.

To serve, cut open the packets. Transfer the chicken to dinner plates and serve with the pasta.

MAKES 2 SERVINGS.

BREADED CHICKEN CUTLETS
WITH POLENTA

3½ cups water
1 cup cornmeal
1 tablespoon olive oil
4 boneless, skinless chicken breast halves

1 egg or ¼ cup fat-free egg substitute
2 tablespoons skim milk
¾ cup dry whole-grain breadcrumbs

¼ cup grated Parmesan cheese
1 teaspoon paprika
¼ teaspoon ground black pepper
¼ teaspoon dried marjoram

In a 3-quart casserole, mix the water, cornmeal, and oil until smooth. Microwave on high for 5 minutes. Stir well, then microwave on high for 5 minutes, or until thickened.

Microwave on high, stirring every 2 minutes, until all of the water has been absorbed and the polenta is the consistency of mashed potatoes. (This will take 4 to 6 minutes.)

Pour the polenta into a wet wooden salad bowl or a deep serving dish and smooth the top with a spatula. Cover with foil and let stand for 15 minutes, until set.

Place each chicken piece between two pieces of wax paper and pound to ¼" thick with a rubber mallet or meat pounder.

In a shallow bowl, beat the egg with the milk until completely blended.

On a piece of wax paper, combine the breadcrumbs, Parmesan, paprika, pepper, and marjoram.

Dip each piece of chicken into the egg mixture, then into the crumb mixture, patting the coating in place with your hands.

Arrange the chicken on a large plate with the thickest sections toward the outside and overlapping the thinner sections. Cover with wax paper and microwave on high for 6 minutes. Turn the chicken over and reposition so the less-cooked areas are toward the outside of the plate. Rotate the plate a half turn. Cover and microwave on high for 4 to 6 minutes, or until the chicken is no longer pink. Cover and let stand for 5 minutes.

Turn the polenta out onto a serving platter (the wet bowl makes this step easier). Cut into slices or wedges and serve with the chicken.

MAKES 4 SERVINGS.

Variation: For Chicken Cutlets with Tomato Sauce and Cheese, *spoon 2 to 3 tablespoons tomato sauce onto each cutlet. Top each with 1 ounce thinly sliced mozzarella cheese. Microwave on medium (50% power) for 2 to 3 minutes, until the sauce is hot and the cheese is melted. Serve with spaghetti topped with tomato sauce.*

TORTILLA CASSEROLE

2 boneless, skinless chicken breast halves

4 flour tortillas

4 scallions, finely chopped

1 cup Super Salsa (page 59)

¼ cup shredded reduced-fat Cheddar cheese

Place the breasts side by side on a microwave-safe plate with the thicker areas facing out. Cover with wax paper and microwave on high for 3 minutes. The breasts should be done, but if they still have pink areas, flip the pieces, rotate the plate a half turn, and microwave on high for 1 minute.

Cover with foil and let stand for 5 minutes. When the chicken is cool enough to handle, shred it with your fingers.

Divide the chicken among the tortillas. Sprinkle with the scallions. Top each with about 2 tablespoons of the salsa. Roll up the tortillas and place in a 7″ × 11″ baking dish. Top with the remaining salsa.

Microwave on high for 3 minutes. Sprinkle with the Cheddar. Microwave on medium (50% power) for 2 to 3 minutes, or until the cheese is melted.

MAKES 2 SERVINGS.

ORIENTAL CHICKEN SALAD

*Although excellent as a chilled salad, this dish
may also be served hot over rice.*

2 boneless, skinless chicken
breast halves

1 medium red onion, thinly
sliced

1 carrot, julienned

1 jalapeño pepper, minced
(wear plastic gloves when
handling)

8 ounces sugar snap peas or
snow peas

1½ cups sliced mushrooms

¼ cup diced sweet red peppers

½ cup sliced water chestnuts

1 teaspoon minced fresh coriander (optional)

½ cup chicken stock

2 tablespoons peanut butter

1 tablespoon soy sauce

1 tablespoon canola oil

1 tablespoon lemon juice

1 tablespoon grated fresh
ginger

1 clove garlic, minced

Pinch of ground red pepper

Place the chicken between two sheets of wax paper and pound with a rubber mallet or meat pounder to an even ¼″ thickness. Remove the paper and transfer the chicken to a large plate. Cover with wax paper and microwave on high for 4 to 5 minutes, or until the chicken is no longer pink. Set aside.

In a 2½-quart casserole, combine the onions, carrots, and jalapeños. Cover with wax paper and microwave on high for 4 minutes, or until the onions are translucent.

Add the peas, mushrooms, and red peppers. Cover with wax paper and microwave on high for 3 minutes, or until the peas are crisp-tender. Allow to cool.

Cut the chicken into thin strips. Add to the vegetable mixture. Stir in the water chestnuts and coriander (if using).

Place the stock in a 2-cup glass measure and microwave on high for 3 minutes. Stir in the peanut butter, soy sauce, oil, lemon juice, ginger, garlic, and ground pepper. Microwave on high for 1 minute, or until heated through. Pour over the salad. Toss well and chill.

MAKES 4 SERVINGS.

Variation: To serve this salad as a hot entrée, after adding the dressing, cover the casserole with wax paper, and microwave on high for 2 to 3 minutes, or until heated through. Serve over hot rice.

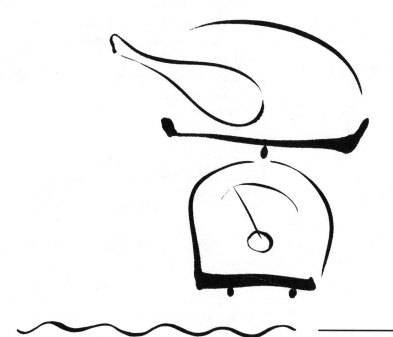

WHITE MEAT IN A FLASH

Want cooked chicken for a picnic salad? Does a casserole recipe require cooked chicken, but you don't have leftovers? Hankering for a chicken sandwich?

Microwaving can give you the cooked chicken breasts you need in minutes. Cut one whole boneless, skinless chicken breast (about 1 pound) in half and rinse it with cold water. Remove any visible fat and gristle.

Place the breast halves side by side on a plate with the thicker areas facing out. Cover with wax paper. Microwave on high for 2 minutes. Rotate the plate a half turn, cover, and microwave on high for 2 to 3 minutes, or until the juices run clear when the flesh is pierced with a fork. Cover the pieces with foil and allow to stand for 5 minutes.

Use cooked chicken as a quick stuffing for tacos, enchiladas, burritos, or pita pockets. Or use it in pasta salads and Italian-style casseroles. You'll be getting excellent protein and next to no fat.

FRY-STYLE CHICKEN
WITH POTATO DUMPLINGS

CHICKEN
- 1 broiler/fryer chicken (3–4 pounds), cut into serving pieces
- ¼ cup skim milk
- ½ cup whole wheat flour
- 1 egg or ¼ cup fat-free egg substitute
- 1 tablespoon canola oil

- 2 cups corn flakes
- ⅓ cup grated Parmesan cheese
- 2 tablespoons ground almonds
- ½ teaspoon paprika
- ½ teaspoon ground black pepper

DUMPLINGS
- 1 cup unbleached flour

- 1 cup cold mashed potatoes
- 1 egg, beaten, or ¼ cup fat-free egg substitute
- 1 tablespoon farina
- 2 tablespoons minced fresh parsley
- 1 teaspoon margarine or butter

To make the chicken: Remove and discard the skin from the chicken. Place the milk in a shallow dish and dip the chicken into it. Dredge the pieces in the flour. Set aside.

Discard all but 1 tablespoon of the milk. Using a fork, beat in the egg and oil.

Place the corn flakes, Parmesan, almonds, paprika, and pepper in a small paper bag. With a rolling pin or by hand, crush the bag to crumble the corn flakes. Shake well. Pour the crumbs into a glass pie plate.

Dip the chicken pieces in the egg mixture, then in the crumbs, turning to coat thoroughly. Arrange the chicken in a shallow oval or 10″ round baking dish with the thickest portions facing the outside of the dish. Cover with paper towels. Microwave on high for 10 to 12 minutes. Rotate the dish a half turn. Microwave on high for 10 to 12 minutes. Rotate the dish again. Microwave on medium (50% power) for 5 minutes, or until the juices run clear when the chicken is pierced with a fork. Cover with foil and let stand for 5 minutes.

To make the dumplings: While the chicken is cooking, bring a large pot of water to a boil.

In a medium bowl, mix the flour, potatoes, egg, and farina until well blended. Take a pinch of the dough and drop it into the boiling water. If it falls apart, beat a little more flour into the potato mixture.

Roll small amounts of dough into finger-size pieces. Drop them in the boiling water and cook for 10 to 15 minutes, or until the dumplings rise to the surface. Remove from the water with a slotted spoon, rinse lightly under warm tap water, and place in a warmed serving bowl. Toss with the parsley and margarine or butter. Serve with the chicken.

MAKES 4 SERVINGS.

CHICKEN WITH BARLEY

1 broiler/fryer chicken (2½–3 pounds)
Paprika
Ground black pepper
2 whole cloves

1 small onion
1½ cups quick-cooking barley
1 cup tomato sauce
1 cup chicken stock

1 cup sliced mushrooms
¼ cup minced onions
½ teaspoon dried marjoram
¼ teaspoon dried thyme

Remove and discard the skin and any visible fat from the chicken. Dust the chicken with paprika and sprinkle the cavity with pepper. Stick the cloves into the onion and place it in the cavity. Tie the legs together with string.

In a 3-quart casserole, combine the barley, tomato sauce, stock, mushrooms, minced onions, marjoram, and thyme. Place the chicken on top. Cover with a lid (use a domed lid if necessary). Microwave on high for 25 to 30 minutes, rotating the dish and stirring the vegetables twice during this time, until the juices run clear when you pierce a thigh with a fork. Let stand for 10 minutes.

Remove the onion from the chicken cavity and discard it. Carve the chicken into serving pieces. Serve with the vegetables.

MAKES 4 SERVINGS.

HONEY-MARINATED CHICKEN WITH PENNE AND VEGETABLES

In this dish, vegetables are quick-cooked with pasta to save both time and nutrients. For best flavor, marinate the chicken for several hours.

¼ cup soy sauce

¼ cup apple juice or pineapple juice

¼ cup rice wine vinegar

3 tablespoons honey

2 cloves garlic, minced

½ teaspoon ground ginger

3 pounds chicken pieces, skin removed

1 carrot

1½ cups penne pasta

½ cup frozen peas, thawed

1 tablespoon minced fresh parsley

1 teaspoon margarine or butter

In a 3-quart casserole, mix the soy sauce, apple juice or pineapple juice, vinegar, honey, garlic, and ginger.

Add the chicken pieces to the dish and turn to coat them on all sides with the sauce. Cover and refrigerate for at least 2 hours.

Remove the chicken and discard the marinade. Arrange the pieces in a 7" × 11" baking dish with the thickest parts facing the outside of the dish. Cover with wax paper. Microwave on high for 20 to 25 minutes, rotating the dish twice during this time and rearranging the pieces so the less cooked portions are toward the outside of the dish. The chicken should be tender and the juices should run clear when the chicken is pierced with a fork. Cover with foil and let stand for 5 minutes.

Using a vegetable peeler, pare very long thin ribbons from the carrot. Set aside.

Cook the pasta in a large pot of boiling water for 6 minutes. Add the carrots and peas to the water. Cook for another 2 minutes, or until the pasta is just tender. Drain and place in a large bowl. Toss with the parsley and margarine or butter. Serve with the chicken.

MAKES 4 SERVINGS.

CHICKEN 'N' CHILI

Chili-simmered chicken breasts, legs, and thighs add an interesting twist to a Mexican-style dinner.

1 carrot, shredded
½ cup finely chopped onions
½ cup diced green peppers
1 clove garlic, minced
1¾ cups canned whole tomatoes, with juice
1½ cups cooked kidney beans

1 cup tomato sauce
1 cup corn
1 tablespoon chili powder
1 teaspoon ground cumin
¼ teaspoon dry mustard
¼ teaspoon ground black pepper

1 broiler/fryer chicken (3½–4 pounds), cut into serving pieces
1½ cups chicken stock
1¼ cups quick-cooking brown rice

In a 2½-quart casserole, combine the carrots, onions, green peppers, and garlic. Microwave on high for 3 minutes.

Add the tomatoes and juice, breaking the tomatoes apart with a wooden spoon. Add the beans, tomato sauce, corn, chili powder, cumin, mustard, and black pepper. Stir well to combine.

Remove and discard the skin from the chicken pieces. Place the pieces over the vegetables. Spoon some of the sauce over the pieces.

Cover with wax paper. Microwave on high for 20 minutes. Stir the vegetables and rearrange the chicken. Rotate the dish a half turn. Cover and microwave on high for 15 minutes, or until the chicken is tender and the juices run clear when the chicken is pierced with a fork. Let stand for 5 minutes.

While the chicken is cooking, bring the stock to a boil in a 2-quart saucepan. Stir in the rice, reduce the heat to low, cover the pan, and simmer for 10 minutes.

Serve the chicken over the rice.

MAKES 4 TO 6 SERVINGS.

95

CHICKEN AND VEGETABLES WITH TARRAGON

2 cups chicken stock
½ cup wild rice
½ cup short-grain brown rice
1 broiler/fryer chicken (3½–4 pounds)
2 teaspoons soy sauce

¼ teaspoon ground black pepper
1 tablespoon fresh tarragon or 1 teaspoon dried tarragon
1 carrot, cut into 3 pieces
1 small onion, quartered

1 celery stalk
3 mushrooms, halved
¾ teaspoon paprika
1 tablespoon cornstarch
½ cup beef stock

In a 2-quart saucepan over medium heat, bring the chicken stock, wild rice, and brown rice to a boil. Reduce the heat to low, cover the pan, and simmer for 45 minutes. Let stand, covered, until ready to serve.

While the rice is cooking, remove and discard the skin and any visible fat from the chicken. Rub the flesh with the soy sauce, pepper, and half of the tarragon. Place the chicken, breast-side up, in a 10″ round baking dish. Arrange the carrots, onions, celery, and mushrooms around the chicken. Cover with wax paper and microwave on high for 15 minutes.

Brush the chicken with the pan juices. Turn the chicken over. Cover with wax paper and microwave on high for 15 minutes, or until the juices run clear when you pierce a thigh with a fork.

Turn the chicken breast-side up and sprinkle with the paprika. Transfer to a warm serving platter and cover with foil. Let stand for 10 to 15 minutes.

Strain the vegetables and juices through a sieve into a 2-cup glass measure. Discard the vegetables.

In a cup, dissolve the cornstarch in the beef stock. Add to the glass measure. Microwave on high for 2 to 3 minutes, or until the sauce boils and thickens slightly. Season with the remaining tarragon.

Arrange the rice around the chicken on the serving platter. Serve the sauce separately.

MAKES 4 SERVINGS.

DIJON CHICKEN WITH SCALLIONS

Serve with a yellow vegetable and a simple salad.

1½ cups chicken stock

1¼ cups quick-cooking brown rice

4 scallions, thinly sliced

½ teaspoon olive oil

1 clove garlic, minced

¼ cup Dijon mustard

2 tablespoons nonalcoholic white wine or white grape juice

1 tablespoon lemon juice

1 teaspoon minced fresh tarragon or ¼ teaspoon dried tarragon

¼ teaspoon ground black pepper

4 boneless, skinless chicken breast halves

In a 2-quart saucepan, bring the stock to a boil. Stir in the rice and half of the scallions. Reduce the heat to low, cover the pan, and simmer for 10 minutes. Keep warm.

Combine the oil, garlic, and remaining scallions in a 10″ glass pie plate. Microwave on high for 2 minutes. Stir in the mustard, wine or grape juice, lemon juice, tarragon, and pepper.

Place the chicken in the sauce, turning the pieces to coat both sides. Arrange the pieces toward the outside of the dish and cover with wax paper. Microwave on high for 3 minutes.

Turn the chicken over and baste with the sauce. Cover with wax paper and microwave on high for 3 to 5 minutes, or until the chicken is no longer pink. Cover and let stand for 5 minutes.

Serve the chicken on the rice with sauce over all.

MAKES 4 SERVINGS.

TURKEY CUTLETS
WITH COUSCOUS RATATOUILLE

*A hybrid of Mediterranean and Middle
Eastern flavors.*

1 onion, thinly sliced

1 small eggplant, cubed

3 cloves garlic, minced

1 teaspoon olive oil

1 sweet red pepper, thinly sliced

1 medium zucchini, halved lengthwise and thinly sliced

3½ cups coarsely chopped canned tomatoes, with juice

¾ cup couscous

½ cup chicken stock

2 teaspoons minced fresh parsley

1 teaspoon minced fresh basil or ½ teaspoon dried basil

½ teaspoon fresh oregano or ¼ teaspoon dried oregano

¼ cup sliced black olives

½ teaspoon ground black pepper

4 turkey breast cutlets

½ lemon

Pinch of paprika

In a 2½-quart casserole, combine the onions, eggplant, garlic, and oil. Cover with a lid and microwave on high for 4 minutes. Add the red peppers and zucchini. Cover and microwave on high for 3 minutes.

Stir in the tomatoes and juice, couscous, stock, parsley, basil, oregano, olives, and black pepper. Cover and microwave on high for 5 minutes. Remove from the microwave and keep warm.

Place each turkey piece between two pieces of wax paper and pound to ¼" thick with a rubber mallet or meat pounder. Arrange the turkey in a shallow 7" × 11" baking dish. Cover with wax paper and microwave on high for 3 minutes.

Rearrange the pieces so the uncooked portions face toward the outside of the dish. Squeeze lemon juice over all, sprinkle with paprika, cover, and microwave on high for 3 to 4 minutes, or until the turkey is no longer pink.

Serve the turkey with the couscous ratatouille.

MAKES 4 SERVINGS.

ORANGE CHICKEN WITH SAVORY PILAF

4 chicken breast halves
¼ cup orange juice
¼ cup grated onions
1 teaspoon grated orange rind
½ teaspoon ground cinnamon
¼ teaspoon ground allspice
¼ teaspoon sherry extract

⅛ teaspoon ground red pepper
1 bay leaf
1 teaspoon margarine or butter
2 tablespoons minced onions
2 tablespoons minced celery
¼ cup shredded carrots

¼ cup raisins
¾ cup long-grain brown rice
¼ cup wild rice
2 cups chicken stock
   Orange slices (garnish)
   Parsley sprigs (garnish)

Remove and discard the skin from the chicken. Place the pieces, bone-side up, in a shallow 2-quart casserole.

In a 1-cup glass measure, combine the orange juice, grated onions, orange rind, cinnamon, allspice, sherry extract, red pepper, and bay leaf. Pour over the chicken. Cover and refrigerate for at least 4 hours.

One hour before serving, melt the margarine or butter in a 2-quart saucepan over medium heat. Stir in the minced onions and celery. Cook until the onions are translucent, about 5 minutes. Stir in the carrots, raisins, brown rice, and wild rice.

Add the stock and bring to a boil over medium-high heat. Reduce the heat to low, cover the pan, and cook for 45 minutes, or until all of the liquid has been absorbed. Let stand, covered, until ready to serve.

About 30 minutes before serving, drain the chicken and discard the marinade (including the bay leaf). Turn the chicken pieces meat-side up and cover with wax paper. Microwave on high for 8 to 15 minutes, rotating the dish twice during this time, until the meat is no longer pink and the juices run clear when the chicken is pierced with a fork. Cover with foil and let stand for 15 minutes.

Fluff the rice and serve with the chicken. Garnish with the orange slices and parsley.

MAKES 4 SERVINGS.

GRILLED TURKEY BREAST WITH CORN ON THE COB

Make an entire turkey breast on the grill in just minutes by precooking it in the microwave. You can even microwave the corn accompaniment.

1 bone-in turkey breast (4½–5 pounds)

8 ears corn, unhusked

Place the turkey breast, skin-side down, in a 7″ × 11″ baking dish. Cover with wax paper and microwave on high for 9 minutes. Turn the breast so it rests on one side. Cover and microwave on medium (50% power) for 15 minutes.

Turn the breast on the other side, cover, and microwave on medium (50% power) for 15 minutes. Turn the turkey skin-side up, cover, and microwave on medium (50% power) for 15 minutes.

Transfer the turkey to a hot grill. Barbecue for 20 to 30 minutes, or until the skin is brown and the juices run clear when the turkey is pierced with a fork.

While the turkey is on the grill, place the ears of corn side by side on the floor of the microwave. Microwave on high for 7 to 10 minutes. Move the center ears to the outside and rotate all the ears so the top half is now facing down. Microwave on high for 8 to 10 minutes, or until the corn is tender.

Using a clean kitchen towel to hold the corn, pull away the husks and tassels. Break off the stem if still attached. Keep the corn warm in a tent of aluminum foil until the turkey is ready to serve.

Serve the corn with the turkey.

MAKES 8 SERVINGS.

Note: If it is necessary to reheat the corn, cover the ears with wax paper and microwave on high for 2 to 3 minutes.

100

SIMPLIFY BARBECUING

Precooking poultry in the microwave cuts down on grilling time and helps avoid those unpleasant instances where the meat is charred outside but undercooked inside. For best results, make sure your coals will be hot when the chicken comes out of the microwave. Here's how to get tender, juicy barbecued chicken in a minimum of time. (The amounts given will serve four.)

Chicken pieces. Cut a 3- to 4-pound broiler/fryer into serving pieces and remove any visible fat. In a 9″ × 13″ baking dish, arrange the pieces with the thickest, meatiest portions toward the outside of the dish. Cover with wax paper. Microwave on high for 5 minutes. Turn and rearrange the pieces to ensure even cooking. Microwave on high for 5 minutes. Transfer to a hot grill. Baste with Barbecue Sauce (page 61). Grill for 15 to 20 minutes, or until the juices run clear when you pierce the thickest areas of the pieces with a fork.

Whole chicken. Remove excess fat from the cavity of a 3- to 4-pound chicken. Tie the legs and fold the wings behind the back. Place the chicken, breast-side down, in a 9″ × 13″ baking dish. Microwave on high for 5 minutes. Then microwave on medium (50% power) for 5 minutes.

Turn the chicken so the breast faces up. Microwave on medium (50% power) for 10 minutes. Transfer the chicken to a foil roasting pan and place it on a hot grill. Cover the grill and cook about 20 to 25 minutes, or until the juices run clear when you pierce the thickest part of a thigh with a fork.

101

RASPBERRY-GLAZED CORNISH HENS WITH PECAN WILD RICE

For special treats, or for the holidays when a turkey seems too much, serve Cornish hens with a delicious side dish of pecans, wild rice, and brown rice.

2 cups chicken stock
¾ cup long-grain brown rice
¼ cup wild rice
¼ cup coarsely chopped pecans
¼ cup minced onions

¼ teaspoon dried tarragon
2 Cornish hens (about 1½ pounds each)
⅓ cup seedless raspberry preserves

1 tablespoon grated orange rind
2 teaspoons lemon juice
1 tablespoon minced fresh parsley
Orange slices (garnish)

In a 2-quart saucepan over medium heat, bring the stock, brown rice, wild rice, pecans, onions, and tarragon to a boil. Reduce the heat to very low and cover the pan tightly. Simmer for 40 minutes, or until the stock has been absorbed. Let stand, covered, until ready to serve.

While the rice is cooking, remove and discard the skin and any visible fat from the hens. Split the hens in half lengthwise. Arrange them, bone-side down, in a shallow 10″ round baking dish, with the thickest portions facing the outside of the dish.

In a small bowl, combine the preserves, orange rind, and lemon juice. Brush the glaze over the hens. Cover with wax paper.

When the rice has cooked for 20 minutes, microwave the hens on high for 10 minutes. Rotate the dish and rearrange the pieces if they appear to be cooking unevenly. Microwave on high for 8 to 10 minutes, or until the juices run clear when you pierce a thigh with a fork. Cover with foil and let stand for 5 minutes.

Toss the parsley with the rice. Serve the hens with the rice. Garnish them with the orange slices.

MAKES 4 SERVINGS.

ROAST CHICKEN WITH VEGETABLES

This dish was a regular favorite at my grand-mother's Pennsylvania Dutch farm. She claimed long roasting gave the vegetables their delicious flavor. I've found that microwaving yields the same succulent meal in less than half the time it took my grandmother.

1 broiler/fryer chicken (about 4 pounds)
6 potatoes, quartered
4 carrots, quartered

2 celery stalks, halved
1 onion, quartered
1½ cups chicken stock

½ teaspoon flour
½ teaspoon paprika
¼ teaspoon ground black pepper

Remove and discard all skin from the chicken, except for that on the wings. Remove and discard all visible fat. Fold the wings back and tie the legs together with string.

In a 3-quart casserole, combine the potatoes, carrots, celery, and onions. Add the stock. Place the chicken, breast-side up, on top of the vegetables. Cover with wax paper and microwave on high for 20 minutes.

Carefully turn the chicken over. Stir the vegetables. Cover and microwave on high for 15 minutes.

Turn the chicken breast-side up. Stir the vegetables.

In a small bowl, combine the flour, paprika, and pepper. Sprinkle over the chicken. Cover and microwave on high for 10 minutes, or until the juices run clear when a thigh is pierced with a fork. Cover with foil and let stand for 10 to 15 minutes.

MAKES 4 SERVINGS.

TURKEY BOLOGNESE SAUCE AND LINGUINE

8 ounces ground turkey
1 carrot, halved
1 small onion, quartered
2 cups tomato sauce

1 clove garlic, minced
¼ teaspoon dried marjoram
¼ teaspoon dried basil
¼ teaspoon dried oregano

¼ teaspoon ground black pepper
1 pound linguine

Place the turkey in a 7″ × 11″ baking dish. Microwave on high for 3 to 4 minutes, or until the turkey is no longer pink. Stir to break up lumps. Transfer the meat to a sieve to drain off any fat.

Using a food processor, finely chop the carrots and onions using on/off turns. Add to the baking dish used for the turkey. Microwave on high for 3 minutes. Stir in the turkey, tomato sauce, garlic, marjoram, basil, oregano, and pepper. Cover with wax paper and microwave on high for 4 minutes.

Cook the linguine in a large pot of boiling water until just tender, about 10 minutes. Drain and serve with the turkey sauce.

MAKES 4 SERVINGS.

TURKEY PICADILLO

1 onion, chopped
1 green pepper, chopped
1 clove garlic, minced
1 teaspoon olive oil
1 pound ground turkey
1½ cups water
1¼ cups quick-cooking brown rice

¼ cup tomato paste
½ cup chicken stock
1 tablespoon soy sauce
1 tablespoon red wine vinegar
½ teaspoon sherry extract
½ teaspoon ground cumin
½ teaspoon dried oregano

½ teaspoon ground black pepper
⅛ teaspoon ground cinnamon
½ cup raisins
⅓ cup slivered almonds
2 tablespoons minced pimento-stuffed olives

In a 2-quart casserole, combine the onions, peppers, garlic, and oil. Microwave on high for 4 minutes. Stir in the turkey. Microwave on high for 2 minutes. Stir to break up lumps. Microwave on high for 3 minutes, or until the turkey is no longer pink.

While the turkey is cooking, bring the water to a boil in a 2-quart saucepan over medium heat. Stir in the rice, reduce the heat to low, cover the pan, and simmer for 10 minutes. Keep warm.

To the turkey, add the tomato paste, stock, soy sauce, vinegar, sherry extract, cumin, oregano, pepper, and cinnamon. Microwave on high for 6 minutes.

Stir in the raisins, almonds, and olives. Microwave on high for 3 to 5 minutes, or until the sauce thickens. Serve over the rice.

MAKES 4 SERVINGS.

CALIFORNIA AVOCADO
AND TURKEY MELT

1 thick slice (1″) whole-grain bread, toasted

3 ounces sliced cooked turkey breast

1 thick slice tomato

1 ounce Muenster cheese

2 thin slices avocado

1 tablespoon Super Salsa (page 59)

Place the bread on a serving plate. Arrange the turkey on the bread and top it with the tomato and Muenster.

Microwave on high for 1 minute, or until the cheese is melted and the turkey is heated through. Top with the avocado and salsa.

MAKES 1 SERVING.

MEXICAN TURKEY SCRAMBLE

This makes a nice lunch or light supper.

1 package (10 ounces) frozen chopped spinach

1 pound ground turkey

4 scallions, chopped

½ sweet red pepper, diced

1 can (4 ounces) sliced mushrooms, drained

1 clove garlic, minced

½ teaspoon ground black pepper

½ teaspoon chili powder

¼ teaspoon dried oregano

5 eggs or 1¼ cups fat-free egg substitute

2 tablespoons skim milk

2 soft corn tortillas, cut into 8 wedges each

1 cup Super Salsa (page 59)

Place the spinach in a 9″ pie plate. Microwave on high for 2 minutes. Rotate the dish a half turn. Microwave on high for 2 to 4 minutes, or until defrosted. Transfer the spinach to a sieve and drain well, pressing with the back of a spoon to remove all excess moisture. Set aside.

Place the turkey in a 7″ × 11″ baking dish. Microwave on high for 3 to 4 minutes, or until the turkey is no longer pink. Stir to break up lumps. Drain off any fat. Stir in the spinach, scallions, red peppers, mushrooms, garlic, black pepper, chili powder, and oregano. Microwave on high for 4 minutes.

In a medium bowl, lightly beat the eggs with the milk. Stir into the turkey mixture. Add the tortillas. Microwave on high for 3 minutes. Stir, pushing the cooked eggs toward the center of the dish. Microwave on high for 3 to 4 minutes, or until the eggs are set.

Place the salsa in a small bowl and microwave it on high for 1 to 2 minutes. Spoon over the eggs.

MAKES 4 SERVINGS.

TURKEY MEAT LOAF
WITH SAUCY SCALLION NOODLES

1½ pounds ground turkey

1 egg or ¼ cup fat-free egg substitute

1 onion, chopped

1 small green pepper, chopped

2 slices whole wheat bread, crumbled

½ teaspoon dried marjoram

¼ teaspoon dried basil

¼ teaspoon dried oregano

¼ teaspoon ground black pepper

⅛ teaspoon dried thyme

1¼ cups tomato sauce

12 ounces (6 cups) broad noodles

4 scallions, thinly sliced

In large bowl, combine the turkey, egg, onions, green peppers, bread, marjoram, basil, oregano, black pepper, and thyme. Stir in ½ cup of the tomato sauce. Mix well.

Pack the mixture into a round 2-quart casserole. Microwave on high for 10 to 12 minutes, or until the meat loaf begins pulling away from the sides of the dish and the loaf has reached an internal temperature of 160°.

While the meat loaf is cooking, cook the noodles in a large pot of boiling water for 5 minutes. Stir in the scallions. Continue cooking until the noodles are just tender, about 4 minutes. Drain. Place in a large bowl. Toss with ¼ cup of the remaining tomato sauce. Set aside and keep warm.

When the meat loaf is ready, pour off any juices. Spoon the remaining ½ cup tomato sauce over the meat loaf and microwave on high for 2 minutes. If necessary, reheat the noodles by microwaving them on medium (50% power) for 1 minute.

MAKES 4 SERVINGS.

ITALIAN-STYLE TURKEY RIGATONI WITH MOZZARELLA

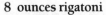

8 ounces rigatoni

1 small onion, quartered

1 small carrot, quartered

1 clove garlic

4 tomatoes, peeled, seeded, and chopped

1 cup sliced mushrooms

⅔ cup tomato paste

½ teaspoon dried basil

½ teaspoon dried marjoram

¼ teaspoon dried oregano

1 pound ground turkey

1 egg white

2 tablespoons grated Parmesan cheese

2 tablespoons dry breadcrumbs

2 tablespoons skim milk

¼ teaspoon paprika

¼ teaspoon ground black pepper

½ cup shredded part-skim mozzarella cheese

Cook the rigatoni in a large pot of boiling water until just tender, about 10 minutes. Drain, rinse with warm water, and set aside.

In a food processor or blender container, combine the onions, carrots, and garlic. Process until finely chopped. Place the mixture in a 2-quart casserole. Microwave on high for 3 minutes.

Stir in the tomatoes, mushrooms, tomato paste, basil, marjoram, and oregano. Cover with a lid and microwave on high for 10 minutes. Stir. Cover and microwave on high for 8 minutes. Set aside, covered.

In a large bowl, mix the turkey, egg white, Parmesan, breadcrumbs, milk, paprika, and pepper. Shape into 18 meatballs, each about 1½" in diameter. Place in a shallow 7" × 11" baking dish. Cover with wax paper. Microwave on high for 3 minutes. Rearrange and turn the meatballs, moving the least cooked ones toward the outside of the dish. Cover and microwave on high for 3 minutes, or until the turkey is no longer pink. Drain off any fat.

Add the rigatoni and sauce to the dish. Combine well. Microwave on high for 2 minutes. Top with the mozzarella. Microwave on medium (50% power) for 2 to 3 minutes, or until the cheese is melted.

MAKES 6 SERVINGS.

TURKEY TOSTADAS

A quick and easy one-dish meal.

TURKEY
- 1 pound ground turkey
- 2 cups tomato sauce
- ½ cup finely chopped onions
- ¼ cup diced canned green chili peppers
- 1 teaspoon ground cumin
- 1 teaspoon chili powder

GUACAMOLE
- 1 large avocado
- 1 tablespoon lime juice
- 1 clove garlic, minced
- ½ teaspoon minced fresh coriander (optional)

TOSTADAS
- 4 large corn tortillas
- ½ head iceberg lettuce, shredded
- 2 medium tomatoes, chopped
- ¾ cup shredded reduced-fat Cheddar cheese
- 1 cup Super Salsa (page 59)

To make the turkey: Place the turkey in a 2-quart casserole and microwave on high for 2 to 3 minutes. Break up the clumps and microwave on high for 1 to 2 minutes, or until the turkey is no longer pink. Drain off any fat.

Stir in the tomato sauce, onions, peppers, cumin, and chili powder. Microwave on high for 4 to 5 minutes.

To make the guacamole: Peel and seed the avocado. Place the flesh in a medium bowl and mash with a fork. Stir in the lime juice, garlic, and coriander (if using).

To make the tostadas: Place the tortillas on individual plates. Top each with one-fourth of the turkey mixture. Sprinkle each with lettuce, tomatoes, and Cheddar. Top with the salsa and a dollop of the guacamole.

MAKES 4 SERVINGS.

Note: Leftover guacamole is excellent for tacos, enchiladas, and other Mexican dishes.

*T*REASURES FROM THE DEEP

*M*icrowave cooking is a perfect match for fish and seafood. The high moisture content of these foods and the microwave's fast cooking times marry to produce flavorful, juicy results. In fact, cooking times are often so brief that it becomes a challenge to find suitably quick-cooking accompaniments!

By microwaving fish and other seafood, you can:

- *Retain fresh, delicious flavors, eliminating the need for salt and other high-sodium seasonings.*
- *Maintain the healthy, low-fat advantage of these foods because microwaving requires no added fat.*

○ Have fresh, vitamin- and mineral-rich meals in less time than it takes to defrost and heat a TV dinner.

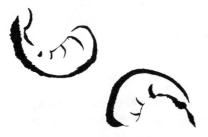

FISHING FOR HEALTH

Your health will certainly benefit from adding more fish to your diet. Seafood is generally low in fat and calories. Although some shellfish contain significant amounts of cholesterol, they're extra low in saturated fat. And many doctors say that saturated fat is far more likely to cause heart disease than cholesterol alone.

Studies have also shown that the omega-3 fatty acids present in many fish can help prevent abnormal blood clots, which could lead to heart attacks or strokes. And high potassium and low sodium levels earn many fish excellent marks for keeping blood pressure within healthy bounds.

Because microwaving fish does not dry it out or subject it to searing heat, both nutrients and flavor are maintained. This means, in part, that you don't need to add salt to bring out flavor: Lemon juice, herbs, or finely chopped vegetables will do the trick!

Microwaved fish just will not stick to cooking dishes, so no added fat is necessary. That means you can reap the benefits of healthful fish oils without counteracting their contributions by using butter or other saturated fats.

Best of all from a cook's point of view, you'll be able to have an entire dinner on the table in 15 minutes or less. And the attractive combinations of fish and pasta, rice, or other accompaniments are sure to pick up your spirits as well as tempt your palate. Prepackaged frozen dinners just can't compete with the freshness, nutrition, and versatility that are yours when you get hooked on microwaving fish.

By the way, many of the fish recipes that follow would work equally well with chicken breasts. A general guideline that I've come up with is that you can replace whole fish fillets with an equal weight of boneless, skinless chicken breasts. Microwaving times for the chicken will be a minute or two longer per pound.

CANCÚN COD
WITH CORIANDER RICE

*For a less spicy dish, reduce the amount of
jalapeño peppers.*

2 tablespoons lime juice

¼ teaspoon ground black
  pepper

2 teaspoons canola oil

4 cod fillets (6 ounces each)

1½ cups chicken stock

1¼ cups quick-cooking brown
  rice

1 tablespoon minced scallions

1 tablespoon minced fresh
  coriander

1 teaspoon minced garlic

1 teaspoon minced jalapeño
  peppers (wear plastic gloves
  when handling)

½ teaspoon ground cumin

½ cup finely chopped onions

½ cup diced sweet red or yellow peppers

3 tablespoons minced fresh
  parsley

Combine the lime juice, black pepper, and 1 teaspoon of the oil in a 9″ glass pie plate. Add the fish and
turn to coat with the marinade. Arrange the fish so the
thickest portions are toward the outside of the dish. Cover
and set aside to marinate for 15 minutes.

In a 2-quart saucepan over medium heat, bring the stock to
a boil. Stir in the rice, reduce the heat to low, cover the pan,
and simmer for 10 minutes. Toss with the scallions and
coriander. Keep warm.

While the rice is cooking, mix the garlic, jalapeños, and
cumin with the remaining 1 teaspoon oil in a 4-cup glass
measure. Microwave on high for 1 minute. Stir in the
onions and red peppers or yellow peppers. Cover with wax
paper and microwave on high for 1 minute. Stir and
microwave on high for 1 minute, or until the peppers are
crisp-tender.

Spoon the peppers over the fish. Cover with wax paper and
microwave on high for 3 minutes. Rotate the dish a half
turn and microwave on high for 2 to 3 minutes, or until the
thickest part of the fish is opaque throughout. Sprinkle
with the parsley and serve with the rice.

MAKES 4 SERVINGS.

HADDOCK AND SHRIMP STIR-FRY

A tasty and colorful one-dish meal. It's also a great way to use leftover cooked pasta. For convenience, you can begin cooking some of the ingredients as you chop the remaining ones.

1 small onion, thinly sliced	
½ teaspoon canola oil	
3 carrots, thinly sliced	
1 large broccoli stalk	
¼ small head cauliflower, coarsely chopped	
8–10 scallions, halved lengthwise and cut into 2½" pieces	

12 ounces haddock fillets
2 tablespoons lemon juice
Pinch of ground red pepper
4 ounces medium shrimp, peeled, deveined, and halved lengthwise
½ cup chicken stock

½ cup pineapple juice
1 tablespoon soy sauce
1 tablespoon cornstarch
1½ cups cooked spaghetti or linguine

In a 2½-quart casserole, combine the onions and oil. Microwave on high for 2 minutes. Add the carrots and microwave on high for 3 minutes.

Cut the florets from the broccoli stem and separate them into bite-size pieces. Peel the stem and thinly slice it. Add the broccoli, cauliflower, and scallions to the casserole. Microwave on high for 4 minutes. Cover and set aside.

Place the fish in a 9" glass pie plate. Sprinkle with the lemon juice and red pepper. Cover with wax paper and microwave on high for 3 minutes. Break the fish apart, pushing uncooked portions to the outside.

Add the shrimp. Cover and microwave on high for 2 to 3 minutes, or until the fish and shrimp are opaque. Add to the casserole dish and set aside.

In a 1-quart saucepan, combine the stock, pineapple juice, soy sauce, and cornstarch. Stir over medium heat until thick and clear. Pour over the fish and vegetables. Add the spaghetti or linguine. Mix well. Microwave on high for 2 to 3 minutes, or until heated through.

MAKES 4 SERVINGS.

SEAFOOD LASAGNA

Here's a new twist on an old favorite.

6 spinach lasagna noodles

2 cups chopped canned tomatoes, with juice

²/₃ cup tomato paste

½ teaspoon grated orange rind

¼ teaspoon fennel seeds

¼ teaspoon dried marjoram

⅛ teaspoon ground red pepper

⅛ teaspoon ground black pepper

1 bay leaf

1 clove garlic, minced

12 ounces haddock fillets, halved

4 ounces medium shrimp, peeled, deveined, and chopped

2 cups part-skim ricotta cheese

2 tablespoons skim milk

2 tablespoons minced fresh parsley

1 tablespoon grated Parmesan cheese

1 can (15½ ounces) salmon, drained and flaked

½ cup shredded part-skim mozzarella cheese

Cook the noodles in a large pot of boiling water until tender, about 12 minutes. Drain, lay the noodles in a single layer on a tray, and set aside.

In a 2-quart casserole, combine the tomatoes and their juice, tomato paste, orange rind, fennel seeds, marjoram, red pepper, black pepper, bay leaf, and garlic. Cover with wax paper and microwave on high for 10 minutes. Stir. Remove and discard the bay leaf. Set aside.

Place the fish in a single layer in an 8″ × 8″ baking dish. Cover with wax paper and microwave on high for 3 minutes. Sprinkle with the shrimp. Cover and microwave on high for 2 to 3 minutes, or until the fish and shrimp are opaque. Drain. Flake the fish and transfer the fish and shrimp to a bowl. Wipe out the baking dish.

In a medium bowl, combine the ricotta, milk, parsley, and Parmesan.

Lay three of the noodles side by side in the bottom of the baking dish. Top with half of the tomato mixture. Sprinkle with half of the salmon and half of the haddock and shrimp mixture. Top with half of the ricotta mixture and half of the mozzarella.

Repeat the layers, ending with the mozzarella.

Microwave on medium-high (70% power) for 20 to 25 minutes, rotating the dish twice during this time, until heated through. Cover and let stand for 10 minutes before serving.

MAKES 8 TO 10 SERVINGS.

BLUEFISH WITH GREEN ONIONS

2 tablespoons pineapple juice
1 tablespoon lemon juice
1 tablespoon soy sauce
12 ounces bluefish fillets

¾ cup chicken stock
⅔ cup quick-cooking brown rice
½ cup finely chopped scallions

2 tablespoons minced fresh parsley
1 tablespoon grated fresh ginger
1 teaspoon margarine or butter

In an 8″ × 8″ baking dish, combine the pineapple juice, lemon juice, and soy sauce. Add the fish, skin-side up. Arrange the fish so the thickest portions are toward the outside of the dish. Set aside to marinate for 30 minutes.

In a 1-quart saucepan over medium heat, bring the stock to a boil. Stir in the rice, reduce the heat to low, cover the pan, and simmer for 10 minutes. Keep warm.

In a cup, combine ¼ cup of the scallions, 1 tablespoon of the parsley, and the ginger.

Flip the fish with a spatula so the skin side is down. Press the scallion mixture into the surface of the fish. Cover with wax paper and microwave on high for 3 minutes, or until the fish is opaque throughout. Let stand, covered.

In a small serving dish, combine the margarine or butter with the remaining ¼ cup scallions and 1 tablespoon parsley. Microwave on high for 30 seconds. Stir in the cooked rice. Microwave on high for 1 to 2 minutes, until the rice is heated through. Serve with the fish.

MAKES 2 SERVINGS.

TUNA STEAKS WITH DIJON SAUCE

2 cups fusilli

4 tuna steaks (6 ounces each)

2 tablespoons lemon juice

½ cup chicken stock

1 teaspoon margarine or butter

1 teaspoon cornstarch

1 teaspoon Dijon mustard

¼ teaspoon grated lemon rind

1 tablespoon minced fresh dill

Cook the pasta in a large pot of boiling water until just tender, about 8 minutes. Drain, transfer to a bowl, and keep warm.

While the pasta is cooking, arrange the fish in a 7″ × 11″ baking dish with the thickest portions facing toward the outside of the dish. Sprinkle with 1 tablespoon of the lemon juice. Cover with wax paper and microwave on high for 6 minutes, or until the fish is just firm and opaque throughout.

In a 1-quart saucepan, combine the stock, margarine or butter, cornstarch, mustard, lemon rind, and the remaining 1 tablespoon lemon juice. Stirring constantly, bring to a boil over medium heat and cook until clear and thickened.

Serve the sauce over the tuna and pasta. Sprinkle with the dill.

MAKES 4 SERVINGS.

MEDITERRANEAN FILLETS WITH SHELLS

1 tablespoon grated Parmesan cheese

¼ teaspoon ground black pepper

¼ teaspoon paprika

4 sole fillets (about 3 ounces each)

2 tomatoes, peeled, seeded, and chopped

¼ cup julienned zucchini

1 tablespoon sliced black olives

½ teaspoon minced garlic

1¼ cups medium pasta shells

In a cup, combine the Parmesan, pepper, and paprika. Sprinkle on the skin side of each fillet. Arrange the fish, skin-side down, in a 9″ glass pie plate. Set aside.

In a small bowl, combine the tomatoes, zucchini, olives, and garlic. Microwave on high for 2 minutes. Spoon the vegetables over the fish. Cover with wax paper and microwave on high for 1 minute. Rotate the dish a half turn and microwave on high for 2½ to 3 minutes, or until the fish is opaque throughout. Cover and let stand for 3 to 5 minutes before serving.

In a large pot of boiling water, cook the shells until just firm-tender, about 10 minutes. Drain. Transfer to a platter and top with the fish and vegetables.

MAKES 4 SERVINGS.

BEST TECHNIQUES
FOR MICROWAVING FISH

You have a variety of preparation techniques at your disposal when it comes to microwaving fish. No matter what method or type of dish you're using, covering the dish with wax paper or a lid helps hold in some steam and thereby helps the seafood cook more evenly.

One thing I really don't recommend is cooking seafood on paper towels, because it may stick to the toweling and be hard to remove. Here are some of the options open to you when preparing fish and other seafood:

◐ Cook it directly on a serving plate. Drain off any accumulated liquid before serving or adding a sauce.

◐ Make parchment packets, which will seal in juices and help blend the flavors of accompanying herbs or vegetables. No oil or butter is needed to prevent fish from sticking to the paper. And you can serve the food right from the paper—just place a packet on each diner's plate. Do be careful when opening packets to avoid releasing built-up steam into your face or onto your hands.

◐ Poach fish in a small amount of flavorful liquid. Choose a shallow casserole dish with a lid for best results.

117

STUFFED BROOK TROUT

If there's a fisherman in the family, you can create an elegant dinner to celebrate the catch!

1 onion, thinly sliced

½ cup diced green peppers

1 teaspoon olive oil

1 tomato, peeled, seeded, and chopped

1 cup sliced fresh mushrooms

¼ cup chicken stock

3 tablespoons quick-cooking brown rice

1 teaspoon soy sauce

⅛ teaspoon celery seeds

4 small brook trout (5–6 ounces each), cleaned

¼ cup tomato sauce

1 teaspoon honey

½ teaspoon paprika

⅛ teaspoon ground black pepper

1 clove garlic, minced

In a 1-quart casserole, combine the onions, peppers, and oil. Microwave on high for 3 minutes. Stir in the tomatoes, mushrooms, stock, rice, soy sauce, and celery seeds. Cover with a lid. Microwave on high for 5 minutes. Let stand, covered, for 5 minutes.

Divide the mixture among the fish, stuffing the body cavities. Arrange the fish in a 7″ × 11″ baking dish, with the backbones toward the outside of the dish and the head end of one fish overlapping the tail of another.

In a cup, combine the tomato sauce, honey, paprika, pepper, and garlic. Baste the fish with the mixture.

Cover with wax paper. Microwave on medium-high (70% power) for 10 to 12 minutes, or until the fish is opaque throughout. Cover with foil and let stand for 4 to 5 minutes before serving.

MAKES 4 SERVINGS.

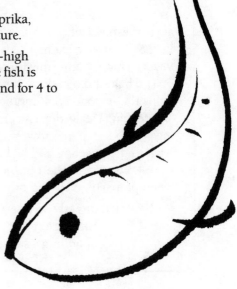

TILEFISH PROVENÇALE WITH SPAGHETTI SQUASH

2 large cloves garlic, minced

2 shallots, minced

1 tablespoon olive oil

1½ pounds tilefish fillets, cut into 2" cubes

2 teaspoons lemon juice

½ spaghetti squash (cut lengthwise), stemmed and seeded

1 large tomato, peeled, seeded, and chopped

1 teaspoon minced fresh basil or ¼ teaspoon dried basil

¼ teaspoon dried marjoram

¼ teaspoon ground black pepper

3 tablespoons minced fresh parsley

Lemon slices (garnish)

In an 8″ × 8″ baking dish, combine the garlic, shallots, and oil. Microwave on high for 1 minute. Add the fish and toss to coat. Sprinkle with the lemon juice and set aside to marinate until the squash is cooked.

Place the squash, cut-side down, on a plate. Microwave on high for 6 to 8 minutes, or until the squash is cooked through and a few strands separate easily when you flake them with a fork. Cover and keep warm.

Cover the fish with wax paper and microwave on high for 2 minutes. Add the tomatoes, basil, marjoram, and pepper; toss to mix. Cover and microwave on high for 3 to 4 minutes, or until the fish is just opaque throughout. Sprinkle with the parsley and toss well.

With a fork, remove the strands of squash from the shell. Transfer to a serving platter. Top with the fish and the lemon slices.

MAKES 4 SERVINGS.

119

BAY SCALLOPS AND PEPPERS

*Low in fat and super nutritious, these scallops
get a flavor and color lift from red and
green peppers.*

1 onion	1 clove garlic, minced	12 ounces bay scallops
1 cup sliced mushrooms	1¼ cups chicken stock	2 teaspoons cornstarch
½ teaspoon olive oil	⅓ cup water	1 tablespoon lemon juice
1 sweet red pepper	1¼ cups quick-cooking brown rice	2 teaspoons soy sauce
1 green pepper		⅛ teaspoon red pepper flakes

Thinly slice the onion crosswise. Mince the top
and bottom slices; set aside. Cut the remaining rings in half
and place in a 2-quart casserole. Add the mushrooms and
oil. Microwave on high for 3 minutes.

Meanwhile, remove the stems and seeds from the red
pepper and green pepper. Cut a slice from the top and
bottom of each pepper; mince and set aside. Cut the rest of
the peppers into ¼″ rings, then cut the rings in half. Add
these half rings to the casserole. Stir in the garlic and 1 tablespoon of the stock. Microwave on high for 5 to 7 minutes,
stirring twice during this time. Cover and keep warm.

In a 2-quart saucepan over medium heat, bring 1 cup of
the remaining stock and the water to a boil. Stir in the rice
and the minced onions and peppers. Reduce the heat to
low, cover the pan, and simmer for 10 minutes. Keep warm.

Arrange the scallops in an 8″ × 8″ baking dish. Cover with
wax paper and microwave on medium (50% power) for
2 minutes. Stir, cover, and microwave on medium (50%
power) for 3 to 4 minutes, or until the scallops just begin to
turn opaque.

Drain the cooking liquid from the vegetables and the
scallops into a 1-quart saucepan. (You should have ½ to
⅔ cup.) Stir the cornstarch into the remaining 3 tablespoons stock until dissolved. Add to the liquid in the pan.
Stir in the lemon juice, soy sauce, and pepper flakes. Cook

over medium heat, stirring constantly, until clear and thickened.

Stir the scallops and sauce into the vegetables. Cover with a lid and microwave on high for 2 minutes, or until heated through.

Fluff the rice and serve with the scallops.

MAKES 4 SERVINGS.

FINISHED IN A FLASH

Fish becomes fast food when made in a microwave. You can make a dish in a matter of minutes!

In all cases, times are based upon using high power and covering the dish with a lid or wax paper. Remember that times can vary a little depending upon the exact size and wattage of your microwave. In general, cook fish until it just flakes easily with a fork, shrimp until they turn pink and opaque, and scallops until white and opaque. It's always wise to rotate the dish a half turn at least once during the cooking time, even if you're using a carousel.

PORTION	TIME: on high (minutes)
Fish	
1 fillet (4 oz., ½" thick)	1
1 fillet (8 oz., ½" thick)	2
1 fillet (8 oz., ¾" thick)	3
1 fillet (8 oz., 1" thick)	3
2 fillets (8 oz. each, 1" thick)	4–5
4 fillets (8 oz. each, 1" thick)	6
1 steak (6 oz., 1" thick)	3
2 steaks (6 oz. each, 1" thick)	4–5
2 steaks (8 oz. each, ¾" thick)	4–5
4 steaks (6 oz. each, 1" thick)	6
4 steaks (8 oz. each, ¾" thick)	8

PORTION	TIME: on high (minutes)
Scallops	
8 oz. sea scallops	2
1 lb. sea scallops	3
8 oz. bay scallops	1½–2
1 lb. bay scallops	2–2½
Shrimp	
4 oz. (shelled medium)	1–2
8 oz. (shelled medium)	2–3
12 oz. (shelled medium)	3–3½
1 lb. (shelled medium)	3½–4

MOROCCAN FISH

Couscous, raisins, and five-spice powder give sole fillets an exotic flavor and lift them out of the ordinary.

1⅓ cups water
⅔ cup couscous
1 tablespoon minced fresh parsley
4 sole fillets (about 3 ounces each)

1 tablespoon lemon juice
¾ cup chicken stock
1 tablespoon soy sauce
2 teaspoons cornstarch

½ teaspoon five-spice powder*
¼ cup raisins
2 tablespoons thinly sliced celery

In a 2-quart saucepan over medium heat, bring the water to a boil. Stir in the couscous and parsley. Remove from the heat, cover the pan, and let stand for at least 5 minutes.

Place the fish in a 9″ glass pie plate, with the thickest portions toward the outside. Sprinkle with the lemon juice. Cover with wax paper. Microwave on high for 2½ to 3 minutes, or until the fish is opaque throughout.

In a 1-quart saucepan, combine the stock, soy sauce, cornstarch, and five-spice powder. Stir to dissolve the cornstarch. Add the raisins and celery. Cook, stirring constantly, over medium heat until thickened, clear, and bubbly. Cook and stir for 1 minute more.

Fluff the couscous with a fork and place on a serving platter. Arrange the fish over the couscous and top with the sauce.

MAKES 4 SERVINGS.

Five-spice powder is available in oriental markets and many large supermarkets.

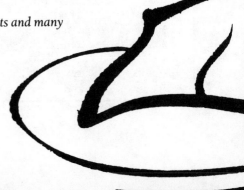

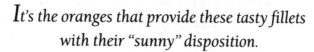

SUNSHINE FISH FILLETS
WITH COUSCOUS PILAF

*It's the oranges that provide these tasty fillets
with their "sunny" disposition.*

1 large navel orange
4 fish fillets (12 ounces total)
2 tablespoons lemon juice
1 tablespoon minced fresh
   parsley

1¼ cups chicken stock
1 teaspoon margarine or
   butter
¼ cup couscous

2 tablespoons currants or
   raisins
2 tablespoons slivered almonds
¼ teaspoon ground coriander

Halve the orange and cut two thin crosswise slices from each half. Squeeze the juice from the remaining orange sections into a small bowl. Set the slices and the juice aside.

Arrange the fish in an 8″ × 8″ baking dish, with the thickest portions toward the outside of the dish. Sprinkle with the lemon juice, parsley, and the reserved orange juice. Top each fillet with an orange slice.

Cover with wax paper and microwave on high for 1 minute. Rotate the dish a half turn and microwave on high for 1½ to 2 minutes, or until the fish is opaque throughout. Let stand, covered, for 2 to 3 minutes.

While the fish is microwaving, bring the stock and margarine or butter to a boil in a 2-quart saucepan over medium heat. Stir in the couscous, currants or raisins, almonds, and coriander. Remove from the heat, cover the pan, and let stand for 5 minutes.

Fluff the couscous with a fork and serve with the fish.

MAKES 4 SERVINGS.

SOMBRERO RED SNAPPER

*For a less fiery dish, eliminate the
jalapeño peppers.*

2 packages (10 ounces each) frozen chopped spinach

1 cup sliced mushrooms

4 scallions, chopped

1 cup Super Salsa (page 59)

1½ pounds red snapper fillets

½ cup shredded reduced-fat Cheddar cheese

1 tablespoon minced canned jalapeño peppers (wear plastic gloves when handling)

6 soft corn tortillas

Remove the spinach from its wrapping and place on a large plate. Microwave on high for 6 minutes. Cover with foil and let stand for 5 minutes to complete thawing. Transfer the spinach to a sieve and drain well, pressing with the back of a spoon to remove all excess moisture.

Spread the spinach in an even layer in a 7″ × 11″ baking dish. Top with the mushrooms and scallions. Pour ½ cup of the salsa over the vegetables.

Lay the fish in a single layer over the vegetables. Top the fish with the remaining ½ cup salsa. Cover with wax paper and microwave on high for 5 to 6 minutes, or until the fish is opaque throughout.

Sprinkle with the Cheddar and jalapeños. Microwave on medium (50% power) for 2 to 3 minutes, or until the cheese is melted.

While the fish is microwaving, bring 1″ of water to a boil in a small frying pan. Reduce the heat to low. Just before serving, dip the tortillas, one at a time, into the water for a few seconds, until limp. Remove with a spatula, allowing the excess water to drain off.

Place the tortillas on individual plates. Top with the fish and vegetables.

MAKES 6 SERVINGS.

STUFFED SOLE WITH PARSLEYED NEW POTATOES

8–12 small red potatoes

1½ tablespoons margarine or butter

⅓ cup minced fresh parsley

¼ cup thinly sliced scallions

¼ cup thinly sliced celery

1½ cups fresh whole wheat breadcrumbs

1 teaspoon minced fresh tarragon or ¼ teaspoon dried tarragon

⅛ teaspoon ground black pepper

8 sole fillets (about 1½ pounds)

⅓ cup chicken stock

2 tablespoons lemon juice

⅛ teaspoon paprika

Scrub the potatoes and peel a band of skin from around the middle of each. Place them in a 3-quart saucepan with cold water to cover. Bring to a boil over medium heat, then reduce the heat and simmer until just tender, about 10 minutes. Drain the potatoes and toss with ½ tablespoon margarine or butter and half of the parsley. Set aside and keep warm.

In a 4-cup glass measure, combine the scallions, celery, and the remaining 1 tablespoon margarine or butter. Microwave on high for 2 minutes. Add the breadcrumbs, tarragon, pepper, and the remaining parsley.

Place the fillets, skin-side down, on a work surface. Divide the stuffing among the fillets, spreading an equal amount on each. Roll up each fillet, beginning at the thicker end. Secure each with a wooden toothpick. Place in a 7″ × 11″ baking dish.

Pour the stock and lemon juice over the fish. Dust with the paprika. Cover with wax paper and microwave on high for 3 minutes. Rotate the dish a half turn and microwave on high for 2 to 3 minutes, or until the fish is opaque throughout.

Place the fish on a platter and serve with the potatoes.

MAKES 4 SERVINGS.

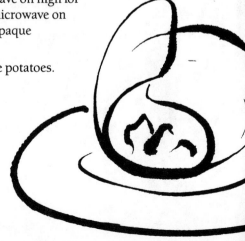

SOLE AND FENNEL WITH ORZO

*The mild licorice flavor of fennel lends exotic flair
to this fish-and-pasta combination.*

1 small fennel bulb
1 small onion, thinly sliced
1 teaspoon olive oil
2 cups packed spinach leaves,
  chopped
4 scallions, chopped

1 large tomato, peeled, seeded,
  and chopped
1 clove garlic, minced
¼ teaspoon ground black
  pepper

1 cup orzo
1 pound sole fillets
1 tablespoon lemon juice

Slice off the fennel bulb's feathery tops, mince
them, and set aside. Thinly slice the fennel bulb. Place in a
7″ × 11″ baking dish. Add the onions and oil. Microwave
on high for 3 minutes.

Add the spinach, scallions, tomatoes, garlic, and pepper.
Microwave on high for 4 minutes.

While the vegetables are microwaving, cook the orzo in
boiling water until tender, about 10 minutes. Drain, place
in a bowl, and keep warm.

Place the fish, skin-side up, over the vegetables in the
baking dish. Cover with wax paper. Microwave on medium
(50% power) for 5 minutes.

Flip the fillets over with a spatula. Sprinkle with the lemon
juice and the reserved minced fennel tops.

Cover and microwave on medium (50% power) for 5 to
6 minutes, or until the fish is opaque throughout. Serve
over the orzo.

MAKES 4 SERVINGS.

HALIBUT WITH VEGETABLES

The convenience of a one-dish meal plus wonder-ful flavor: a winning combination!

1 small onion, thinly sliced
1 cup sliced mushrooms
1 leek, chopped
2 carrots, thinly sliced
1 zucchini, diced
2 cups chopped canned tomatoes, with juice

¾ cup quick-cooking brown rice
¼ cup minced fresh parsley
⅓ cup orange juice
½ teaspoon fennel seeds
½ teaspoon grated orange rind

⅛ teaspoon ground black pepper
Pinch of ground red pepper
4 halibut steaks (6 ounces each)
Lemon slices (garnish)
Parsley sprigs (garnish)

In a 7″ × 11″ baking dish, combine the onions and mushrooms. Microwave on high for 3 minutes.

Add the leeks and carrots. Microwave on high for 2 minutes. Add the zucchini. Microwave on high for 2 minutes.

Stir in the tomatoes and their juice, rice, parsley, orange juice, fennel, orange rind, black pepper, and red pepper. Cover with a lid or wax paper and microwave on high for 3 minutes. Rotate the dish a half turn and microwave on high for 3 minutes. Stir well.

Arrange the fish in a layer on top of the vegetables with the thickest portions toward the outside of the dish. Cover with wax paper and microwave on medium (50% power) for 6 minutes.

Flip the fish over with a spatula. Cover and microwave on medium (50% power) for 6 minutes, or until the fish is opaque throughout. Garnish with the lemons and parsley.

MAKES 4 SERVINGS.

SAVORY FISH
WITH CORN ON THE COB

Dinner for one? Don't let it be boring! This easy combination treats you the way you deserve to be treated.

1 teaspoon margarine or butter	2 tablespoons dry breadcrumbs	⅛ teaspoon dried oregano
1–2 ears corn, unhusked	¼ teaspoon dried marjoram	⅛ teaspoon ground black pepper
1 fish steak (6 ounces)		

Place the margarine or butter in a 1-cup glass measure. Microwave on high for 30 seconds or until melted.

Place the corn on a plate and microwave on high for 4 minutes for one ear, 7 minutes for two ears. Wrap in a kitchen towel to keep the corn warm until the fish is ready.

While the corn is cooking, brush the melted margarine or butter on the fish. In a small bowl, combine the breadcrumbs, marjoram, oregano, and pepper. Sprinkle 1 tablespoon of the seasoned crumbs on each side of the fish and pat to help the crumbs adhere.

Place the fish diagonally on a large square of parchment paper, fold the corners across the fish, and place on a plate with the folded edges down. Microwave on high for 2 to 3 minutes, or until the fish is opaque throughout. Let stand while husking the corn.

Using a clean kitchen towel to hold the corn, pull away the husks and tassles. Break off the stem.

Unwrap the fish and serve with the corn.

MAKES 1 SERVING.

FISH STEAKS WITH CURRIED RICE

1 tablespoon margarine or
   butter
1 teaspoon canola oil
1 small onion, finely chopped
1 small carrot, finely chopped
2 teaspoons curry powder

1⅓ cups long-grain white rice
2⅔ cups chicken stock
   3 scallions, thinly sliced
   2 tablespoons nonfat yogurt
   4 halibut steaks
      (6 ounces each)

2 tablespoons chutney
1 tablespoon water
1 teaspoon lemon juice
¼ teaspoon finely grated lemon
   rind

In a 2-quart saucepan over medium heat, heat the margarine or butter until melted. Add the oil, onions, carrots, and curry powder. Cook, stirring frequently, until the onions are wilted, about 5 minutes.

Add the rice and stir until it is well coated with seasonings. Add the stock and bring to a boil. Reduce the heat to low, cover the pan, and simmer until the rice is tender, about 15 minutes.

In a small bowl, combine the scallions and yogurt. Stir them into the rice. Spread the rice in an even layer in a 7″ × 11″ baking dish. Arrange the fish on top of the rice, with the thickest portions toward the outside of the dish.

In a small bowl, stir together the chutney, water, lemon juice, and lemon rind. Spoon over the fish. Cover with wax paper and microwave on high for 3 minutes. Rotate the dish a half turn and microwave on high for 2 to 3 minutes, or until the fish is opaque throughout.

MAKES 4 SERVINGS.

GARLIC SHRIMP WITH CAPELLINI

The thin strands of pasta, herbs, garlic, and shrimp make a succulent dish for two.

4 ounces capellini

2–3 cloves garlic, minced

2 tablespoons olive oil

2 tablespoons chicken stock

⅛ teaspoon paprika

12 ounces large shrimp, peeled and deveined

2 tablespoons lemon juice

¼ cup minced fresh parsley

2 teaspoons minced fresh basil

Lemon slices (garnish)

Cook the capellini in a large pot of boiling water until just tender, about 3 minutes. Drain, place in a bowl, and keep warm.

In an 8″ × 8″ baking dish, combine the garlic and oil. Microwave on high for 1 minute. Add the stock and paprika. Microwave on high for 1 minute.

Add the shrimp and lemon juice; toss to combine. Cover with wax paper and microwave on high for 1 minute. Stir, cover, and microwave on high for 2 to 3 minutes, or until the shrimp just begin to turn opaque.

Toss the capellini, parsley, and basil with the shrimp. Garnish with the lemon slices.

MAKES 2 SERVINGS.

SWORDFISH WITH TOMATOES AND COUSCOUS

2 large tomatoes

⅓ cup chicken stock

½ teaspoon margarine or butter

¼ cup couscous

8 large fresh basil leaves

2 swordfish steaks (8 ounces each)

1 tablespoon lemon juice

¼ teaspoon minced fresh basil

Cut two thick slices from each tomato and place the slices in pairs in a 7″ × 11″ baking dish. Set aside.

Seed and finely chop the rest of the tomatoes. Place in a 1-quart saucepan and add the stock and margarine or butter. Bring to a boil over medium heat. Stir in the couscous. Remove from the heat, cover the pan, and let stand for at least 5 minutes.

Top each of the tomato slices in the baking dish with a basil leaf. Position each fish steak so it covers two tomato slices. Top with the remaining four basil leaves. Sprinkle with the lemon juice. Cover with wax paper and microwave on high for 4 to 5 minutes, or until the fish is opaque throughout.

Fluff the couscous with a fork and place on a platter. Top with the fish and tomatoes. Sprinkle with the minced basil.

MAKES 2 SERVINGS.

SEA FOODS: KNOW WHERE THEY STAND

As with other types of food, how fish and seafood are arranged in the microwave is essential for even cooking. Remember, too, that it's better to err on the side of caution. After all, you can always return seafood to the microwave for additional time, but you can't rescue it if it's overcooked.

Fish fillets should be arranged in spoke fashion whenever possible, with the thickest sections toward the outside of the dish. The narrow, thin ends of fillets can be tucked under to give more uniform thickness to the fish.

Fish steaks should likewise be positioned in a circle with their thickest areas facing outward. If using a side-by-side arrangement, alternate the pieces so the thick parts don't all face the same way.

Shrimp and lobster should be arranged in spoke fashion with their tails pointing inward.

Scallops should be evenly placed around the outer edges of a dish, with a little space between the pieces. Cover them to retain moisture and microwave them only until they turn white and nearly opaque so they don't become rubbery. Cover and let stand for a few minutes to finish cooking.

Clams and mussels in the shell should be scrubbed well (snip any beards from the mussels), then arranged around the rim of a large plate with their hinges facing outward. Microwave until the shells open.

HERBED SALMON
WITH SPINACH FETTUCCINE

A delight to the eye as well as the palate. If you're using dried pasta rather than fresh, begin cooking it before microwaving the fish.

1 medium carrot, julienned

1 celery stalk, julienned

2 salmon steaks (5 ounces each)

2 tablespoons thinly sliced scallions

2 tablespoons minced fresh parsley

2 teaspoons minced fresh dill

8 ounces fresh spinach fettuccine

2 teaspoons margarine or butter

1 tablespoon grated Parmesan cheese

Tear off two (10″ × 14″) sheets of parchment. Fold each in half and trim the edges to form a half-moon shape. Open the parchment and coat the top of each with no-stick spray.

Divide the carrots and celery between the papers, positioning them to one side of the crease on each wrapper. Top with the fillets. Sprinkle each with half of the scallions, parsley, and dill. Fold the parchment over the fish, fold up the edges securely, and crimp them to seal well.

Place the packets on a plate and microwave on high for 3 to 4 minutes, or until the fish is opaque throughout.

While the fish is microwaving, cook the fettuccine in a large pot of boiling water until just tender, about 3 minutes. Drain and place in a large bowl. Toss with the margarine or butter and then with the Parmesan.

Cut open the tops of the parchment wrappers to expose the fish. Serve with the fettuccine.

MAKES 2 SERVINGS.

JABMALAYA

Serve this Cajun specialty with a tossed salad and crusty bread.

2 cups chicken stock
1 cup long-grain white rice
2 tablespoons canola oil
2 tablespoons flour
1½ cups finely chopped onions
½ cup finely chopped green peppers

1 teaspoon minced garlic
2 cups canned tomatoes, with juice
12 ounces medium shrimp, peeled and deveined

¼ teaspoon hot pepper sauce
¼ teaspoon ground black pepper
1 cup diced cooked ham

In a 2-quart saucepan over medium heat, bring the stock to a boil. Stir in the rice, reduce the heat to low, cover the pan, and simmer for 25 minutes, or until the rice is tender and all of the liquid has been absorbed. Set aside, covered.

In a 3-quart casserole, stir together the oil and flour until smooth. Microwave on high for 4 to 6 minutes, stirring every 2 minutes during this time, until the mixture is medium brown in color.

Add the onions, peppers, and garlic. Cover with a lid and microwave on high for 2 minutes. Stir, then cover and microwave on high for 1 to 2 minutes, or until the onions are tender.

Add the tomatoes and their juice and chop them up slightly with a spoon. Add the shrimp, hot pepper sauce, and black pepper. Cover and microwave on high for 2 minutes. Stir, then cover and microwave on high for 2 to 3 minutes, or until the shrimp just begin to turn opaque.

Stir in the ham and cooked rice. Cover and microwave on high for 2 minutes, or until heated through.

MAKES 4 SERVINGS.

SEAFOOD TOSTADAS

A colorful, delicious Tex-Mex dish.

- 1 small onion, chopped
- 1 teaspoon canola oil
- 1 large tomato, peeled, seeded, and diced
- 1 yellow summer squash, diced
- ½ jalapeño pepper, minced (wear plastic gloves when handling)

- 2 cloves garlic, minced
- ¼ teaspoon dried oregano
- 12 ounces medium shrimp, peeled and deveined
- 4 tostada shells

- 1½ cups shredded lettuce
- ¼ cup sour cream
- 1 tablespoon sliced black olives

In an 8″ × 8″ baking dish, combine the onions and oil. Microwave on high for 3 minutes.

Add the tomatoes and squash. Microwave on high for 3 minutes. Add the jalapeños, garlic, and oregano. Microwave on high for 2 minutes.

Stir in the shrimp. Cover with wax paper and microwave on high for 1 minute. Stir, then cover and microwave on high for 2 to 3 minutes, or until the shrimp just begin to turn opaque.

While the shrimp is microwaving, crisp the tostadas in a 275° oven according to package directions.

To serve, place the tostada shells on warmed plates. Top with some lettuce, a mound of shrimp and vegetables, a dollop of sour cream, and a sprinkling of black olives.

MAKES 4 SERVINGS.

SHRIMP FRITTATA

*Good for brunch or a quick supper with soup
and crusty rolls.*

1 small onion, thinly sliced

½ teaspoon olive oil

½ green pepper, thinly sliced

½ sweet red pepper, thinly sliced

½ cup chopped scallions

¼ cup chopped mushrooms

8 ounces medium shrimp, peeled and deveined

6 eggs or 1½ cups fat-free egg substitute

2 tablespoons skim milk

2 tablespoons shredded reduced-fat Monterey Jack cheese

1 tablespoon minced fresh parsley

¼ teaspoon dried tarragon

⅛ teaspoon ground black pepper

Coat an 8″ × 8″ baking dish with no-stick spray. Add the onions and oil. Microwave on high for 2 minutes.

Stir in the green peppers, red peppers, scallions, and mushrooms. Microwave on high for 1 minute. Add the shrimp. Microwave on high for 1 to 2 minutes. Stir, then microwave on high for 2 to 3 minutes, or until the shrimp just begin to turn opaque.

If using whole eggs, discard two yolks. In a medium bowl, lightly beat the eggs with the milk, Monterey Jack, parsley, tarragon, and black pepper. Pour over the shrimp and vegetables; stir.

Microwave on high for 3 minutes. Rotate the dish a half turn. Microwave on medium (50% power) for 7 to 9 minutes, or until the eggs are set.

MAKES 4 SERVINGS.

SEAFOOD SALAD SUPREME

A glamorous main-dish salad.

1 pound medium shrimp, peeled and deveined

¼ cup lemon juice

1 pound small red potatoes, quartered

2 tablespoons water

8 ounces green beans, halved

2 cups cooked chick-peas

1 small sweet red pepper, thinly sliced

¼ cup halved ripe olives

¼ cup low-fat mayonnaise

¼ cup nonfat yogurt

3 tablespoons buttermilk

1 tablespoon Dijon mustard

¼ teaspoon ground black pepper

⅛ teaspoon dried oregano

⅛ teaspoon dried basil

In a 10″ round casserole, arrange the shrimp with their tails pointing toward the center. Sprinkle with 2 tablespoons of the lemon juice. Cover with a lid and microwave on high for 3 to 4 minutes, or until the shrimp just begin to turn opaque. Let stand for 1 to 2 minutes. Drain and chill.

In a 1-quart casserole, combine the potatoes and water. Cover with a lid. Microwave on high for 4 minutes. Stir, cover, and microwave on high for 3 to 5 minutes, or until tender. Using a slotted spoon, transfer the potatoes to a colander; reserve the liquid in the casserole. Rinse the potatoes with cold water, drain well, and place in a large serving bowl.

Add the beans to the water remaining in the casserole. Cover with a lid and microwave on high for 2 minutes. Stir, cover, and microwave on high for 2 to 3 minutes, or until crisp-tender. Transfer to a colander, rinse with cold water, and drain well. Add to the bowl with the potatoes. Stir in the chick-peas, red peppers, olives, and shrimp.

In a small bowl, whisk together the mayonnaise, yogurt, buttermilk, mustard, black pepper, oregano, basil, and the remaining 2 tablespoons lemon juice.

Pour over the shrimp mixture and toss gently to coat.

MAKES 6 SERVINGS.

Variation: When you don't have shrimp on hand, try the less glitzy—but still delicious—Tuna Salad Supreme: Replace the shrimp with 2 cans (6½ ounces each) of water-packed tuna. Drain it well and flake before adding to the salad. Eliminate the 2 tablespoons lemon juice used to cook the shrimp.

CURRIED SHRIMP AND VEGETABLE SALAD

1 small onion, thinly sliced
2 cups broccoli florets
1 carrot, shredded
1 clove garlic, minced
1 tablespoon honey
1 tablespoon canola oil
1 teaspoon lemon juice

1 teaspoon soy sauce
½ teaspoon curry powder
¼ teaspoon paprika
⅛ teaspoon whole cumin seeds
⅛ teaspoon ground black pepper

Pinch of ground red pepper
1 pound large shrimp, peeled and deveined
¼ cup peanuts
Lettuce leaves

Place the onions in a 2-quart casserole. Cover with a lid and microwave on high for 2 minutes, or until translucent. Stir in the broccoli, carrots, and garlic.

In a cup, combine the honey, oil, lemon juice, soy sauce, curry powder, paprika, cumin seeds, black pepper, and red pepper. Pour over the vegetables. Cover with a lid and microwave on high for 2 minutes. Stir, cover, and microwave on high for 2 to 3 minutes, or until the vegetables are crisp-tender. Uncover and set aside to cool.

Place the shrimp in a 1½-quart casserole. Cover with a lid and microwave on high for 2 minutes. Stir, then cover and microwave on high for 1½ to 2 minutes, or until the shrimp just begin to turn opaque. Drain.

Add to the vegetables. Cover and chill, stirring occasionally. Add the peanuts just before serving. Serve on a platter lined with the lettuce leaves.

MAKES 4 SERVINGS.

SINGAPORE LOBSTER AND SHRIMP

Mildly spiced curried seafood—accompanied with small bowls of mango chutney, raisins, and almonds—makes an elegant dinner-party showpiece.

2 tablespoons canola oil
4 teaspoons curry powder
2 cups sliced onions
1 tablespoon soy sauce
1½ cups chicken stock
1¼ cups quick-cooking brown rice
1 tablespoon minced fresh parsley

1 small frozen lobster tail, thawed and shell removed
1 pound large shrimp, peeled and deveined
1 cup pineapple chunks, with juice
1 tablespoon cornstarch

1 cup mung bean sprouts
Pinch of ground red pepper
Raisins
Sliced almonds
Mango chutney

In a 3-quart casserole, combine the oil and curry powder. Microwave on high for 1 minute. Stir in the onions and soy sauce. Cover with a lid and microwave on high for 6 to 9 minutes, stirring twice during this time, until the onions are tender.

While the onions are microwaving, bring the stock to a boil in a 2-quart saucepan over medium heat. Stir in the rice, reduce the heat to low, cover the pan, and simmer for 10 minutes. Stir in the parsley. Keep warm.

Slice the lobster tail into eight pieces. Stir the lobster and shrimp into the onions. Cover and microwave on high for 3 to 4 minutes, or until the shrimp just begin to turn opaque. Cover and set aside.

In a small bowl, mix the juice from the pineapple with the cornstarch until smooth. Microwave on high for 30 seconds. Stir and microwave on high for 30 seconds to 1½ minutes, or until slightly thickened.

Stir into the seafood. Add the pineapple, bean sprouts, and red pepper. Cover and microwave on high for 2 minutes, or

until the mixture is heated through. Serve over the rice.
Sprinkle with the raisins and almonds and accompany
with small spoonfuls of the chutney.

MAKES 4 SERVINGS.

SUCCESS WITH SHRIMP

Considering how expensive shrimp are, you
owe it to yourself to select, prepare, and cook
them with care. The last thing you want to do
is overcook or otherwise ruin these luscious
crustaceans. And you won't if you follow some
basic guidelines:

- Select only dry, firm shrimp. They
  should have a "briny" aroma, not a
  fishy smell.
- Peel shrimp before microwaving. Believe
  me, you'll be doing yourself a favor.
  The shells tend to stick fast to the
  shrimp after microwaving, making
  them difficult to remove. You may,
  however, leave the small tail section of
  the shell attached for a more decorative appearance.
- If you choose to devein your shrimp,
  as I always do, use a sharp paring knife

to remove the black intestine that runs
along the back of the shrimp. Make a
shallow lengthwise cut down the middle of the back and gently pull out the
vein. Rinse the shrimp and proceed
with the recipe.

- My recipes generally call for medium
  or large shrimp. Medium shrimp come
  25 to 30 to a pound; large, 16 to 20;
  and jumbo, 10 to 15. You may inter-
  change sizes as long as you remember
  to alter the microwaving time accord-
  ingly. Naturally, the thicker, larger
  shrimp will require more time.
- To avoid overcooking shrimp in the
  microwave, do them only until they
  turn pink and are not quite opaque
  throughout. Let stand briefly to finish
  cooking.

SCALLOP MANICOTTI

8 manicotti shells
1 pound bay scallops
1 small zucchini, diced
¼ cup thinly sliced scallions
1 clove garlic, minced
1 tablespoon tomato paste
¼ teaspoon grated lemon rind

⅛ teaspoon ground black pepper
2 cups low-fat cottage cheese
¼ cup minced fresh parsley
2 tablespoons grated Parmesan cheese

1 tablespoon minced fresh dill
⅓ cup nonfat yogurt
1 large tomato, peeled, seeded, and chopped
8 lemon slices (garnish)

Cook the manicotti in a large pot of boiling water according to the package directions. Drain and set aside.

In a 9″ glass pie plate, combine the scallops, zucchini, scallions, and garlic. Cover with wax paper and microwave on high for 2 minutes. Stir, then cover and microwave on high for 2 to 3 minutes, or until the scallops just begin to turn opaque.

Add the tomato paste, lemon rind, and pepper. Stir in 1 cup of the cottage cheese, 2 tablespoons of the parsley, 1 tablespoon of the Parmesan, and 1½ teaspoons of the dill.

Stuff the manicotti with the scallop mixture. Arrange the shells in a 7″ × 11″ baking dish. Cover with a lid or wax paper. Microwave on high for 5 minutes.

Using a food processor or blender, process the yogurt and the remaining 1 cup cottage cheese, 1 tablespoon Parmesan, and 1½ teaspoons dill until smooth.

Spoon the sauce over the shells. Cover and microwave on medium (50% power) for 2 to 3 minutes. Rotate the dish a half turn and microwave on high for 2 to 3 minutes, or until the shells are heated through.

In a small bowl, combine the tomatoes and the remaining 2 tablespoons parsley. Sprinkle over the shells. Garnish with the lemon slices.

MAKES 4 SERVINGS.

MARVELOUS VEGETARIAN MEALS

As more and more people elect to cut back on meat, vegetarian cuisine is rising in popularity. Now the mainstay of many diets, it has certainly evolved from the days when the words conjured up images of plain brown rice and scrawny vegetables. Today, exciting, colorful vegetable entrées— accompanied by a wide range of pastas, grains, and beans—are so appealing that you can relish them often, without the fear of boredom setting in. And your microwave can pitch in to make preparation of these meals easier. Here are some of the terrific vegetarian dishes you can have on the table in no time.

- Italian delights like eggplant Parmesan, lasagna, and pasta primavera—all much lower in fat than traditional recipes.
- Quiches that cook in easy microwave crusts.
- Vegetable or tofu stir-fries that are ready in the time it takes to make a side dish of quick-cooking brown rice, bulgur, or couscous.
- Crêpes—the fillings are ready in a flash.

SLIMMING INTERNATIONAL FAVORITES

I really love to serve ethnic dishes, and here are some of the ways I've discovered that my microwave can help me to slash the fat in them: Eggplant Parmigiana, an Italian favorite, generally requires up to ½ cup of oil for frying the eggplant. I can make the same dish in the microwave (see page 162) without one drop of oil. I can soften tortillas in the microwave for all sorts of Mexican dishes using just water, not oil. I can microwave Pasta Primavera (page 156)—a succulent combination of vegetables in a low-fat creamy sauce—without the ½ cup of butter that traditional recipes use to sauté the vegetables.

And here's a real time-saver: When using a microwave—rather than a wok, for example—to make vegetable-rich recipes, you can avoid having to prep all of your ingredients before you can even start cooking. That means you can slice just the longest-cooking veggies first and pop them into the microwave, then you can work on the other ingredients while the first ones cook.

A real plus to vegetable main dishes is that they're higher in fiber than most standard meat, poultry, and fish entrées. And because they are often less "dense" (that is, they have fewer calories per ounce), you can eat more without gaining weight—yet the fiber will satisfactorily appease your hunger.

I often use tofu, which is low in fat and high in protein, in ethnic-style dishes. Among the ones featured here are Cheese and Tofu Stuffed Shells (page 166), Tofu Stir-Fry with Spinach (page 172), and Indonesian Tofu in Peanut Sauce (page 144).

For a quick kid-pleaser, try Pita Pizza (page 170)—my son's favorite. Made with whole wheat pita bread, they're a nice source of fiber and can be microwaved in less than a minute!

CREAMY HERBED FETTUCCINE

12 ounces fettuccine	1 cup minced fresh parsley	¾ cup skim milk
1 onion, finely chopped	¼ cup minced fresh basil	½ cup chicken stock
1 tablespoon margarine or butter	⅛ teaspoon grated nutmeg	1 tablespoon cornstarch
2 cloves garlic, minced	⅛ teaspoon ground black pepper	2 tablespoons grated Parmesan cheese

Cook the fettuccine in a large pot of boiling water until just tender, about 10 minutes. Drain, transfer to a large bowl, and keep warm.

Meanwhile, in a 1½-quart casserole, combine the onions and margarine or butter. Microwave on high for 1 minute, or until the fat is melted. Stir in the garlic. Microwave on high for 2 to 3 minutes, or until the onions are tender.

Add the parsley, basil, nutmeg, and pepper. Microwave on high for 2 minutes, or until the parsley is wilted.

In a 1-quart saucepan, mix the milk, stock, and cornstarch until smooth. Cook over medium heat, stirring constantly, until the mixture comes to a boil and thickens. Add to the casserole. Stir in the Parmesan.

Pour over the fettuccine and toss well to combine.

MAKES 4 SERVINGS.

ENCORE PASTA

The microwave is perfect for reheating left-over pasta dishes. You'll find that the pasta retains its tenderness and flavor. The micro-wave is especially convenient if someone in your family will be late for dinner. Just be sure to refrigerate the reserved portion rather than leaving it at room temperature until needed. That way harmful bacteria won't have a chance to grow. For best results, follow these tips.

- ◗ Place the food in a small casserole and cover it with a lid.
- ◗ For 1 cup of pasta, microwave on high for 1 minute. Stir, replace the cover, and microwave on high for ½ to 1½ minutes, or until hot.
- ◗ For 2 cups of pasta, microwave on high for 1½ minutes. Stir, replace the cover, and microwave on high for 1½ to 2 minutes, or until hot.

INDONESIAN TOFU IN PEANUT SAUCE

For a change-of-pace meal, try this spicy and exotic tofu dish.

1 onion, thinly sliced

2 tablespoons minced fresh ginger

3 cloves garlic, minced

2 hot green chili peppers, seeded and minced (wear plastic gloves when handling)

1 teaspoon canola oil

1 cup thinly sliced scallions

1 sweet red pepper, thinly sliced

1½ cups chicken stock

1¼ cups quick-cooking brown rice

1 bay leaf

⅔ cup chunky peanut butter

1½ cups water

1 pound tofu, cubed

¼–½ teaspoon red pepper flakes (optional)

½ cup sliced scallion greens

1 tablespoon lemon juice

1 tablespoon soy sauce

1 tablespoon molasses

In a 2½-quart casserole, combine the onions, ginger, garlic, chili peppers, and oil. Microwave on high for 3 minutes, or until the onions are crisp-tender. Stir in the scallions. Microwave on high for 2 minutes.

Add the red peppers. Microwave on high for 3 minutes, or until the peppers are crisp-tender.

Meanwhile, in a 2-quart saucepan over medium heat, bring the stock to a boil. Stir in the rice and bay leaf, reduce the heat to low, cover the pan, and simmer for 10 minutes. Keep warm.

Stir the peanut butter into the vegetables. Add the water and mix well. Microwave on high for 5 minutes, or until the vegetables are tender. Add the tofu and pepper flakes (if using). Microwave on high for 3 minutes, or until heated through.

Stir in the scallion greens, lemon juice, soy sauce, and molasses. Microwave on high for 1 to 2 minutes, to heat through.

Fluff the rice with a fork. Discard the bay leaf. Transfer the rice to a platter. Serve the vegetables over the rice.

MAKES 6 SERVINGS.

TOFU AND VEGETABLES WITH COUSCOUS

1 medium onion, thinly sliced
1 clove garlic, minced
¼ teaspoon sesame oil
¼ teaspoon minced fresh ginger
1 pound tofu, cut into ¾" cubes
1½ cups water

1 teaspoon margarine or butter
1 cup couscous
2 cups sliced mushrooms
1 can (8 ounces) bamboo shoots, rinsed and drained
12 asparagus spears
½ cup thinly sliced scallions

½ cup pineapple juice
2 tablespoons lemon juice
1 tablespoon soy sauce
1 tablespoon cornstarch
½ teaspoon molasses
Pinch of ground red pepper

In a 2½-quart casserole, combine the onions, garlic, oil, and ginger. Microwave on high for 3 minutes. Add the tofu. Microwave on high for 2 minutes.

Meanwhile, in a 1-quart saucepan, bring the water and margarine or butter to a boil. Stir in the couscous. Cover and remove from the heat. Keep warm.

Add the mushrooms and bamboo shoots to the tofu mixture. Microwave on high for 3 minutes.

Trim tough ends from the asparagus. If desired, lightly peel the stalks with a vegetable peeler. Slice diagonally into 1½" lengths.

Stir the asparagus and scallions into the tofu mixture. Microwave on high for 2 minutes. Stir and microwave on high for 2 to 3 minutes, or until the asparagus is crisp-tender. Carefully drain off and discard any liquid.

In a 1-quart saucepan, combine the pineapple juice, lemon juice, soy sauce, cornstarch, molasses, and pepper. Stir over medium heat until the sauce thickens and becomes translucent. Pour over the tofu mixture and toss until coated.

Fluff the couscous with a fork. Place on a platter. Top with the tofu mixture.

MAKES 4 SERVINGS.

SPINACH PIE

A no-roll piecrust makes this quiche extra easy.

2 packages (10 ounces each) frozen chopped spinach

¾ cup whole wheat pastry flour

½ cup cooked brown rice

3 tablespoons buttermilk

2 tablespoons olive oil

1 tablespoon grated Parmesan cheese

¾ cup part-skim ricotta cheese

⅓ cup evaporated skim milk

2 eggs or ½ cup fat-free egg substitute

1 teaspoon lemon juice

½ teaspoon dried basil

¼ teaspoon grated nutmeg

Remove the spinach from its wrapping and place on a large plate. Microwave on high for 6 minutes. Cover with foil and let stand for 5 minutes to complete thawing. Transfer the spinach to a sieve and drain well, pressing with the back of a spoon to remove all excess moisture. Place in a medium bowl and set aside.

Place the flour, rice, buttermilk, oil, and Parmesan in a 10″ glass pie plate. Toss with a fork until thoroughly combined. Press the dough in the bottom and up the sides of the plate to form a crust.

Place the pie plate on an inverted saucer and microwave on high for 4 to 6 minutes, or until the crust appears dry.

To the spinach, add the ricotta, milk, eggs, lemon juice, basil, and nutmeg. Spread the filling evenly over the crust. Microwave on high for 5 minutes. Rotate the dish a half turn. Microwave on medium (50% power) for 10 minutes. Rotate the dish a half turn. Microwave on medium (50% power) for 5 to 10 minutes, or until the center of the pie is set.

MAKES 6 SERVINGS.

TOMATO-CHEESE QUICHE

Delicious for a luncheon, especially if served with a big green salad.

1 cup whole wheat pastry flour

1 tablespoon yellow cornmeal

3 tablespoons canola oil

3 tablespoons buttermilk

1 cup part-skim ricotta cheese

½ cup low-fat cottage cheese

⅓ cup shredded reduced-fat Cheddar cheese

2 eggs or ½ cup fat-free egg substitute

1 tablespoon flour

¼ teaspoon dried oregano

Pinch of ground red pepper

1 tomato, thinly sliced

1 tablespoon grated Parmesan cheese

1 tablespoon minced fresh parsley

1 teaspoon minced fresh basil

In a 9″ pie plate, place the whole wheat flour, cornmeal, oil, and buttermilk. Toss with a fork until thoroughly combined. Press the dough in the bottom and up the sides of the plate to form a crust. Microwave on high for 2 minutes. Rotate the plate a half turn. Microwave on high for 2 to 3 minutes, or until the crust appears dry.

In a medium bowl, combine the ricotta, cottage cheese, Cheddar, eggs, flour, oregano, and pepper. Spread evenly in the crust.

Set the pie plate on a inverted saucer and microwave on medium (50% power) for 12 to 18 minutes, rotating the plate a quarter turn every 3 minutes during this time, until the center is soft-set.

Top with the tomatoes and sprinkle with the Parmesan. Microwave on medium (50% power) for 2 minutes, or until the tomatoes are heated through. Sprinkle with the parsley and basil.

MAKES 6 SERVINGS.

SAUCY EGGPLANT CASSEROLE

Most recipes for eggplant require lots of oil—but those done in the microwave are just perfect without all the fat.

1 eggplant (about 1 pound)
2 tablespoons water
2 cups cooked chick-peas
1½ teaspoons fennel seeds

2 cloves garlic, minced
2 cups Basic Tomato Pasta Sauce (page 161)
½ cup crumbled feta cheese

¼ cup sliced ripe olives
2 tablespoons pine nuts or chopped walnuts

Peel the eggplant if the skin is tough. Cut into ½"-thick slices; halve the slices crosswise. Place the slices in a 7" × 11" baking dish in an even layer. Sprinkle with the water. Microwave on high for 4 minutes, or until the eggplant is crisp-tender. Drain well.

Spoon the chick-peas over the eggplant. Stir the fennel and garlic into the tomato sauce. Pour over the chick-peas. Microwave on high for 5 minutes, or until the eggplant is tender.

Sprinkle with the feta, olives, and pine nuts or walnuts. Microwave on medium (50% power) for 2 to 3 minutes, or until the toppings are heated through.

MAKES 4 SERVINGS.

ZUCCHINI-CHEESE CASSEROLE

½ cup chopped onions
½ teaspoon olive oil
3 medium zucchini, thinly sliced on the diagonal
1 pound low-fat cottage cheese

1 egg or ¼ cup fat-free egg substitute
1 tablespoon chopped fresh basil or 1 teaspoon dried basil

1 teaspoon chopped fresh oregano or ½ teaspoon dried oregano
2 large tomatoes, sliced
3 tablespoons grated Parmesan cheese

In a 1½-quart casserole, combine the onions and oil. Microwave on high for 2 minutes. Add the zucchini. Microwave on high for 4 minutes, or until crisp-tender. Drain off and discard any liquid. Transfer the zucchini mixture to a bowl and set aside. Wipe out the casserole with a paper towel.

In a blender or food processor, blend the cottage cheese, egg, basil, and oregano until smooth.

Place about a third of the zucchini in the casserole. Top with a third of the cottage cheese and a third of the tomatoes. Repeat twice to use all of the ingredients.

Sprinkle with the Parmesan. Microwave on high for 10 minutes, or until heated through. Cover and let stand for 5 minutes before serving.

MAKES 6 SERVINGS.

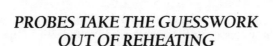

PROBES TAKE THE GUESSWORK OUT OF REHEATING

If your microwave has a probe, you can reheat foods—especially casseroles that can't be stirred—with ease. You won't have to guess how much time is needed, and you won't overcook or dry out the food.

To use, simply insert the probe so that its tip is in the center of the food, not touching the container. Set the probe at 160°, then set your oven to the desired power level.

Most casseroles can be reheated on high.

Cover with wax paper or a lid to keep in moisture and promote even heating. Where practical, stir the food occasionally. When that's not possible (as with lasagna), use the medium (50% power) setting. Also use a medium setting for delicate egg or cheese casseroles, which might curdle at a higher power. In any case, the food should be steaming and very hot to the touch before it's served.

SPAGHETTI SQUASH RIVIERA

To maximize your use of time, microwave the spaghetti squash while preparing the vegetables for the sauce.

1 spaghetti squash (2 pounds)
1 onion, thinly sliced
1 green pepper, thinly sliced
1 sweet red pepper, thinly sliced
1 teaspoon olive oil
2 small zucchini, thinly sliced on the diagonal

1 cup loosely packed spinach, chopped
¼ cup chopped fresh basil
2 tablespoons minced fresh parsley

1 cup cooked chick-peas
1 cup tomato sauce
¼ teaspoon ground black pepper
¼ cup grated Parmesan cheese

Halve the spaghetti squash lengthwise and remove the seeds. Place each half, cut-side down, on a plate. Microwave each half on high for 7 minutes, or until tender. Keep warm.

In a 2½-quart saucepan, combine the onions, green peppers, red peppers, and oil. Microwave on high for 3 minutes, or until crisp-tender. Stir in the zucchini. Microwave on high for 3 minutes, or until the zucchini is crisp-tender.

Stir in the spinach, basil, and parsley. Microwave on high for 2 minutes, or until the spinach is wilted. Stir in the chick-peas, tomato sauce, and black pepper. Microwave on high for 3 to 4 minutes, or until heated through.

Using a fork, flake the spaghetti squash into strands. Place the strands on a serving platter. Top with the vegetables. Sprinkle with the Parmesan.

MAKES 6 SERVINGS.

CURRIED VEGETABLES WITH RICE

This beautiful dish combines an array of nutrient-dense vegetables, including carrots, cauliflower, and peppers. For a really simple, delicious meal, just add a salad and fresh bread.

1½ cups chicken stock

1¼ cups quick-cooking brown rice

1 medium onion, thinly sliced

3 carrots, thinly sliced

1 teaspoon minced fresh ginger

1 clove garlic, minced

2 cups cauliflower florets

½ sweet red pepper, thinly sliced

½ green pepper, thinly sliced

1 cup frozen peas

1 teaspoon soy sauce

1 tablespoon canola oil

1½ teaspoons curry powder

¼ cup peanuts

2 scallions, thinly sliced (garnish)

4 thin lemon slices (garnish)

In a 2-quart saucepan over medium heat, bring the stock to a boil. Stir in the rice, reduce the heat to low, cover the pan, and simmer for 10 minutes. Keep warm.

In a 2½-quart casserole, combine the onions, carrots, ginger, and garlic. Microwave on high for 3 minutes. Add the cauliflower. Microwave on high for 3 minutes.

Add the red peppers and green peppers. Microwave on high for 2 minutes. Stir in the peas and soy sauce.

In a cup, stir together the oil and curry powder. Add to the vegetables. Microwave on high for 2 minutes. Stir well. Microwave on high for 2 minutes. Stir in the peanuts.

Fluff the rice with a fork. Place on a serving platter. Top with the vegetables. Garnish with the scallions and lemon slices.

MAKES 4 SERVINGS.

LENTIL LOAF SURPRISE

What's the surprise? This loaf tastes so good that even people who "can't stand" lentils want more. Another surprise—the loaf is table-ready in less than half the time of conventionally baked loaves.

3 cups hot water
1 cup lentils
½ bay leaf
½ cup chopped walnuts
½ cup fresh whole-grain breadcrumbs
½ cup skim milk

1 egg or ¼ cup fat-free egg substitute
1 onion, chopped
1 carrot, chopped
½ celery stalk, chopped
1 tablespoon soy sauce

1 teaspoon ground cumin
½ clove garlic, minced
¼ teaspoon dried thyme
¼ teaspoon ground black pepper
¼ cup tomato sauce

In a 2-quart casserole, combine the water, lentils, and bay leaf. Microwave on high for 20 minutes. Drain. Remove and discard the bay leaf.

Transfer the lentils to the bowl of a food processor. Add the walnuts, breadcrumbs, milk, egg, onions, carrots, celery, soy sauce, cumin, garlic, thyme, and pepper. Process with on/off turns until well mixed and smooth.

Coat an 8″ × 8″ baking dish with no-stick spray. Add the lentil mixture and smooth the top with a spatula. Spread the tomato sauce over the top of the loaf. Microwave on high for 10 to 12 minutes, or until cooked through. Let cool slightly before serving.

MAKES 6 SERVINGS.

Note: Leftovers make delicious sandwiches. Thinly slice the lentil loaf and slip the pieces into pita pockets. Top with shredded cheese, chopped scallions, chopped tomatoes, sprouts, and a dollop of nonfat yogurt.

MICROWAVE BEAN CUISINE

Let me say right off that I don't really recommend cooking dried beans in the microwave. They require long, slow simmering for best results, and the stove is really a more appropriate appliance. Besides, microwaving beans takes just about as long as regular preparation. That said, I do find the microwave a handy tool for quickly soaking dried beans as well as thawing and reheating cooked ones.

Rather than soaking dried beans overnight, let your microwave rehydrate them in 30 minutes. To do this, rinse and pick over 1 pound of dried beans, such as kidney, navy, or pink. Place in a 2½-quart casserole and cover generously with cold water. Microwave on high for 15 minutes. Stir, cover, and let stand until the beans have swelled up, about 15 minutes. Proceed with your regular recipe.

When freezing cooked beans, choose a microwave-safe container. To defrost, simply remove the lid and cover the beans with wax paper. Microwave on the defrost setting until the beans are nearly thawed but still icy in the center. (The time will vary according to the amount of beans and the exact power setting used.) Remove the container from the microwave and let stand at room temperature for 4 to 5 minutes to finish thawing.

To reheat cooked beans, place in a dish and cover with wax paper or a lid. Beans may explode when reheated on high, so choose medium (50% power) or whatever setting the manufacturer recommends in your microwave handbook. Heating time will vary with the amount of beans. Stir at least once while reheating, and allow to stand for 4 to 5 minutes before serving to distribute the heat evenly.

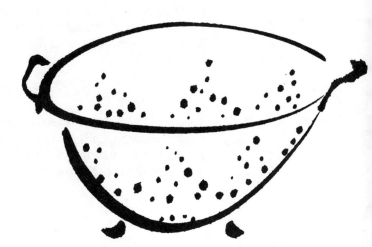

GARDEN-STYLE BURRITOS

Make this attractive dish by wrapping savory mixed vegetables and cheese in flour tortillas and topping them with hot tomato salsa.

1 small onion, thinly sliced

½ cup sliced mushrooms

½ teaspoon canola oil

½ cup diced green peppers

½ cup diced zucchini

½ cup chopped tomatoes

½ cup chopped broccoli florets

1 cup loosely packed spinach, chopped

1 tablespoon nonfat yogurt

4 flour tortillas

½ cup shredded reduced-fat Cheddar cheese

¾ cup Super Salsa (page 59)

¼ cup thinly sliced scallions (garnish)

In a 1½-quart casserole, combine the onions, mushrooms, and oil. Microwave on high for 3 minutes. Stir in the peppers and zucchini. Microwave on high for 2 minutes, or until almost tender.

Add the tomatoes and broccoli. Microwave on high for 2 minutes, or until the broccoli is crisp-tender. Drain off and discard any liquid.

Add the spinach and yogurt. Microwave on high for 1 to 2 minutes, or until the spinach is wilted.

To warm the tortillas, microwave each on a plate on high for 15 seconds. Sprinkle with the Cheddar. Divide the vegetable mixture among the tortillas. Roll up and place, seam-side down, on a platter. Top with the salsa. Garnish with the scallions.

MAKES 4 SERVINGS.

Variation: For Garden-Style Pita Sandwiches, omit the tortillas and salsa. Cut 4 pitas in half. Place 1 tablespoon shredded cheese in each pocket. Top with the vegetables. Sprinkle with more cheese and the scallions.

BEAN BURRITOS DELUXE

Serve with a big green salad.

1 small onion, chopped
2 scallions, thinly sliced
1 jalapeño pepper, minced (wear plastic gloves when handling)
½ teaspoon canola oil
2 cups cooked pinto beans, mashed

1 tablespoon chili powder
½ teaspoon ground cumin
¼ teaspoon dried oregano
Pinch of ground black pepper
6 flour tortillas
¾ cup shredded reduced-fat Cheddar cheese

1 cup shredded lettuce
½ cup peeled, seeded, and chopped tomatoes
1 tablespoon minced fresh coriander
1 cup Super Salsa (page 59)

In a medium bowl, combine the onions, scallions, jalapeños, and oil. Microwave on high for 4 minutes, or until tender.

Add the beans, chili powder, cumin, oregano, and black pepper.

Place the tortillas between two paper towels. Microwave on high for 20 seconds to soften. Spoon ⅓ cup of the bean filling down the center of each tortilla. Fold in the sides and roll up the tortillas. Place, seam-side down, in a 7″ × 11″ baking dish. Cover with a paper towel.

Microwave on high for 5 minutes, or until hot throughout. Sprinkle with the Cheddar. Microwave on medium (50% power) for 2 minutes, or until the cheese is melted.

Sprinkle with the lettuce, tomatoes, and coriander. Serve with the salsa.

MAKES 6 SERVINGS.

PASTA PRIMAVERA

This lower-fat version of classic pasta primavera is an elegant—but easy—main dish. One way that I reduced the fat was by replacing the traditional heavy-cream sauce with a light variation.

1 onion, finely chopped

1 tablespoon margarine or butter

1 carrot, halved lengthwise and thinly sliced

8 large mushrooms, sliced

2 cloves garlic, minced

12 ounces linguine

1 cup cauliflower florets

1 small zucchini, halved lengthwise and thinly sliced

5 scallions, thinly sliced on the diagonal

8 ounces asparagus, cut into 1" pieces

1 cup peas

½ cup milk

½ cup chicken stock

1 tablespoon cornstarch

¼ cup grated Parmesan cheese

2 tablespoons minced fresh basil

In a 2½-quart casserole, combine the onions and margarine or butter. Microwave on high for 30 seconds. Add the carrots, mushrooms, and garlic. Microwave on high for 3 minutes, or until the carrots are crisp-tender.

Cook the linguine in a large pot of boiling water until just tender, about 10 minutes. Drain, transfer to a bowl, and keep warm.

Meanwhile, add the cauliflower, zucchini, and scallions to the onion mixture. Microwave on high for 4 minutes, or until the zucchini is crisp-tender. Add the asparagus and peas. Microwave on high for 4 to 5 minutes, or until the asparagus is crisp-tender.

In a 1-quart saucepan, combine the milk, stock, and cornstarch. Stir over medium heat until thickened.

Sprinkle the vegetables with the Parmesan and basil. Add the sauce. Toss well to combine. Serve over the pasta.

MAKES 4 SERVINGS.

MIDDLE EASTERN OMELET

Flavored with feta cheese, this vegetable omelet is a wonderful surprise.

½ medium red onion, thinly sliced

½ sweet red pepper, thinly sliced

½ teaspoon olive oil

½ cup seeded and chopped tomatoes

2 tablespoons minced fresh parsley

3 tablespoons crumbled feta cheese

3 eggs or ¾ cup fat-free egg substitute

1 teaspoon margarine or butter
Parsley sprigs (garnish)

In an 8″ × 8″ baking dish, combine the onions, peppers, and oil. Microwave on high for 3 minutes. Add the tomatoes and 1 tablespoon of the minced parsley. Microwave on high for 3 minutes. Stir in the feta.

In a small bowl, lightly beat the eggs with the remaining 1 tablespoon minced parsley. Place an omelet pan or medium skillet over medium heat. Add the margarine or butter and wait until it's melted and the foam subsides. Add the eggs and swirl the pan slightly to distribute the eggs.

Continue to swirl the pan, pulling the cooked edges of the omelet toward the center with a fork and allowing the uncooked eggs to run toward the outside of the pan. When the omelet is no longer runny but is still slightly soft on top, place the vegetables over half of the surface. Fold the omelet in half to cover the vegetables. Serve garnished with the fresh parsley sprigs.

MAKES 2 SERVINGS.

PLEASANT PEASANT PASTA

Delicate, aromatic sauce—flavored with cheese and cauliflower—nicely complements the pasta in this simple dish.

12 ounces linguine
1 onion, finely chopped
1 teaspoon margarine or butter
1 carrot, shredded
2 cloves garlic, minced
3 cups coarsely chopped cauliflower

2½ cups Basic Tomato Pasta Sauce (page 161)
½ cup shredded reduced-fat Colby or Monterey Jack cheese
⅛ teaspoon ground black pepper

⅛ teaspoon grated nutmeg
1 tablespoon grated Parmesan cheese

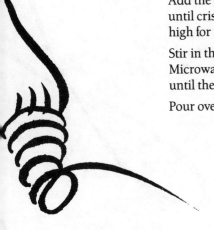

Cook the linguine in a large pot of boiling water until just tender, about 10 minutes. Drain, transfer to a bowl, and keep warm.

In a 2½-quart casserole, combine the onions and margarine or butter. Microwave on high for 1 minute. Stir in the carrots and garlic. Microwave on high for 2 minutes, or until the vegetables are softened.

Add the cauliflower. Microwave on high for 5 minutes, or until crisp-tender. Add the tomato sauce. Microwave on high for 8 minutes, or until the cauliflower is tender.

Stir in the Colby or Monterey Jack, pepper, and nutmeg. Microwave on medium (50% power) for 3 to 4 minutes, or until the cheese is melted. Stir in the Parmesan.

Pour over the linguine and toss to combine.

MAKES 4 SERVINGS.

LEMON-BROCCOLI CURRY WITH CASHEWS

1½ cups chicken stock

1¼ cups quick-cooking brown rice

1 small onion, finely chopped

2 teaspoons margarine or butter

1 teaspoon curry powder

2 cloves garlic, minced

1 medium carrot, julienned

1 large bunch broccoli

¼ cup lemon juice

2 tablespoons water

2 teaspoons soy sauce

1 teaspoon cornstarch

1 teaspoon honey

½ teaspoon grated lemon rind

¼ cup chopped cashews

In a 2-quart saucepan over medium heat, bring the stock to a boil. Stir in the rice, reduce the heat to low, cover the pan, and simmer for 10 minutes. Keep warm.

In a 2½-quart casserole, combine the onions and margarine or butter. Microwave on high for 1 minute. Stir in the curry powder and garlic. Microwave on high for 2 minutes. Add the carrots. Microwave on high for 2 minutes.

Cut the broccoli florets from the stems and separate them into small pieces. Peel the stems and julienne them. Add all the broccoli to the casserole. Microwave on high for 3 to 4 minutes, or until the broccoli is crisp-tender.

In a 1-quart saucepan, combine the lemon juice, water, soy sauce, cornstarch, honey, and lemon rind in a small saucepan. Stir over medium heat until the mixture comes to a boil and thickens. Pour over the vegetables. Stir in the cashews. Microwave on high for 2 minutes, or until the broccoli is tender.

Fluff the rice with a fork and place on a platter. Serve the vegetables over the rice.

MAKES 4 SERVINGS.

LAZY LASAGNA

Easily assembled and quickly microwaved, this lasagna for eight is a breeze. If you're serving fewer, wrap the leftovers in individual portions and freeze them for later instant meals.

9 lasagna noodles

8 ounces part-skim mozzarella cheese, shredded

¼ cup grated Parmesan cheese

2 cups Basic Tomato Pasta Sauce (opposite page)

1¾ cups part-skim ricotta cheese

Cook the noodles in a large pot of boiling water until just tender, about 12 minutes. Drain and place in a single layer on a tray.

In a small bowl, combine the mozzarella and Parmesan.

Spoon about 3 tablespoons of the tomato sauce in the bottom of a 7″ × 11″ baking dish. Top with three lasagna noodles in a single layer. Spoon on a third of the remaining sauce, spread with half of the ricotta cheese, and sprinkle with a third of the mozzarella mixture.

Repeat with another layer of noodles, sauce, ricotta, and mozzarella. Top with the remaining noodles. Coat with the remaining sauce.

Place the casserole on an inverted saucer. Microwave on high for 4 minutes. Rotate the dish a half turn. Microwave on high for 4 to 6 minutes, or until the lasagna is hot and bubbly.

Sprinkle with the remaining mozzarella. Microwave on medium (50% power) for 6 to 8 minutes, or until the cheese is melted. Let stand for 3 to 4 minutes before serving.

MAKES 8 SERVINGS.

SAUCY TALK

Here's a basic topping for the magnificent array of pastas available. You can make this versatile sauce as plain or fancy as you like, adding anything from a sprinkle of Parmesan to a generous helping of meat, chicken, or seafood.

BASIC TOMATO PASTA SAUCE

1 carrot, coarsely chopped	2 cups crushed tomatoes	¼ teaspoon dried basil
1 celery stalk, coarsely chopped	1 clove garlic, minced	¼ teaspoon dried oregano
1 onion, coarsely chopped	1 tablespoon minced fresh parsley	¼ teaspoon ground black pepper
1 teaspoon oil		

In a food processor, process the carrots, celery, and onions with on/off turns until finely chopped. Transfer to a lightly oiled 8″ × 8″ baking dish. Add the oil and stir well. Microwave for 2 minutes.

Stir in the tomatoes, garlic, parsley, basil, oregano, and pepper. Cover with a lid and microwave on high for 4 minutes.

MAKES ABOUT 3 CUPS.

Variations: Add any one of the following: 1 cup cooked kidney beans or lentils, 1 cup cubed tofu, 1 cup cooked mushrooms, 1 cup cooked mixed vegetables (such as peppers, onions, and mushrooms), ¼ cup grated Parmesan cheese, or ¼ cup chopped nuts.

EGGPLANT PARMIGIANA

1 eggplant (about 1 pound)

1 egg or ¼ cup fat-free egg substitute

2 tablespoons skim milk

⅔ cup dry breadcrumbs

¼ teaspoon dried marjoram

¼ teaspoon dried oregano

¼ teaspoon dried basil

⅛ teaspoon ground black pepper

2½ cups Basic Tomato Pasta Sauce (page 161)

¼ cup grated Parmesan cheese

6 ounces part-skim mozzarella cheese, shredded

Peel the eggplant if the skin is tough. Cut it into ¼" to ½" slices.

In a shallow dish, lightly whisk together the egg and milk.

On a sheet of wax paper, combine the breadcrumbs, marjoram, oregano, basil, and pepper.

Dip the eggplant into the egg mixture, then into the breadcrumbs. Transfer to two large plates, arranging the eggplant in single layers as much as possible. Microwave each on high for 5 to 6 minutes, or until the eggplant is slightly tender.

Place 3 tablespoons of the tomato sauce in the bottom of a 7" × 11" baking dish. Arrange one layer of eggplant in the dish, cutting the slices as necessary to fit. Sprinkle with half of the Parmesan. Top with half of the remaining tomato sauce and half of the mozzarella. Repeat with the remaining eggplant, Parmesan, and tomato sauce.

Microwave on high for 10 to 12 minutes, or until the eggplant is tender. Sprinkle with the remaining mozzarella. Microwave on medium (50% power) for 2 to 3 minutes, or until the mozzarella is melted.

MAKES 4 TO 6 SERVINGS.

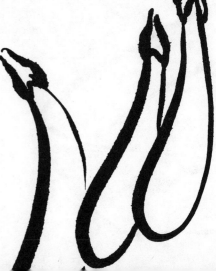

QUICK LENTIL CHILI

A delicious no-meat chili, ready in next to no time! Prepare the vegetables while the lentils cook.

- 3 cups hot water
- 1 cup lentils
- 1 bay leaf
- 2 onions, chopped
- 2 carrots, thinly sliced
- 5 cloves garlic, minced
- 1 hot chili pepper, seeded and minced (wear plastic gloves when handling)
- 1 teaspoon olive oil
- 2 celery stalks, sliced
- 1 tomato, seeded and chopped
- ½ green pepper, cubed
- ½ sweet red pepper, cubed
- 3½ cups chopped canned tomatoes, with juice
- 1¾ cups Basic Tomato Pasta Sauce (page 161)
- ¼ cup minced fresh parsley
- 2 teaspoons chili powder
- 1 teaspoon ground cumin
- 1 teaspoon dried marjoram
- 1 teaspoon dried oregano

In a 1½-quart casserole, combine the water, lentils, and bay leaf. Microwave on high for 10 minutes. Stir well, then microwave on high for 10 minutes. Cover, set aside, and keep warm.

In a 2½-quart casserole, combine the onions, carrots, garlic, chili peppers, and oil. Microwave on high for 3 minutes, or until crisp-tender. Stir in the celery, fresh tomatoes, green peppers, and red peppers. Microwave on high for 5 minutes, or until the peppers are crisp-tender.

Drain the lentils and discard the bay leaf. Add the lentils to the cooked vegetables. Stir in the canned tomatoes and their juice, tomato sauce, parsley, chili powder, cumin, marjoram, and oregano. Microwave on high for 8 minutes. Stir and microwave on high for 7 to 12 minutes, or until heated through and the vegetables are tender.

MAKES 6 SERVINGS.

HERBED VEGETABLE AND BROWN RICE CASSEROLE

If you keep cooked rice in the refrigerator or freezer, casseroles like this will be a snap.

1 cup sliced mushrooms

1 small zucchini, thinly sliced

4 scallions, thinly sliced

1 large tomato, seeded and chopped

½ cup low-fat cottage cheese

⅓ cup part-skim ricotta cheese

¼ cup buttermilk

1 egg or ¼ cup fat-free egg substitute

2 tablespoons minced fresh parsley

1 teaspoon minced fresh basil or ½ teaspoon dried basil

½ teaspoon dried marjoram

2 cups cooked brown rice

2 teaspoons grated Parmesan cheese

½ cup Basic Tomato Pasta Sauce (page 161)

In a 9″ pie plate, combine the mushrooms and zucchini. Microwave on high for 4 minutes, or until slightly tender. Drain off any liquid. Add the scallions and tomatoes. Microwave on high for 3 minutes, or until the scallions are crisp-tender.

In a food processor or blender, combine the cottage cheese, ricotta, buttermilk, egg, parsley, basil, and marjoram. Process until smooth.

In a 1-quart casserole, layer half of the rice. Press down lightly. Top with half of the vegetables and half of the cheese mixture. Repeat with the remaining rice, vegetables, and cheese mixture. Sprinkle with the Parmesan.

Cover with a lid. Microwave on high for 4 minutes. Then microwave on medium (50% power) for 12 to 15 minutes, rotating the dish twice during this time, until the casserole is heated through. Let stand for 3 to 4 minutes.

Place the tomato sauce in a 1-cup glass measure. Microwave on high for 1 minute. Top each serving of casserole with 2 tablespoons of the sauce.

MAKES 4 SERVINGS.

RICE AND THE MICROWAVE

When it comes to rice, you've got a lot of choices. I most often cook rice on the stove while more complicated main dishes cook in the microwave. But many people swear by rice turned out in the microwave, even if there's no significant savings in time. So here are some easy microwave recipes.

White rice: In a 3-quart casserole, combine 1 cup long-grain rice with 1¾ to 2 cups stock or water. Cover with a lid and microwave on high for 5 minutes. Microwave on medium (50% power) for 12 to 15 minutes, or until the liquid has been absorbed and the rice is tender. Let stand, covered, for 5 minutes. This amount makes four servings.

Brown rice: In a 3-quart casserole, combine 1 cup long-grain rice with 1¾ to 2 cups stock or water. Cover with a lid and microwave on high for 5 minutes. Then microwave on medium (50% power) for 30 to 35 minutes, or until almost all the liquid has been absorbed and the rice is tender. Let stand, covered, for 5 minutes. Fluff with a fork. If you prefer sticky rice, as for Chinese meals, use short-grain brown rice—1 cup with 2 to 2¼ cups stock or water. Both recipes serve four.

Risotto: You can make delicious risotto in the microwave—without the constant stirring required by stove-top methods. Place 1 tablespoon margarine or butter in a 7″ × 11″ baking dish and microwave on high for 1 minute. Stir in ¾ cup finely chopped onions and microwave on high for 3 minutes. Stir in 1 cup short-grain brown rice; microwave on high for 4 minutes. Stir in 3½ cups stock. Micro-wave on high for 15 minutes. Stir, then microwave on medium (50% power) for 15 minutes. Stir again, then microwave on medium (50% power) for another 10 to 15 minutes, or until all the liquid has been absorbed. Cover with foil and let stand for 5 minutes. This recipe serves four.

You may notice that many of my recipes use the new quick-cooking brown rice. It has as much fiber as regular brown, but it's ready in one-third of the time. Whether you microwave or boil it, it's done in 10 to 15 minutes. I often find that it's most efficient to let the rice simmer on the stove while the main course cooks in the microwave.

If you still prefer regular, long-cooking brown rice, you may cook up a batch at your leisure, then refrigerate or freeze it in small amounts. For best results, make sure the rice is cool before storing it. To freeze, place 1 to 2 cupfuls in a freezer bag. Press out the air and flatten the rice into an even layer. Seal the bag and freeze it flat.

To reheat frozen rice, break off as much as you need and place on a serving plate or in a microwave-safe bowl. Sprinkle with 2 tablespoons of water for each cup of rice. Microwave 1 cup on high for 3 to 4 minutes; do 2 cups for 4 to 7 minutes, stirring midway through the period. Stir again, cover, and let stand for a minute or so.

To reheat refrigerated rice, sprinkle with 2 tablespoons of water per cup of rice. Microwave 1 cup on high for 1 to 2 minutes; do 2 cups for 2 to 3 minutes.

CHEESE AND TOFU STUFFED SHELLS

20 jumbo pasta shells

1 egg or ¼ cup fat-free egg substitute

2 cups low-fat small-curd cottage cheese

½ cup drained, crumbled tofu

3 tablespoons minced fresh parsley

1 teaspoon minced fresh tarragon or ¼ teaspoon dried tarragon

½ teaspoon minced fresh oregano or ¼ teaspoon dried oregano

¼ teaspoon ground black pepper

⅛ teaspoon grated nutmeg

½ cup grated Parmesan cheese

2 cups Basic Tomato Pasta Sauce (page 161)

½ cup shredded part-skim mozzarella cheese

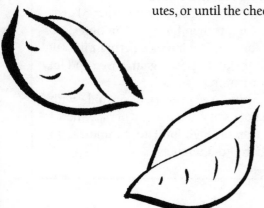

Cook the shells in a large pot of boiling water until just tender, about 12 minutes. Drain well and place in a single layer on a tray.

In a medium bowl, combine the egg, cottage cheese, tofu, parsley, tarragon, oregano, pepper, and nutmeg. Add ¼ cup of the Parmesan.

Spoon about 2 tablespoons of the mixture into each shell.

Spread ½ cup of the tomato sauce in the bottom of a 7" × 11" baking dish. Add the shells in a single layer. Top with the remaining 1½ cups of sauce.

Microwave on high for 10 to 12 minutes, rotating the dish a quarter turn three times during this time, until the casserole is bubbly.

Sprinkle with the remaining ¼ cup Parmesan and the mozzarella. Microwave on medium (50% power) for 5 minutes, or until the cheese is melted.

MAKES 4 SERVINGS.

FLORENTINE CRÊPES

These delicate crêpes have a creamy spinach-ricotta filling. They're excellent for an elegant Sunday brunch or a special dinner.

1 package (10 ounces) frozen chopped spinach

1½ cups part-skim ricotta cheese

1 egg white

¼ cup grated Parmesan cheese

3 tablespoons minced fresh parsley

1 teaspoon minced fresh basil or ½ teaspoon dried basil

⅛ teaspoon grated nutmeg

⅛ teaspoon ground black pepper

8 Whole Wheat Crêpes (page 169)

½ cup Basic Tomato Pasta Sauce (page 161)

Place the spinach in a 9″ pie plate. Microwave on high for 2 minutes. Rotate the dish a half turn. Microwave on high for 2 to 4 minutes, or until defrosted. Transfer the spinach to a sieve and drain well, pressing with the back of a spoon to remove all excess moisture.

In a medium bowl, combine the ricotta, egg white, Parmesan, parsley, basil, nutmeg, and pepper. Add the spinach and mix well.

Divide the filling among the crêpes, positioning it along one side. Roll to enclose the filling.

Coat a 7″ × 11″ baking dish with no-stick spray. Arrange the crêpes, seam-side down, in the dish. Spoon the sauce over the crêpes. Cover the dish with wax paper. Microwave on medium (50% power) for 5 minutes. Rotate the dish a half turn. Microwave on medium (50% power) for 5 to 7 minutes, or until heated through.

MAKES 4 SERVINGS.

FANCY CRÊPES—IN A MICROSECOND

When you think of stuffed crêpes, you probably envision a fancy restaurant where the culinary creations are out of this world—and so are the prices (not to mention the calories and fat). What you may not realize is that crêpes are quite easy to make at home.

You can even prepare the basic crêpes (see the opposite page) ahead of time and store a batch in the freezer. For ease in separating the pieces later, place squares of wax paper between them. Seal the stack inside a freezer bag. To use, remove the desired number from the bag. Thaw at room temperature or microwave on the defrost setting until pliable (keep the crêpes covered with wax paper to prevent drying). Exact times will depend on the number of crêpes involved and the precise power setting used.

Then, with the help of your microwave, you can whip up luscious fillings and toppings in minutes (see below). Your guests will be so impressed. They'll think you've been slaving in the kitchen all day!

Spoon your choice of filling onto the crêpes and roll them up. Place, seam-side down, in a shallow, lightly oiled microwave-safe casserole dish. If desired, top with a sauce.

Cover the baking dish with wax paper. Microwave on medium (50% power), rotating the dish occasionally, until heated through. Eight crêpes, which will serve four, take about 10 to 12 minutes.

Here are some quick crêpe stuffings:

- Lightly seasoned microwaved fish, shellfish, or poultry, flaked or chopped into bite-size pieces.
- Microwaved vegetables, plain or in a low-fat cream sauce.
- Leftovers such as the vegetables from Pasta Primavera (page 156).
- Part-skim ricotta cheese or low-fat cottage cheese flavored with fresh herbs.
- For dessert: stewed dried fruits, sliced fresh fruits, or applesauce.

These are some of my favorite crêpe sauces, followed by an all-purpose crêpe recipe:

- Basic Tomato Pasta Sauce (page 161) or spaghetti sauce.
- Low-fat cream sauce (with or without vegetables, poultry, or fish).
- Super Salsa (page 59) for crêpes with a Mexican flair.
- Leftover sauce from Creamy Herbed Fettuccine (page 142).
- Reduced-fat sour cream thinned with yogurt (if desired, flavor with fresh herbs).
- For dessert: applesauce or fresh fruits blended with maple syrup.

WHOLE WHEAT CRÊPES

1 cup skim milk

1 egg or ¼ cup fat-free egg substitute

1 egg white

¾ cup whole wheat flour

Place the milk, egg, and egg white in a blender container. Process on medium speed until combined. Add the flour and process on medium speed until smooth, stopping and scraping down the sides of the container as needed.

Coat a crêpe pan or medium no-stick frying pan with no-stick spray. Set the pan over medium heat until heated to the point where water sprinkled on the surface dances and sputters.

For each crêpe, add 2 to 3 tablespoons of the batter to the pan. Immediately swirl the pan gently to distribute the batter in a thin layer. Cook the crêpe until the surface appears dry, about 1 minute.

Turn the crêpe out of the pan onto a clean kitchen towel draped over a wire rack. Allow to cool, then stack the crêpes, separating them with wax paper.

MAKES 10 CRÊPES.

Note: I usually recommend whisking or reblending the batter before making each crêpe so the solids don't settle. If the batter becomes too thick near the end, thin it with a bit of milk.

VEGETABLE PIZZA

Using flour tortillas in place of regular pizza crust lets you have individual pizzas anytime.

2 mushrooms, thinly sliced
2 tablespoons diced green or sweet red peppers
1 scallion, thinly sliced
1/4 teaspoon olive oil

1 flour tortilla
1 tablespoon tomato paste
1/8 teaspoon dried basil
1/8 teaspoon dried oregano

Pinch of ground black pepper
1/4 cup shredded part-skim mozzarella cheese

In a small bowl, combine the mushrooms, peppers, scallions, and oil. Microwave on high for 2 minutes, or until the vegetables are crisp-tender.

Prick the surface of the tortilla all over with a fork. Place between two paper towels. Microwave on high for 1 1/2 minutes, or until somewhat crisp.

Place the tortilla on a plate. Spread with the tomato paste. Sprinkle with the basil, oregano, and pepper. Top with the vegetables and sprinkle with the cheese.

Microwave on high for 30 to 45 seconds, or until the cheese is melted.

MAKES 1 SERVING.

PITA PIZZA

1 whole wheat pita
1 tablespoon tomato paste

1/8 teaspoon dried basil
1/8 teaspoon dried oregano

1/4 cup shredded part-skim mozzarella cheese

Broil the pita on one side only for about 3 minutes, or until crisp but not browned. Flip and spread the soft top with the tomato paste. Sprinkle with the basil and oregano, then with the mozzarella.

Place the pita on a plate and microwave on high for
30 seconds to 1 minute, or until the cheese is melted.

MAKES 1 SERVING.

Variation: For Vegetable Pita Pizza: *In a small bowl, combine
1 tablespoon thinly sliced onions, 2 mushrooms (sliced), 2 tablespoons diced green peppers, and ¼ teaspoon olive oil.
Microwave on high for 1 to 2 minutes, or until tender. Arrange
the vegetables over the herbs and tomato paste. Sprinkle with the
mozzarella. Microwave on high for 30 to 45 seconds, or until
the cheese is melted.*

VEGETARIAN MACARONI CASSEROLE

1¾ cups elbow macaroni

½ cup chopped onions

½ cup chopped green peppers

1 clove garlic, minced

½ cup sliced mushrooms

2 cups chopped canned tomatoes, drained

¾–1 cup shredded reduced-fat Cheddar cheese

1 tablespoon minced fresh parsley

1 teaspoon minced fresh basil or ¼ teaspoon dried basil

¼ teaspoon grated lemon rind

Cook the macaroni in a large pot of boiling water
until just tender, about 5 to 6 minutes. Drain, rinse with
cold water, place in a bowl, and set aside.

In a 2-quart casserole, combine the onions, peppers, and
garlic. Microwave on high for 3 minutes, or until crisp-
tender. Stir in the mushrooms. Microwave on high for
3 minutes. Drain off and discard any liquid.

Add the macaroni, tomatoes, Cheddar, parsley, basil, and
lemon rind. Cover with a lid and microwave on high for
4 minutes. Remove the lid and microwave on medium
(50% power) for 8 to 10 minutes, or until the vegetables
are cooked through and the cheese is melted.

MAKES 4 SERVINGS.

171

TOFU STIR-FRY WITH SPINACH

Freezing the tofu before cooking it gives it a chewy, almost meaty texture.

8 ounces tofu, cut into slices ¼" thick

1½ cups water

1¼ cups quick-cooking brown rice

1 onion, thinly sliced

2 carrots, thinly sliced on the diagonal

½ teaspoon sesame oil

1 celery stalk, thinly sliced on the diagonal

1 yellow pepper, thinly sliced

1 sweet red pepper, thinly sliced

½ cup sliced mushrooms

8 ounces spinach, torn into bite-size pieces

½ cup chicken stock

½ cup pineapple juice

1 tablespoon ginger juice*

1 tablespoon soy sauce

1 tablespoon cornstarch

1 teaspoon honey

1 teaspoon lemon juice

¼ teaspoon hot pepper flakes

¼ teaspoon ground coriander

3 tablespoons roasted peanuts

1 teaspoon toasted sesame seeds

Place the tofu on a baking sheet in a single layer. Freeze for several hours or overnight. Remove from the freezer and set aside to thaw just before beginning this dish.

In a 2-quart saucepan over medium heat, bring the water to a boil. Stir in the rice, reduce the heat to low, cover the pan, and simmer for 10 minutes. Keep warm.

In a 2-quart casserole, combine the onions, carrots, and oil. Microwave on high for 3 minutes, or until the onions are slightly tender. Stir in the celery, yellow peppers, red peppers, and mushrooms. Microwave on high for 4 minutes, or until the celery begins to soften.

Stir in the spinach. Cover with wax paper and microwave on high for 1 minute. Stir, cover, and microwave on high for 1 to 2 minutes, or until the spinach wilts. Drain off and discard any liquid.

In a 1-quart saucepan, combine the stock, pineapple juice, ginger juice, soy sauce, cornstarch, honey, lemon juice, pepper flakes, and coriander. Stir over medium heat until the mixture comes to a boil and thickens.

Place the peanuts and sesame seeds in blender. Chop finely. Stir into the sauce. Pour over the vegetables and stir to combine. Cube the tofu and add. Microwave on high for 2 minutes, or until heated through.

Fluff the rice with a fork. Place on a platter. Top with the vegetables.

MAKES 4 SERVINGS.

To make ginger juice, shred enough fresh ginger to obtain about ¼ cup. Place in a piece of cheesecloth and twist to squeeze out the liquid.

MACARONI AND CHEESE

1½ cups elbow macaroni

¾–1 cup shredded reduced-fat Cheddar cheese

1 cup Basic Tomato Pasta Sauce (page 161)

⅓ cup skim milk

⅛ teaspoon paprika

⅛ teaspoon ground black pepper

2 tablespoons grated Parmesan cheese

Cook the macaroni in a large pot of boiling water until just tender, about 5 to 6 minutes. Drain and place in a 1½-quart casserole. Add the Cheddar and toss well.

Stir in the tomato sauce, milk, paprika, and pepper. Sprinkle with the Parmesan. Cover with wax paper and microwave on high for 5 to 6 minutes, or until heated through and the cheese is melted. Let stand for 5 minutes before serving.

MAKES 4 SERVINGS.

Variations: To the macaroni mixture, add either ½ cup cooked mushrooms, 1 tablespoon grated onions, or 2 tablespoons minced fresh parsley.

RAREBIT POTATOES WITH VEGETABLES

4 large baking potatoes
1 small onion, chopped
1 clove garlic, minced
½ teaspoon olive oil
2 carrots, thinly sliced

1 celery stalk, thinly sliced
1 broccoli stalk
1 cup peas
2 tablespoons margarine or butter

2 tablespoons whole wheat pastry flour
1¾–2 cups skim milk
⅓ cup shredded reduced-fat Cheddar cheese

Scrub and dry the potatoes. Pierce several times with a fork. Place in a square pattern on a paper towel. Microwave on high for 15 minutes, turning and rearranging the potatoes twice during this time, until the potatoes are just tender enough to pierce with a sharp knife.

Transfer to a 350° oven, placing the potatoes directly on the rack.

In a 2-quart casserole, combine the onions, garlic, and oil. Microwave on high for 2 minutes. Stir in the carrots and celery. Microwave on high for 4 minutes, or until the carrots are crisp-tender.

Cut the florets from the broccoli stalk and separate them into bite-size pieces. Peel the stem and thinly slice. Add the broccoli and peas to the casserole. Microwave on high for 4 to 5 minutes, or until the broccoli is crisp-tender.

In a 1-quart saucepan over medium heat, melt the margarine or butter. Add the flour and stir over heat for 1 minute.

Whisk in 1½ cups of the milk. Cook, stirring, until the sauce is bubbly and begins to thicken. Add the Cheddar, remove from the heat, and stir until the cheese is melted. Add enough of the remaining milk to make the sauce the consistency of light cream.

Pour the sauce over the cooked vegetables and stir to combine. Slit open the baked potatoes. Spoon the sauce over them.

MAKES 4 SERVINGS.

TIJUANA TORTILLAS

*If you don't have fresh coriander, omit it altogether.
There's just no substitute.*

1 cup shredded zucchini

1 medium tomato, seeded and chopped

⅓ cup finely chopped green peppers

¼ cup finely chopped onions

1 clove garlic, minced

4 corn tortillas

½ cup part-skim ricotta cheese

1 teaspoon minced fresh coriander (optional)

¼ teaspoon chili powder

⅛ teaspoon ground cumin

⅔ cup shredded reduced-fat Cheddar cheese

1 cup Super Salsa (page 59)

In a 1-quart casserole, combine the zucchini, tomatoes, peppers, onions, and garlic. Microwave on high for 2 minutes. Stir and microwave on high for 2 to 4 minutes, or until the onions are crisp-tender. Cover and let stand.

In a medium frying pan, bring ½″ of water to a simmer. Place the tortillas, one at a time, in the water for 10 to 20 seconds, or until just pliable. Remove with a spatula. Drain and set aside to cool.

In a small bowl, combine the ricotta, coriander (if using), chili powder, and cumin. Stir in ⅓ cup of the Cheddar.

Drain the vegetables, pressing them with a spoon to remove excess moisture. Add ½ cup of the salsa.

To assemble the tortillas, spread about ¼ cup of the cheese mixture on each tortilla. Place about ⅓ cup of the vegetables in the center of each tortilla. Roll the tortillas to enclose the filling.

Arrange, seam-side down, in an 8″ × 8″ baking dish. Pour the remaining ½ cup salsa over the tortillas. Cover with wax paper.

Microwave on high for 2 minutes. Rotate the dish a half turn. Microwave on high for 2 minutes. Sprinkle with the remaining ⅓ cup Cheddar. Microwave on medium (50% power) for 3 to 4 minutes, or until the cheese is melted.

MAKES 4 SERVINGS.

NORTH AFRICAN COUSCOUS PILAF

This unique dish is guaranteed to win raves. It blends the piquant aroma of roasted coriander and cumin seeds with the sweet flavors of fresh fennel, raisins, and red peppers.

1 teaspoon coriander seeds

1 teaspoon cumin seeds

½ cup pine nuts

1 onion, thinly sliced

1 clove garlic, minced

2 teaspoons olive oil

1 small fennel bulb (about 8 ounces), julienned

2 sweet red peppers, thinly sliced

2½ cups water or chicken stock

1 tablespoon margarine or butter

1¾ cups couscous

1½ cups cooked chick-peas

¾ cup raisins

In a 1-cup glass measure, combine the coriander and cumin. Microwave on high for 1 minute. Let cool, then grind the spices with a mortar and pestle or a spice mill.

Spread the pine nuts on a plate. Microwave on high for 2 to 3 minutes, or until just golden and aromatic.

In a 2½-quart casserole, combine the onions, garlic, and 1 teaspoon of the oil. Microwave on high for 2 minutes, or until the onions are crisp-tender.

Add the fennel and the remaining 1 teaspoon oil. Microwave on high for 3 minutes, or until the fennel is crisp-tender. Add the peppers. Microwave on high for 2 minutes, or until the peppers are crisp-tender.

Meanwhile, in a 2-quart saucepan over medium heat, bring the stock and margarine or butter to a boil. Stir in the couscous. Cover the pan, remove it from the heat, and let stand for 5 minutes.

Add the chick-peas and raisins to the casserole. Microwave on high for 3 minutes, or until heated through.

Fluff the couscous with a fork. Place in a large serving bowl. Sprinkle with the spices and pine nuts. Add the vegetables and toss to combine.

MAKES 6 SERVINGS.

176

EASY GRAIN SIDE DISHES

These two fast-cooking grains add versatility and interesting texture to meals, vegetarian or not. If you can't find them in your supermarket, take a trip to the health-food store. Make sure the bags you buy are individually labeled, so you know what you have once you get home.

Couscous: One of the fastest grain dishes to prepare, couscous is essentially a form of pasta. Made from precooked and dried hard white semolina wheat, it's very popular in North African dishes. For four servings, combine 1½ cups water and ½ teaspoon oil, margarine, or butter in a 1-quart bowl. Microwave on high for 5 minutes, or until boiling. Stir in 1 cup couscous. Cover with a lid or foil and let stand for 5 minutes. Fluff with a fork before using.

Bulgur: Though not quite as fast to prepare as couscous, bulgur is still amazingly handy. And because it's made from whole wheat kernels that have been minimally processed—steamed, dried, and crushed—it's higher in fiber than couscous. It comes in fine, medium, and coarse grinds. Medium seems to work best for vegetarian dishes. To serve four, place 2 cups water in a 1-quart bowl. Microwave on high for 6 minutes, or until boiling. Stir in 1 cup bulgur. Cover with a lid or foil and let stand for 10 to 15 minutes, or until the water has been absorbed and the bulgur is soft. Fluff with a fork before using.

SOUPS, STEWS & STOCKS

When you look to your microwave for help in preparing healthy dishes, you will never find it more versatile than with soups. That's because:

- You can use the microwave to make really fast stocks that are low in sodium.

- Vegetables retain their own rich flavors as they cook, so you don't need to add a lot of salt or fat to perk up your soups and stews.

- Traditionally long-cooking vegetables that make excellent soup, such as sweet potatoes, potatoes, and winter squash, cook quickly in the microwave.

❍ The microwave's quick cooking time helps foods retain important nutrients that would be lost during the extensive simmering required for stove-top soups.

Soups can contribute to a healthy lifestyle in many ways. For starters, they're an ally when it comes to losing weight or keeping off unwanted pounds. Doctors have found that beginning a meal with a bowl of hot soup helps people consume fewer calories later in the meal. That's because it takes *time* to eat hot soup—time that your appetite control center needs to start registering your calorie intake so you don't overeat.

Soup is also nutrient dense. You can get a lot of nutritional mileage out of a bowl. Many vegetables that you—or your children—might ignore when served by themselves are heartily accepted when incorporated into a tasty soup. Spinach, kale, broccoli, leeks, and squash come to mind as good examples.

One very important contribution the microwave makes is control over sodium and fat levels in soup. If you read the labels on many commercial soups, you'll notice that sodium levels are sky-high. If you have high blood pressure, you should think twice about eating such soups. But it's easy to make low-sodium stocks and soups in the microwave. By the same token, you can cut fat levels considerably by microwaving soup. That's because you don't have to sauté your vegetables in a lot of butter or oil as you might with stove-top preparation.

TAKING STOCK

Making stock is so easy with a microwave. I've included four basic recipes in this chapter—chicken, beef, fish, and seafood—that can serve as the base for most soups, stews, and sauces. Homemade stock is also very inexpensive when you save up all sorts of meat and poultry bones and vegetable trimmings.

If you bone your own chicken breasts, you'll have a nice supply of bones (along with any meat that clings to them) for stock. Just store them in the freezer until you have enough for stock. Add necks, gizzards, and hearts from whole birds. (Don't save skin or chicken livers for stock.) Likewise, you can save any beef bones you might remove from steaks or roasts.

And set aside the trimmings from vegetables. Although those from cabbage, broccoli, brussels sprouts, and cauliflower might be too strong for stock, many other trimmings are perfect. Celery leaves, root ends of scallions, pea pods, carrot trimmings, parsley stems, spinach stems, mushroom stems, tomato peels, potato peels, leek tops, sweet red pepper trimmings, and the tips of green beans and summer squash are all perfectly acceptable. Just be sure not to save any pieces that are spoiled or that have been waxed (such as the skin from some winter squash).

If your fish purveyor fillets fish for you, be sure to request the trimmings. Or ask about buying trimmings. I prefer the trimmings of lean white fish, such as cod, haddock, red snapper, and bass. Flat fish, such as flounder and sole, can give the broth a bitter taste. Fattier fish, such as salmon and mackerel, make a stronger-flavored stock that's best for dishes containing these fish. As with other trimmings, you may freeze these until you collect enough for stock.

If company arrives for dinner on short notice, you can fashion a fine meal from soup. If you have small quantities of several soups in the freezer, you can often combine them with good results. Some of the soups in this book that complement each other and that you can combine to make a delicious new soup are: Pagoda Chicken Soup (page 201) and Snappy Corn Soup (page 191); Chicken-Barley Soup (page 200) and Cream of Cauliflower Soup (page 198); Vegetable and Ground Beef Soup (page 205) and Quick Curried Tomato Soup (page 194); Vichyssoise (page 193) and Creamy Clam Chowder (page 198).

To extend a single soup, try adding tomato juice, canned tomatoes, buttermilk, yogurt, mashed potatoes, mashed winter squash, or pureed corn. The beauty of soup is that it's infinitely variable. You'll never run out of tasty combinations.

CHICKEN STOCK

When you see how easy it is to make your own chicken stock—and how delicious the final product is—you won't want to buy the canned version again.

1½ pounds chicken bones
4 cups water
2 celery stalks, thickly sliced

2 carrots, thickly sliced
1 small onion, quartered

3 parsley sprigs
1 bay leaf

In a 2½-quart casserole, combine the bones, water, celery, carrots, onions, parsley, and bay leaf. Cover with a lid. Microwave on high for 30 minutes. Let stand for 10 minutes. Strain through a sieve into a large bowl.

Refrigerate until the fat that rises to the top congeals. Remove the fat before using the stock. (If you will not be using the stock within two days, freeze it in single-serving-size containers.)

MAKES 1 QUART.

Variations: You may substitute other herbs, such as dill, rosemary, or chives, for the parsley. You may substitute 1 small leek for the onion. If you choose to make the stock without vegetables, increase the bones to 2 pounds.

CHICKEN-VEGETABLE SOUP

Bursting with vegetables and rich flavor, this soup makes a hit with kids and grown-ups alike.

1 onion, chopped
1 celery stalk, thinly sliced
2 cloves garlic, minced
1 teaspoon olive oil
1 broccoli stalk
3 carrots, thinly sliced
2 boneless, skinless chicken breast halves

3 small tomatoes, peeled and cut into thin wedges
3½ cups chicken stock
2 tablespoons minced fresh parsley
1 teaspoon soy sauce

1 teaspoon lemon juice
¼ teaspoon dried marjoram
⅛ teaspoon ground black pepper
Pinch of ground red pepper

In a 2½-quart casserole, combine the onions, celery, garlic, and oil. Cover with wax paper and microwave on high for 4 minutes, or until the onions are translucent.

Cut the florets from the broccoli stem and separate into small pieces; set aside.

Peel the broccoli stem and thinly slice; add to the onion mixture. Stir in the carrots. Cover with wax paper and microwave on high for 4 to 6 minutes, or until the carrots are crisp-tender.

While the vegetables are cooking, slice the chicken into thin, short strips. Add to the carrots. Stir in the tomatoes, 1 cup of the stock, and the reserved broccoli florets. Cover with a lid and microwave on high for 4 to 5 minutes. Stir and microwave on high for 4 to 5 minutes, or until the chicken is just opaque.

Add the parsley, soy sauce, lemon juice, marjoram, black pepper, red pepper, and the remaining 2½ cups stock. Cover with a lid and microwave on high for 4 to 5 minutes, or until heated through.

MAKES 6 SERVINGS.

BEEF STOCK

*Broiling the beef bones and onions gives rich
flavor and color to this stock.*

2 pounds beef neck or marrow
  bones

2 small onions, quartered

4 cups water

1 small carrot, thickly sliced

Place the bones and onions in a single layer in a
roasting pan. Broil 6″ from the heat, stirring occasionally,
for about 30 minutes, or until well browned.

Transfer to a 4-quart casserole. Use a little of the water to
loosen any baked-on particles from the roasting pan; add
to the casserole. Stir in the rest of the water and the carrots.

Microwave on high for 30 minutes. Cover the casserole and
let stand for 10 minutes. Strain through a sieve into a large
bowl.

Refrigerate until any fat that rises to the top congeals.
Remove the fat before using the stock. (If you will not be
using the stock within two days, freeze it in single-serving-
size containers.)

MAKES 1 QUART.

FISH STOCK

Use as a base for fish or seafood soups.

1 pound fish bones and heads
  (without gills)

4 cups water

2 tablespoons lemon juice

1 celery stalk, thickly sliced
1 carrot, thickly sliced
1 small onion, quartered

3 parsley sprigs
1 bay leaf
2 peppercorns

In a 3-quart casserole, combine the fish bones and heads, water, lemon juice, celery, carrots, onions, parsley, bay leaf, and peppercorns. Cover with a lid. Microwave on high for 20 minutes. Let stand for 10 minutes.

Strain through a fine sieve lined with cheesecloth. Refrigerate or freeze until needed.

MAKES 1 QUART.

SEAFOOD STOCK

The next time you prepare shrimp, save the shells for a delicious stock. If you won't be making the stock right away, freeze the shells. The amount of shells called for in this recipe is what you'd get from 1 pound of whole shrimp.

2–3 ounces shrimp shells	1 celery stalk, thickly sliced	1 bay leaf
3½ cups water	1 carrot, thickly sliced	1 lemon slice
1 leek or onion, coarsely chopped	3 parsley sprigs	

In a 4-quart casserole, combine the shells, water, leeks or onions, celery, carrots, parsley, bay leaf, and lemon. Cover with a lid. Microwave on high for 20 minutes. Let stand for 5 minutes.

Strain through a fine sieve lined with cheesecloth. Refrigerate or freeze until needed.

MAKES 1 QUART.

CREAM OF THE CROP

You can make wonderful low-fat "cream" soups in the microwave. They're fast and infinitely variable according to what vegetables are in season. I find that the basic recipe below works for all sorts of vegetables, from asparagus to zucchini. To use it, choose a vegetable from the chart on the opposite page and cut it into uniform pieces. (For more even cooking of asparagus and broccoli, peel the stems before using them.) The chart gives cooking times and suggested seasonings for each vegetable.

CREAM OF FRESH VEGETABLE SOUP

½ cup chopped onions
1 clove garlic, minced
1 tablespoon margarine or butter

Vegetable (see chart)
2 tablespoons unbleached flour
1 cup low-fat milk

1½ cups chicken stock
Seasonings (see chart)

In a 2½-quart casserole, combine the onions, garlic, and margarine or butter. Microwave on high for 1 minute, or until the margarine or butter is nearly melted. Stir and add your choice of vegetable.

Cover with wax paper and microwave on high for the time indicated on the chart, or until the vegetables are tender. Stir in the flour.

Transfer to a blender. Add the milk and puree until smooth.

Return the mixture to the casserole. Add the stock and the seasonings from the chart. Microwave on high for 5 to 6 minutes, or until heated through.

MAKES 3 TO 4 SERVINGS.

VEGETABLE	AMOUNT (cups)	COOKING TIME (minutes)	SEASONINGS
ASPARAGUS	2	4–5	1 tsp. lemon juice ⅛ tsp. ground mace
BROCCOLI	2	4–5	½ tsp. dried basil 1 small bay leaf (remove before serving)
CARROTS	1½	4–5	⅛ tsp. grated nutmeg
CAULIFLOWER	2	5–6	½ tsp. curry powder
GREEN BEANS AND LEEKS	1½ ½	6–8	½ tsp. dried savory
PEAS	1½	3–4	¼ cup shredded lettuce 2 Tbsp. diced lean ham ⅛ tsp. dried sage
ZUCCHINI	1½	3–4	⅛ tsp. grated nutmeg

CHILI BEAN SOUP

Using a combination of beans—choose from among black, white, pinto, and pink or red kidney beans—gives added taste and visual interest to this spicy soup. If I'm really pressed for time, I use canned beans (three of the 19-ounce size gives about 6 cups of cooked beans).

1 onion, chopped

1 celery stalk, thinly sliced

1 jalapeño pepper, seeded and minced (wear plastic gloves when handling)

1 clove garlic, minced

1 tablespoon olive oil

6 cups cooked beans, with liquid

½ cup chicken stock

½ cup Super Salsa (page 59)

2 ounces diced smoked turkey or lean ham

2 teaspoons chili powder

1 teaspoon ground cumin

¼ teaspoon dried oregano

⅓ cup shredded reduced-fat Cheddar cheese

2 scallions, thinly sliced

In a 3-quart casserole, combine the onions, celery, jalapeños, garlic, and oil. Cover with wax paper and microwave on high for 5 minutes, or until the onions are translucent.

Add the beans with their liquid, stock, salsa, turkey or ham, chili powder, cumin, and oregano. Cover with a lid and microwave on high for 5 minutes. Stir, cover, and microwave on high for 5 to 10 minutes, or until all of the ingredients are hot.

Ladle into bowls and sprinkle with the Cheddar and scallions.

MAKES 6 SERVINGS.

DUTCH SPLIT-PEA SOUP

3 cups water
1 cup dried green or yellow split peas
4 cloves garlic
1 bay leaf
1 large onion, quartered

2 celery stalks, coarsely chopped
2 carrots, coarsely chopped
4 cups chicken stock
½ teaspoon dried basil
½ teaspoon ground coriander

⅛ teaspoon ground allspice
1 cup skim milk
1 tablespoon soy sauce
Minced fresh parsley

In a 2½-quart casserole, combine the water, split peas, garlic, and bay leaf. Microwave on high for 30 minutes (do not stir during this time). Remove and discard the bay leaf.

Transfer the mixture to a blender. Process on medium speed until smooth, stopping to scrape down the sides of the container as needed. Pour back into the casserole.

Place the onions, celery, and carrots in the blender container with ½ cup of the stock. Process on medium speed until smooth, scraping down the sides of the container as needed.

Add the onion mixture to the casserole. Stir in the basil, coriander, allspice, and 2½ cups of the remaining stock. Microwave on high for 10 minutes, then stir. Repeat twice for a total of 30 minutes of cooking time.

Stir in the remaining 1 cup stock and the milk. Microwave on high for 7 minutes, then stir. Repeat twice for a total of 21 minutes of cooking time. Stir in the soy sauce and sprinkle with the parsley.

MAKES 6 SERVINGS.

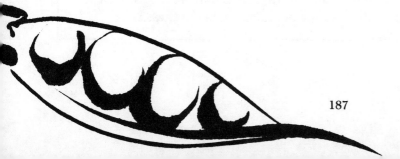

SIMPLE TOMATO SOUP

2 cups chopped canned plum tomatoes, with juice

2 cups chicken stock

2 cloves garlic, minced

1 teaspoon soy sauce

¼ teaspoon dried basil

⅛ teaspoon ground black pepper

In a 2-quart casserole, combine the tomatoes, stock, garlic, soy sauce, basil, and pepper. Microwave on high for 10 minutes.

MAKES 4 SERVINGS.

Variation: For Cheddar Tomato Soup: *Stir ½ cup shredded reduced-fat Cheddar cheese into the finished soup. Microwave on medium (50% power) for 2 to 3 minutes, or until the cheese is melted. Stir. Serve hot, garnished with croutons.*

QUICK AND EASY CROUTONS

You can make terrific croutons in the microwave. They're much less expensive than store-bought ones, and they're an excellent way to use up leftover bread. White, whole wheat, rye, and most other loaves work well. It's particularly nice to do a mixture. My family likes the combination of herbs in the recipe below, but you should feel free to experiment with your favorite seasonings. For instance, sage and thyme make tasty croutons, as do dill and summer savory.

To make the croutons, place 2 tablespoons margarine or butter in a 2-quart casserole. Microwave on high for 1 minute, or until melted. Stir in 2 tablespoons grated Parmesan cheese, ½ teaspoon dried marjoram, ½ teaspoon dried basil, ¼ teaspoon dried oregano, ⅛ teaspoon celery seeds, and a pinch of ground black pepper. (If you'd like, you can also add some minced garlic.)

Add 2 cups stale bread cubes and stir to coat them well with the herb mixture. Microwave on high for 1 minute. Stir well and repeat until the croutons are lightly browned and sizzling. Total microwaving time will be from 3 to 5 minutes.

Spread out on a double thickness of paper towels and let stand until crisp and cool. Store in the refrigerator in a tightly closed container to maintain crispness.

MINESTRONE

I like to use whole wheat macaroni in soups because I find it doesn't become soggy like the white variety sometimes does. It even stands up to storing, freezing, and reheating. This hearty soup makes a great main dish for quick suppers. Serve with a salad and crusty whole-grain rolls.

1 large onion, chopped
2 cloves garlic, minced
1 teaspoon olive oil
2 carrots, thinly sliced
2 cups chicken stock
2 cups chopped canned tomatoes, with juice

½ cup whole wheat elbow macaroni
½ teaspoon dried basil
½ teaspoon dried marjoram
¼ teaspoon dried oregano

2 cups cooked kidney beans
2 cups thinly sliced fresh spinach
¼ cup minced fresh parsley

In a 3-quart casserole, combine the onions, garlic, and oil. Cover with wax paper and microwave on high for 4 minutes, or until the onions are translucent. Add the carrots, cover with wax paper, and microwave for 5 to 6 minutes, or until crisp-tender.

Stir in the stock, tomatoes with juice, macaroni, basil, marjoram, and oregano. Cover with a lid and microwave on high for 15 to 18 minutes, or until the macaroni is nearly tender.

Stir in the beans, spinach, and parsley. Cover with a lid and microwave on high for 3 to 4 minutes, or until the spinach is wilted. Let stand for 2 to 5 minutes, or until the macaroni is tender.

MAKES 4 SERVINGS.

CABBAGE SOUP

½ cup chopped onions

¼ cup chopped celery

2 cloves garlic, minced

1 teaspoon olive oil

2 cups shredded cabbage

1 small zucchini, cubed

2 cups chopped canned tomatoes, with juice

1 cup chicken stock

¼ cup minced fresh parsley

½ teaspoon ground coriander

½ teaspoon ground cumin

½ teaspoon dried oregano

¼ teaspoon dried thyme

¼ teaspoon ground black pepper

¼ cup nonfat yogurt

In a 2-quart casserole, combine the onions, celery, garlic, and oil. Cover with wax paper and microwave on high for 4 minutes, or until the onions are translucent. Add the cabbage and zucchini. Cover with wax paper and microwave on high for 7 to 8 minutes, or until the cabbage is tender.

Set aside 1 cup of the vegetables. Transfer the remainder to a blender or food processor and puree until smooth. Pour into the casserole. Stir in the tomatoes, stock, parsley, coriander, cumin, oregano, thyme, and pepper. Add the reserved vegetables.

Microwave on high for 8 to 10 minutes, or until heated through. Ladle into bowls and serve with a dollop of yogurt.

MAKES 4 TO 6 SERVINGS.

FRENCH-STYLE ONION SOUP

4 large Spanish onions, thinly sliced

2 teaspoons margarine or butter

2 teaspoons olive oil

3 cloves garlic, minced

1 tablespoon whole wheat flour

4 cups chicken stock

1 tablespoon soy sauce

4–6 slices French bread

¾ cup shredded reduced-fat Swiss or Gruyère cheese

In a 3-quart casserole, combine the onions, margarine or butter, and oil. Microwave for 3 to 4 minutes, or until the margarine or butter is melted. Stir in the garlic.

Cover with wax paper and microwave on high for 10 to 15 minutes, or until the onions are tender. Sprinkle with the flour and stir well. Stir in the stock and soy sauce. Cover with a lid and microwave on high for 15 minutes.

Divide the bread among individual bowls. Add soup and sprinkle with the Swiss or Gruyère. Microwave two bowls at a time on medium (50% power) for 3 to 4 minutes, or until the cheese is melted.

MAKES 4 TO 6 SERVINGS.

SNAPPY CORN SOUP

Fast, low-fat, delicious! This is a terrific meal starter.

¼ cup diced sweet red or green peppers
¼ cup sliced scallions
1½ cups chicken stock

½ cup corn
1 bay leaf
1 teaspoon lemon juice

¼ teaspoon ground coriander
Pinch of ground red pepper
Scallion tops, cut on the diagonal (garnish)

In a 1½-quart casserole, combine the red peppers or green peppers and sliced scallions. Cover with wax paper and microwave on high for 3 minutes, or until the peppers are crisp-tender.

Add the stock, corn, bay leaf, lemon juice, coriander, and red pepper. Cover with a lid and microwave on high for 3 to 5 minutes, or until the vegetables are crisp-tender. Remove and discard the bay leaf. Sprinkle the soup with the scallion tops.

MAKES 2 SERVINGS.

WINTER-SQUASH SOUP

Butternut squash makes an excellent base for soup. But baking one of these winter squash can take an hour in a conventional oven. The microwave slashes that time to 12 minutes—making it convenient to serve this vegetable often.

1 butternut squash (about 2 pounds)

1 leek, white part only, chopped

1 tart green apple, chopped

1 tablespoon margarine or butter

2 cups chicken stock

¼ teaspoon grated orange rind

½ cup buttermilk or nonfat yogurt

4 orange slices (garnish)

Pierce the squash deeply in several places with a sharp knife. Place on a double layer of paper towels and microwave on high for 6 minutes. Turn the squash over. Microwave on high for 6 to 7 minutes, or until the squash is easily pierced with a knife and gives under gentle pressure. Let stand for 5 minutes.

In a 2-quart casserole, combine the leeks, apples, and margarine or butter. Cover with wax paper and microwave on high for 2 minutes, or until the margarine or butter is melted. Stir, cover with wax paper, and microwave on high for 4 to 6 minutes, or until the apples are crisp-tender.

Cut the squash in half lengthwise. Remove and discard the seeds. Scoop the pulp from the shell and add to the apple mixture; stir in the stock and orange rind. Working in batches, transfer to a blender and puree until smooth.

Return the mixture to the casserole. Cover with a lid and microwave on high for 5 to 7 minutes, or until heated through. Remove from the microwave and let stand for 2 minutes.

Place the buttermilk or yogurt in a small bowl. Microwave on high for 30 seconds. Stir into the soup, then ladle into bowls and garnish with the orange slices.

MAKES 4 SERVINGS.

VICHYSSOISE

This version of the classic soup is lighter than most because I've jettisoned the heavy cream, but it's still velvety smooth. If you serve it hot, feel free to call it Leek and Potato Soup.

2 leeks, white part only, thinly sliced

1 small onion, chopped

1 tablespoon margarine or butter

2 large baking potatoes, peeled and diced

4 cups chicken stock

1 cup low-fat milk

¼ teaspoon ground white pepper

Minced fresh chives

In a 3-quart casserole, combine the leeks, onions, and margarine or butter. Microwave on high for 2 minutes, or until the margarine or butter is melted. Stir and microwave on high for 3 to 4 minutes, or until the onions are translucent.

Add the potatoes and 2 cups of the stock. Cover with a lid and microwave on high for 15 minutes, or until the potatoes are quite tender. Transfer to a blender and puree on medium speed until just smooth (do not overprocess or the potatoes will become gummy).

Pour back into the casserole. Stir in the milk, pepper, and remaining 2 cups stock. Cover and chill thoroughly. Sprinkle with the chives.

MAKES 6 SERVINGS.

Note: If you prefer to serve this soup hot, puree the vegetables and return them to the casserole. Stir in the remaining stock. Microwave on high for 5 minutes, or until heated through. Add the milk and pepper, cover with a lid, and microwave on high for 5 minutes. Sprinkle with the chives.

QUICK CURRIED TOMATO SOUP

3 cups tomato juice
3 cups chicken stock
4 whole cloves
1 small onion
1 tablespoon lemon juice

2 teaspoons molasses
¼–½ teaspoon curry powder
⅛ teaspoon ground black pepper

½ cup shredded reduced-fat Monterey Jack cheese
½ cup thinly sliced scallion tops

In a 3-quart casserole, combine the tomato juice and stock. Stick the cloves into the onion and add to the casserole. Microwave on high for 7 to 8 minutes, or until the mixture comes to a simmer.

Stir in the lemon juice, molasses, curry powder, and pepper. Cover with a lid and microwave on high for 5 minutes. Remove and discard the onion. Ladle into bowls and sprinkle with the Monterey Jack and scallions.

MAKES 6 SERVINGS.

LENTIL SOUP

3 cups hot water
1 cup dried lentils
1 bay leaf
4 whole cloves
1 clove garlic
1 cup chopped onions

1 cup chopped celery
1 tablespoon minced garlic
1 tablespoon olive oil
4 carrots, thinly sliced
2 cups beef or chicken stock
¼ cup minced fresh parsley

2 tablespoons soy sauce
⅛ teaspoon grated nutmeg
⅛ teaspoon ground black pepper
1 tomato, seeded and quartered

In a 1½-quart casserole, combine the water, lentils, and bay leaf. Stick the whole cloves into the garlic for easy retrieval later; add to the casserole. Microwave on high for 20 minutes. Cover tightly and set aside for 10 minutes. Remove and discard the bay leaf and clove of garlic.

In a 4-quart casserole, combine the onions, celery, minced garlic, and oil. Cover with wax paper and microwave on high for 6 minutes, or until the onions are translucent. Stir in the carrots. Cover with wax paper and microwave on high for 6 to 8 minutes, or until the carrots are tender.

Take 1 cup of the cooked lentils and add to the carrot mixture. Add the stock, parsley, soy sauce, nutmeg, and pepper. Set aside.

Transfer the remaining lentils, with their liquid, to a blender. Add the tomatoes. Puree on medium speed until smooth. Add to the carrot mixture. Microwave on high for 5 minutes, or until heated through.

MAKES 6 SERVINGS.

THE SECOND TIME AROUND

Most of the soup recipes in this book serve four, some even six or eight. If you have leftovers, consider freezing them for future quick meals. Soup freezes very well and may even taste better when reheated because the flavors will have had more time to blend. You might even want to whip up a few batches of different soups when you have extra time so you can put them aside for really busy days.

Freeze soup in 1- or 2-cup portions. If the container is microwave-safe, you can defrost and reheat the soup right in the container. Alternatively, you can pop the frozen block out of the container into a soup bowl (running hot tap water over the outside of the container makes this easier). In either case, cover the soup with wax paper. Microwave 1 cup of frozen soup on high for 2 minutes; stir if possible and microwave for another 2 minutes, or until the soup is hot. For 2 cups of frozen soup, microwave on high for 4 to 6 minutes, stirring twice during this time.

Naturally, it's easy to reheat soups that have simply been refrigerated. For one serving, place 1 cup of soup in a bowl and microwave on high for 2 minutes. For two servings, place 2 cups of soup in a 4-cup glass measure and microwave on high for 2 minutes; stir, then microwave for another 1 to 2 minutes, or until hot. For four servings, ladle 4 cups of soup into a 1½-quart casserole and microwave on high for 2 minutes; stir, then microwave for another 2 to 3 minutes, or until heated through.

HOLIDAY SWEET-POTATO SOUP

Sweet potatoes are long-cooking vegetables that become very convenient when done in the microwave. Rich in cancer-preventing beta-carotene, they're a flavorful base for a delicately spiced soup.

2 large sweet potatoes (about 1½ pounds total)

½ cup minced onions

½ cup minced celery

1 tablespoon margarine or butter

1 tart green apple, peeled and diced

2 cups chicken stock

½ teaspoon ground cinnamon

¼ teaspoon ground coriander

⅛ teaspoon grated nutmeg

⅛ teaspoon ground ginger

1 cup low-fat milk

Pierce the sweet potatoes with a knife in several places. Arrange side by side on a paper towel in the microwave. Microwave on high for 4 to 5 minutes. Flip and rearrange, then microwave on high for 4 to 5 minutes, or until tender. Set aside.

In a 3-quart casserole, combine the onions, celery, and margarine or butter. Microwave on high for 2 minutes, or until the margarine or butter is melted. Stir in the apples. Microwave on high for 4 minutes, or until the apples are crisp-tender.

Peel and quarter the sweet potatoes. Place in a blender with 1 cup of the stock and the cinnamon, coriander, nutmeg, and ginger. Process on medium speed until smooth. Stir in the milk and the remaining 1 cup stock. Pour back into the casserole.

Cover with a lid and microwave on high for 5 to 6 minutes, or until heated through.

MAKES 6 SERVINGS.

NEW-ENGLAND ACORN-SQUASH SOUP

Made easy with the microwave, this elegant soup is suitable for the fanciest entertaining.

- 2 acorn squash (about 1¼ pounds each)
- 1 large onion, chopped
- ¼ cup thinly sliced celery

- 1 tablespoon margarine or butter
- 2 cups chicken stock
- ½ cup low-fat milk

- ⅛ teaspoon grated nutmeg
- 2 tablespoons maple syrup
- ⅓ cup nonfat yogurt

Pierce each squash several times with a knife. Arrange on a large plate and microwave on high for 10 minutes. Turn the squash over, then microwave on high for 8 to 10 minutes, or until tender. Halve, let cool, then remove and discard the seeds.

In a 3-quart casserole, combine the onions, celery, and margarine or butter. Microwave on high for 2 minutes, or until the margarine or butter is melted. Stir, then microwave on high for 4 minutes, or until the onions are crisp-tender.

Scoop the flesh from the squash shells and transfer to a food processor. Add the onion mixture. Puree until smooth. Return to the casserole. Stir in the stock, milk, nutmeg, and 1 tablespoon of the maple syrup. Microwave on high for 5 to 7 minutes, or until the mixture comes to a simmer. Ladle into bowls.

In a cup, combine the yogurt with the remaining 1 tablespoon maple syrup. Drizzle over each serving.

MAKES 6 SERVINGS.

CREAM OF CAULIFLOWER SOUP

1 small onion, finely chopped
½ celery stalk, finely chopped
½ clove garlic, minced
2 tablespoons margarine or butter

2 tablespoons unbleached flour
4 cups chicken stock
1 large head cauliflower, coarsely chopped

½ cup low-fat milk
⅛ teaspoon grated nutmeg
Minced fresh chives

In a 2½-quart casserole, combine the onions, celery, garlic, and margarine or butter. Microwave on high for 1 to 2 minutes, or until the margarine or butter is melted. Stir in the flour.

Add the stock and cauliflower. Cover with a lid and microwave on high for 10 to 15 minutes, or until the cauliflower is tender. Let stand for 10 minutes.

Working in batches, puree in a food processor or blender on medium speed until smooth. Return to the casserole and stir in the milk and nutmeg. Microwave on high for 2 to 3 minutes, or until hot. Sprinkle with the chives.

MAKES 4 TO 6 SERVINGS.

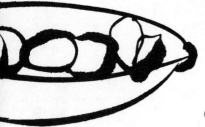

CREAMY CLAM CHOWDER

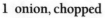

1 onion, chopped
2 celery stalks, thinly sliced
1 tablespoon margarine or butter
2 tablespoons unbleached flour

¼ teaspoon dried oregano
¼ teaspoon dried thyme
⅛ teaspoon ground black pepper
1 cup clam juice or Fish Stock (page 182)

3 carrots, shredded
3 medium baking potatoes, diced
2 cups low-fat milk
2 cans (6½ ounces each) minced clams, with liquid

In a 3-quart casserole, combine the onions, celery, and margarine or butter. Microwave on high for 2 minutes, or until the margarine or butter is melted. Stir, cover with

wax paper, and microwave on high for 3 minutes, or until the onions are translucent.

Stir in the flour, oregano, thyme, and pepper. Add the clam juice or stock. Microwave on high for 3 minutes. Stir, then microwave on high for 2 to 3 minutes, or until the mixture comes to a simmer.

Add the carrots, potatoes, and 1 cup of the milk. Cover with wax paper and microwave on high for 12 to 14 minutes, or until the potatoes are tender. Stir in the remaining 1 cup milk and the clams with liquid. Microwave on high for 4 to 5 minutes, or until heated through.

MAKES 4 SERVINGS.

THICKENING SOUPS THE LOW-FAT WAY

Creamy, rich soups often get their velvety texture from butter and heavy cream. But you can make really satisfying creamy soups without those unhealthy additions. Here are some wonderful low-fat ingredients I use to give soups a smooth, thick consistency.

Rice. I cook white rice until it's nice and soft, then puree it with some of the cooking liquid from the soup. To make the rice, combine 1½ cups rice and 3½ cups water in a 2½-quart casserole. Microwave on high for 20 minutes without stirring. Cover and let stand for 5 to 10 minutes, or until all water has been absorbed. For *each serving,* transfer ½ cup liquid from the soup and ¼ cup of the rice to a blender. Puree until smooth. Stir into the soup and reheat if needed.

To make things easier, freeze the soft-cooked rice for future use. Coat a baking sheet with no-stick spray. Place ¼ cup mounds of the rice on the sheet. Freeze until solid. Store in freezer bags.

Potatoes. Cook your favorite type of potatoes until tender. (Cook them as you wish—in the microwave, on the stove, or in a conventional oven.) Peel and chop. Place in a blender or food processor with some of the liquid from the soup you wish to thicken. Puree just until smooth. Do not overprocess the potatoes or they will become gummy. Stir them into the soup.

Vegetables. Various other vegetables make good thickeners, and they're the basis for my Cream of Fresh Vegetable Soup (page 184). When making other types of soup, you can remove some of the vegetables from the soup and simply puree them in a blender or food processor. Use enough of the soup liquid to facilitate the blending. Stir the vegetables back into the soup.

CHICKEN-BARLEY SOUP

1 onion, chopped
1 cup sliced mushrooms
1 clove garlic, minced
2 carrots, julienned
1 large celery stalk, julienned

½ cup quick-cooking barley
4 cups chicken stock
8 ounces boneless, skinless chicken breast, cut into thin strips 1½″ long

½ cup peas
2 tablespoons minced fresh parsley
1 tablespoon minced fresh chives

In a 3-quart casserole, combine the onions, mushrooms, and garlic. Cover with wax paper and microwave on high for 5 minutes, or until the onions are translucent. Stir in the carrots and celery. Cover with wax paper and microwave on high for 3 to 4 minutes, or until the vegetables are crisp-tender.

Add the barley and 2 cups of the stock. Cover with a lid and microwave on high for 15 minutes, or until the barley is nearly tender.

Add the chicken, peas, and remaining 2 cups stock. Cover with a lid and microwave on high for 3 to 4 minutes, or until the chicken is no longer pink. Stir in the parsley and chives. Cover and let stand for 3 to 4 minutes.

MAKES 4 SERVINGS.

MANHATTAN CLAM CHOWDER

1 onion, chopped
½ cup thinly sliced celery
1 carrot, diced
1 clove garlic, minced
2 teaspoons olive oil
2 large baking potatoes, diced
1 cup clam juice or Fish Stock (page 182)

1 bay leaf
2 cups chopped canned plum tomatoes, with juice
2 cans (6½ ounces each) minced clams, with liquid
¼ cup minced fresh parsley

1 teaspoon lemon juice
¼ teaspoon dried marjoram
¼ teaspoon dried thyme
Pinch of ground black pepper
Pinch of ground red pepper

In a 3-quart casserole, combine the onions, celery, carrots, garlic, and oil. Cover with a lid and microwave on high for 5 minutes, or until the onions are translucent.

Add the potatoes, clam juice or stock, and bay leaf. Cover with a lid and microwave on high for 10 minutes. Stir, cover, and microwave on high for 5 to 10 minutes, or until the potatoes are quite tender.

Stir in the tomatoes with juice, clams with liquid, parsley, lemon juice, marjoram, thyme, black pepper, and red pepper. Cover and microwave on high for 4 to 5 minutes, or until just heated through. Remove and discard the bay leaf.

MAKES 4 SERVINGS.

PAGODA CHICKEN SOUP

2 cups chicken stock

6 thin slices fresh ginger

3 cloves garlic, minced

1 bay leaf

½ small jalapeño pepper, minced (wear plastic gloves when handling)

4 ounces boneless, skinless chicken breast, cut into ½" cubes

2 tablespoons thinly sliced scallions

2 teaspoons lemon juice

½ cup cooked spaghetti, cut up

1 tablespoon minced fresh coriander or parsley

2 teaspoons soy sauce

In a 2-quart casserole, combine the stock, ginger, garlic, bay leaf, and jalapeños. Microwave on high for 8 minutes.

Add the chicken, scallions, and lemon juice. Microwave on high for 2 to 4 minutes, or until the chicken is no longer pink.

Stir in the spaghetti, coriander or parsley, and soy sauce. Microwave on high for 1 minute, or until heated through. Remove and discard the bay leaf and ginger slices.

MAKES 4 SERVINGS.

CREAM OF SPINACH SOUP

Delicious, easy, and beautiful!

2 boxes (10 ounces each) frozen chopped spinach

1 onion, chopped

2 cloves garlic, minced

1 tablespoon margarine or butter

1½ tablespoons unbleached flour

¼ teaspoon grated nutmeg

2 cups low-fat milk

2 cups chicken stock

¼ teaspoon dried tarragon

Remove the spinach from the boxes and place on a large plate. Microwave on high for 6 minutes. Cover with foil and let stand for 5 minutes to complete thawing.

In a 2½-quart casserole, combine the onions, garlic, and margarine or butter. Microwave on high for 2 minutes, or until the margarine or butter is melted. Stir, then microwave on high for 2 minutes, or until the onions are translucent. Stir in the flour and nutmeg.

Transfer the spinach to a sieve and drain well, pressing with the back of a spoon to remove all excess moisture. Place the spinach in a blender or food processor. Add the onion mixture and 1 cup of the milk. Puree until smooth. Pour back into the casserole.

Stir in the stock, tarragon, and remaining 1 cup milk. Microwave on high for 4 to 5 minutes. Stir, then microwave on high for 4 to 5 minutes, or until heated through.

MAKES 6 SERVINGS.

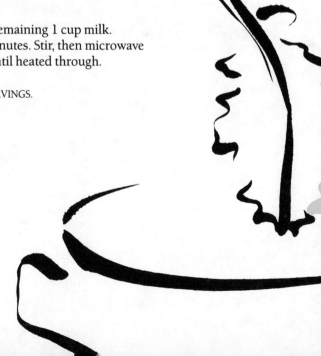

CIOPPINO

Pronounced "chuh-PEE-noh," this Italian seafood stew is delicious in any language. I like it best spooned over linguine. Fresh sourdough bread and a big green salad are admirable accompaniments.

2 cups chopped onions

1 tablespoon minced garlic

1 tablespoon olive oil

1 cup diced green peppers

½ cup diced sweet red peppers

3½ cups chopped canned tomatoes, with juice

1 cup tomato sauce

1 cup clam juice or Fish Stock (page 182)

1 tablespoon minced fresh basil

½ teaspoon dried oregano

¼ teaspoon ground black pepper

⅛ teaspoon ground red pepper

1½ pounds haddock or cod, cut into 2" pieces

½ cup minced fresh parsley

1 pound medium shrimp, peeled and deveined

Minced fresh parsley

Grated Parmesan cheese

In a 4-quart casserole, combine the onions, garlic, and oil. Microwave on high for 4 to 5 minutes, stirring once, or until the onions are translucent.

Stir in the green peppers and red peppers. Microwave on high for 4 to 5 minutes, or until the peppers are crisp-tender. Add the tomatoes with juice, tomato sauce, clam juice or stock, basil, oregano, black pepper, and red pepper.

Microwave on high for 15 minutes. Stir and microwave on high for 15 to 20 minutes, or until the vegetables are tender. Add the haddock or cod and ½ cup parsley. Microwave on high for 3 to 4 minutes, or until the fish begins to turn opaque.

Add the shrimp and microwave on high for 2 minutes, or until the shrimp begin to turn opaque. Cover and let stand for 5 minutes, or until the fish and shrimp are opaque throughout. Ladle into bowls and sprinkle with the parsley and Parmesan.

MAKES 4 TO 6 SERVINGS.

COQUINA-FISH STEW

*Coquinas are little periwinkle clams native to
Florida and are difficult for most of us to come by.
Canned baby clams are readily available and
produce a very agreeable dish.*

1 onion, chopped

2 cloves garlic, minced

1 tablespoon olive oil

2 celery stalks, thinly sliced

1 green pepper, diced

1 can (10 ounces) whole baby clams, with liquid

1½–2 cups clam juice or Fish Stock (page 182)

3½ cups crushed tomatoes

1 bay leaf

½ teaspoon dried marjoram

½ teaspoon dried thyme

⅛ teaspoon ground black pepper

⅛ teaspoon ground red pepper

1½ pounds haddock fillets, cut into bite-size pieces

12 ounces medium shrimp, peeled and deveined

2 tablespoons minced fresh parsley

In a 4-quart casserole, combine the onions, garlic, and oil. Cover with wax paper and microwave on high for 4 minutes, or until the onions are translucent.

Add the celery and peppers. Cover with wax paper and microwave on high for 4 to 6 minutes, or until the vegetables are crisp-tender.

Drain the clams, reserving the liquid. Set the clams aside. Pour the liquid into a glass measure and add enough clam juice or stock to equal 2½ cups. Pour into the casserole.

Stir in the tomatoes, bay leaf, marjoram, thyme, black pepper, and red pepper. Cover with a lid and microwave on high for 15 to 20 minutes, stirring the stew and rotating the dish twice during this period.

Stir in the haddock. Cover with a lid and microwave on high for 4 minutes. Add the shrimp, parsley, and clams. Cover with a lid and microwave on high for 3 to 4 minutes, or until the fish and shrimp are cooked through. Remove and discard the bay leaf.

MAKES 6 TO 8 SERVINGS.

VEGETABLE
AND GROUND BEEF SOUP

*Popular with kids, this soup combines a healthful
selection of vegetables they might otherwise
ignore. With a salad and hearty bread, you've
got a meal.*

1 pound extra-lean ground beef
1 onion, chopped
1 clove garlic, minced
3 celery stalks, thinly sliced
5 carrots, thinly sliced
1/3 cup long-grain white rice

4 cups beef stock or chicken stock
3½ cups crushed tomatoes
2 cups finely chopped spinach or Swiss chard
1/4 cup minced fresh parsley

1 teaspoon dried basil
1/2 teaspoon dried marjoram
1/4 teaspoon dried thyme
1/4 teaspoon dried oregano
1/8 teaspoon ground black pepper

In a 4-quart casserole, combine the beef, onions, and garlic. Microwave on high for 2 minutes. Stir and microwave on high for 2 to 3 minutes, or until the meat is no longer pink. Drain off any fat.

Add the celery, carrots, rice, and 1 cup of the stock. Cover with a lid and microwave on high for 7 minutes. Stir well and rotate the dish a half turn. Cover and microwave on high for 8 minutes, or until the vegetables are tender.

Add the tomatoes and the remaining 3 cups stock. Microwave on high for 5 minutes, or until heated through. Stir in the spinach or Swiss chard, parsley, basil, marjoram, thyme, oregano, and pepper. Microwave on high for 5 to 6 minutes, or until the spinach is cooked through.

MAKES 8 SERVINGS.

BEEF STEW

The cooking time on this stew is a little longer than you might expect for a microwave recipe, but it gives the same wonderful slow-simmered flavor you get from conventional beef stews.

1 large onion, chopped

3 cloves garlic, minced

1 tablespoon margarine or butter

3 large carrots, thinly sliced

1 celery stalk, thinly sliced

6 mushrooms, sliced

1 pound lean beef, trimmed of all visible fat and cut into ½" cubes

2 cups beef stock or chicken stock

1 cup tomato sauce

1 teaspoon dried basil

½ teaspoon dried marjoram

¼ teaspoon dried tarragon

¼ teaspoon ground black pepper

3 large baking potatoes, cubed

1 tablespoon minced fresh parsley

In a 3-quart casserole, combine the onions, garlic, and margarine or butter. Microwave on high for 2 minutes, or until the margarine or butter is melted. Stir, cover with wax paper, and microwave on high for 4 minutes, or until the onions are translucent.

Add the carrots, celery, and mushrooms. Cover with wax paper and microwave on high for 8 minutes, or until the carrots are crisp-tender.

Add the beef, stock, tomato sauce, basil, marjoram, tarragon, and pepper. Cover with a lid and microwave on high for 45 minutes, or until the beef and vegetables are tender.

About 30 minutes before serving, place the potatoes in a 3-quart saucepan with cold water to cover. Bring to a boil and cook for 25 minutes, or until tender. Drain, cover, and keep warm until the stew is ready. Just before serving, stir in the parsley.

If desired, stir the potatoes into the stew. Otherwise, serve the stew over them.

MAKES 4 SERVINGS.

SHRIMP BISQUE

A delicately seasoned, deliciously light way to start a meal.

¾ cup chopped celery
1 cup chopped leeks or onions
2 cloves garlic, minced
1 tablespoon margarine or butter

1 cup diced potatoes
1 tablespoon unbleached flour
1 cup Fish Stock (page 182) or chicken stock

12 ounces medium shrimp, peeled and deveined
1½ cups low-fat milk
¼ teaspoon dried tarragon
⅛ teaspoon grated nutmeg

In a 2-quart casserole, combine the celery, leeks or onions, garlic, and margarine or butter. Microwave on high for 2 minutes, or until the margarine or butter is melted.

Stir in the potatoes. Cover with wax paper and microwave on high for 5 to 6 minutes, or until the potatoes are crisp-tender. Stir in the flour. Transfer to a blender. Add the stock and process on medium speed until smooth. Return the mixture to the casserole.

Leave half of the shrimp whole; cut the rest into ½″ pieces. Add the shrimp to the casserole. Cover with a lid and microwave on high for 2 to 3 minutes, or until the shrimp just begin to turn opaque.

Stir in the milk, tarragon, and nutmeg. Cover with a lid and microwave on high for 5 to 6 minutes, or until the soup is heated and the shrimp are delicately cooked.

MAKES 4 SERVINGS.

CREAM OF CARROT SOUP

¼ cup minced onions

1 tablespoon minced celery

1 teaspoon margarine or butter

¾ cup thinly sliced carrots

½ clove garlic, minced

1½ cups chicken stock

½ cup low-fat milk

½ teaspoon maple syrup

Pinch of ground cinnamon

Pinch of grated nutmeg

2 tablespoons nonfat yogurt (garnish)

In a 1½-quart casserole, combine the onions, celery, and margarine or butter. Microwave on high for 1 minute, or until the margarine or butter is melted. Stir in the carrots and garlic. Cover with wax paper and microwave on high for 3 minutes, or until the carrots are crisp-tender.

Transfer to a blender with ½ cup of the stock. Process on medium speed until smooth. Return to the casserole. Add the milk, maple syrup, cinnamon, nutmeg, and the remaining 1 cup stock.

Cover with a lid and microwave on high for 3 to 4 minutes, or until heated through. Ladle into bowls and serve garnished with the yogurt.

MAKES 2 SERVINGS.

Note: This soup is also delicious served chilled. Refrigerate after adding the milk and spices. Serve garnished with the yogurt.

VEGETABLES & COMPANY

When it comes to waging a campaign for good health, fresh vegetables are among your best allies. They're low in fat and calories, while high in vitamins and fiber. The challenge is to make sure you serve vegetables every day. One way is to expand your repertoire beyond a few tried-and-true favorites so your family will really relish vegetables. And the microwave can help in several important ways.

First, vegetables cook so quickly in the microwave that their colors, textures, and flavors stay at their peak. That makes them more appealing—even to fussy eaters—without the addition of fatty or

salty sauces. Second, those vegetables that usually require long cooking, such as winter squash, baking potatoes, and sweet potatoes, can be ready in minutes. That means you can serve these nutrient-dense favorites any night of the week.

Here are a few of the vegetable dishes and other accompaniments that you can prepare with ease using a microwave:

- Potatoes in every guise, from scalloped and stuffed to potato salad and herb-flavored "fries."
- "Specialty" vegetables such as artichokes, asparagus, and tiny pumpkins that you might otherwise overlook.
- Ethnic salads such as tabbouleh, antipasto, and taco salad.
- Quick pilafs and vegetable medleys.

FRESHNESS IS FOREMOST

For best flavor and nutrition, choose the freshest produce you can find. Look for vegetables that are firm and have good color. When you can, avoid peeling thin-skinned types such as carrots and potatoes. Just scrub them thoroughly (removing any eyes from potatoes) so you can take advantage of the nutrients that lie just below the skin. Do, however, peel and discard the skins of vegetables that may have been waxed, such as cucumbers, winter squash, and rutabagas.

As with most other foods done in the microwave, vegetables should be slightly undercooked. They'll continue to cook for a few minutes after being removed from the microwave, and you don't want them to turn out mushy. You can always pop them back into the appliance for a few more seconds if needed.

Many types of winter squash have particularly tough skins. The microwave can help you cut right through them. If you want to cut acorn squash, for instance, pierce it in several places with a sharp knife. Place on a paper towel and microwave on high for 1 to 2 minutes. (Do two squash for 2 to 3 minutes.) That will soften the skin just enough to facilitate cutting. Do butternut and other squash the same way. The time will vary according to the size and variety. A nice-size butternut, for instance, takes 4 to 5 minutes.

The easiest way ever to cook corn on the cob is in the microwave. You don't even have to shuck the ears or remove the corn silk. In fact, the silk lends valuable moisture that keeps the corn from drying out. And the silk is more easily removed once the corn is cooked than when it is raw. You can do up to four ears at a time with this basic technique: Place the ears directly on the floor of the microwave. Cook on high power, turning the ears and rearranging them halfway through the cooking period. (Do one ear for a total of 3 to 4 minutes; two ears for 5 to 6 minutes; three ears for 7 to 8 minutes; four ears for 9 to 11 minutes.) Then use pot holders to hold the hot corn as you remove the husk and silk.

Other vegetables fare equally well in the microwave. The recipes in this chapter cover the most common vegetables. I've tried to cook them in ways that will give you ideas for similar dishes so you can use the same basic techniques. I've included in this chapter some of my other favorite side dishes, such as Rice Pilaf (page 228), Cranberry-Apple Relish (page 230), Acorn-Squash Pancakes (page 224), and a variety of salads.

ARTICHOKES WITH CURRY SAUCE

When steamed, artichokes need up to 45 minutes to become tender. Microwaving cuts that time down to 10 minutes, so you can make these interesting vegetables a more frequent part of your diet.

2 artichokes

2 tablespoons nonfat yogurt

1 tablespoon low-fat mayonnaise

¼ teaspoon curry powder

⅛ teaspoon ground coriander

Trim the artichoke stems to within ½″ of the bottoms. Snap off the tough bottom row of leaves. Using kitchen shears, cut the top quarter from each remaining leaf. Rinse well and shake off excess water.

Wrap each artichoke in wax paper. Place each upright in a small dish or ramekin. Microwave on high for 9 to 11 minutes, or until tender.

In a small bowl, combine the yogurt, mayonnaise, curry, and coriander.

To eat, use your fingers to remove one leaf at a time. Dip the lower end in the curry sauce. Draw that portion of the leaf through your teeth to eat the tender part of the leaf; discard the remainder of the leaf. When you get to the center, remove the small interior leaves; scoop out and discard the fuzzy choke area. Eat the remaining heart with a knife and fork, dipping sections into the sauce.

MAKES 2 SERVINGS.

ASPARAGUS

*A simple recipe for a simply delicious vegetable.
And you don't have to worry about the tips
overcooking before the stems are done, as you
might with standard cooking methods.*

1 pound fresh asparagus	1 teaspoon lemon juice

Snap the tough stem bottoms from the asparagus spears. Using a vegetable peeler, remove a thin layer of peel from the stalks, starting about 1″ below the tips. Rinse but do not drain.

Arrange the spears, spoke fashion, in an oval baking dish with the tips at the center of the dish. Cover with wax paper.

Microwave on high for 5 to 6 minutes, or until the spears are crisp-tender. Cover with foil and let stand for 2 minutes. Drain. Serve drizzled with the lemon juice.

MAKES 4 SERVINGS.

BEETS WITH ORANGE SAUCE

*These beets get added pizzazz from citrus. Great
when company's coming.*

1 pound small beets, stems trimmed to 1″	⅓ cup orange juice	½ teaspoon maple syrup
½ cup water	½ teaspoon cornstarch	

In a 2-quart casserole, combine the beets and water. Cover with a lid and microwave on high for 9 minutes. Stir, cover, and microwave on high for 9 to 11 minutes, or until tender.

In a small bowl, combine the orange juice, cornstarch, and maple syrup. Microwave on high for 1 minute, or until thickened.

Trim and peel the beets. Slice or quarter. Place in a large bowl. Add the sauce and mix well.

MAKES 4 SERVINGS.

BROCCOLI WITH CHEDDAR SALSA

1 bunch broccoli (about 1 pound)

1 tomato, coarsely chopped

2 scallions, coarsely chopped

1 jalapeño pepper, coarsely chopped (wear plastic gloves when handling)

¼ cup shredded reduced-fat Cheddar cheese

Trim the broccoli to remove leaves and tough portions of the stems. Cut the broccoli lengthwise into spears. In a 7″ × 11″ baking dish, arrange the spears with the florets facing the center of the dish. Cover with wax paper. Microwave on high for 3 minutes. Rearrange the spears so they cook evenly. Cover with wax paper and microwave on high for 3 to 5 minutes, or until crisp-tender. Let stand for 3 minutes.

In a blender or food processor, combine the tomatoes, scallions, and jalapeños. Process until combined but not totally pureed. Transfer to a medium bowl. Microwave on high for 3 minutes. Add the Cheddar and stir until melted.

Serve the sauce with the broccoli.

MAKES 4 SERVINGS.

SWEET-AND-SOUR RED CABBAGE

When cooked in the microwave, cabbage retains its shape and texture. That gives a new light and delicious slant to sweet-and-sour cabbage.

1 medium red cabbage (about 1½ pounds)

1 tart apple, diced

¼ cup red wine vinegar or cider vinegar

2 tablespoons honey

1 teaspoon soy sauce

1 tablespoon margarine or butter

Shred the cabbage, discarding the core. Place in a 3-quart casserole. Add the apple and toss to combine. Stir in the vinegar, honey, and soy sauce. Dot with the margarine or butter.

Cover with a lid and microwave on high for 5 minutes. Stir. Cover and microwave on high for 5 to 10 minutes, or until just tender.

MAKES 6 SERVINGS.

GLAZED CARROTS AND PARSNIPS

3 carrots, thinly sliced or julienned

2 small parsnips, thinly sliced or julienned

¼ cup water

Minced fresh parsley

2 tablespoons maple syrup

1 tablespoon margarine or butter

¼ teaspoon ground cinnamon

In a 1-quart casserole, combine the carrots, parsnips, and water. Cover with a lid and microwave on high for 3 minutes. Stir, cover, and microwave on high for 2 to 4 minutes, or until crisp-tender.

Let stand for 3 minutes. Drain and sprinkle with the parsley.

In a small bowl, combine the maple syrup, margarine or butter, and cinnamon. Microwave on high for 45 seconds, or until the margarine or butter is melted. Stir well. Pour over the vegetables and toss gently.

MAKES 4 SERVINGS.

Note: This glaze works well with all sorts of vegetables and gives holiday flair to everyday meals. Try it on sweet potatoes, rutabagas, beets, or winter squash. It's also delicious on cooked fruit, such as apples or pears.

ITALIAN-STYLE BROCCOLI

1 bunch broccoli (about 1 pound)
1 tablespoon olive oil
1 clove garlic, minced

⅛ teaspoon dried oregano
⅛ teaspoon ground black pepper

1 jar (4 ounces) whole pimentos, drained and cut into thin strips
2 teaspoons lemon juice

Trim the broccoli to remove leaves and tough portions of the stems. Cut the broccoli lengthwise into spears. In a 7″ × 11″ baking dish, arrange the spears with the florets facing the center of the dish.

In a small cup, combine the oil, garlic, oregano, and pepper. Spoon over the broccoli. Cover with wax paper. Microwave on high for 3 minutes. Rearrange the spears so they cook evenly. Cover with wax paper and microwave on high for 3 to 5 minutes, or until crisp-tender. Let stand for 3 minutes.

In a small bowl, combine the pimentos and lemon juice. Spoon over the broccoli. Cover with wax paper and microwave on high for 30 seconds. Serve hot or cold.

MAKES 4 SERVINGS.

SUMMER-SQUASH CASSEROLE

3 medium zucchini, thinly sliced

3 medium yellow summer squash, thinly sliced

¼ cup water

1 teaspoon minced garlic

¼ teaspoon dried marjoram

¼ teaspoon dried oregano

⅛ teaspoon ground black pepper

1 tablespoon margarine or butter

½ cup finely chopped sweet red peppers

5 scallions, thinly sliced

⅔ cup seasoned dry breadcrumbs

2 eggs or ½ cup fat-free egg substitute

½ cup shredded reduced-fat Cheddar cheese

¼ cup chopped fresh parsley

In a deep 3-quart casserole, combine the zucchini, squash, water, garlic, marjoram, oregano, and black pepper. Cover with a lid and microwave on high for 5 minutes. Stir the mixture and rotate the dish a half turn. Cover with a lid and microwave on high for 7 to 9 minutes, or until the squash is almost tender. Let stand for 5 minutes.

Transfer to a colander and gently press on the mixture with the back of a large spoon to extract excess liquid. Place the drained squash in a food processor. Process with on/off turns until the mixture is chunky.

Place the margarine or butter in the casserole dish. Microwave on high for 30 to 45 seconds, or until melted. Stir in the red peppers and scallions. Cover with wax paper and microwave on high for 3 to 4 minutes, or until crisp-tender.

Set aside 2 tablespoons of the breadcrumbs for a topping. Stir the eggs, Cheddar, parsley, and remaining breadcrumbs into the scallion mixture. Add the squash puree and mix well. Smooth the top and sprinkle with the reserved breadcrumbs.

Cover with a lid and microwave on high for 5 minutes. Rotate the dish a half turn.

Cover with wax paper and microwave on medium (50% power) for 4 to 5 minutes, or until the mixture is set around the edges. Replace the wax paper with a lid. Let stand for 5 minutes, or until the center is set.

MAKES 6 SERVINGS.

Let stand for 3 minutes. Drain and sprinkle with the parsley.

In a small bowl, combine the maple syrup, margarine or butter, and cinnamon. Microwave on high for 45 seconds, or until the margarine or butter is melted. Stir well. Pour over the vegetables and toss gently.

MAKES 4 SERVINGS.

Note: This glaze works well with all sorts of vegetables and gives holiday flair to everyday meals. Try it on sweet potatoes, rutabagas, beets, or winter squash. It's also delicious on cooked fruit, such as apples or pears.

ITALIAN-STYLE BROCCOLI

1 bunch broccoli (about 1 pound)

1 tablespoon olive oil

1 clove garlic, minced

⅛ teaspoon dried oregano

⅛ teaspoon ground black pepper

1 jar (4 ounces) whole pimentos, drained and cut into thin strips

2 teaspoons lemon juice

Trim the broccoli to remove leaves and tough portions of the stems. Cut the broccoli lengthwise into spears. In a 7″ × 11″ baking dish, arrange the spears with the florets facing the center of the dish.

In a small cup, combine the oil, garlic, oregano, and pepper. Spoon over the broccoli. Cover with wax paper. Microwave on high for 3 minutes. Rearrange the spears so they cook evenly. Cover with wax paper and microwave on high for 3 to 5 minutes, or until crisp-tender. Let stand for 3 minutes.

In a small bowl, combine the pimentos and lemon juice. Spoon over the broccoli. Cover with wax paper and microwave on high for 30 seconds. Serve hot or cold.

MAKES 4 SERVINGS.

SUMMER-SQUASH CASSEROLE

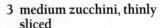

3 medium zucchini, thinly sliced

3 medium yellow summer squash, thinly sliced

¼ cup water

1 teaspoon minced garlic

¼ teaspoon dried marjoram

¼ teaspoon dried oregano

⅛ teaspoon ground black pepper

1 tablespoon margarine or butter

½ cup finely chopped sweet red peppers

5 scallions, thinly sliced

⅔ cup seasoned dry breadcrumbs

2 eggs or ½ cup fat-free egg substitute

½ cup shredded reduced-fat Cheddar cheese

¼ cup chopped fresh parsley

In a deep 3-quart casserole, combine the zucchini, squash, water, garlic, marjoram, oregano, and black pepper. Cover with a lid and microwave on high for 5 minutes. Stir the mixture and rotate the dish a half turn. Cover with a lid and microwave on high for 7 to 9 minutes, or until the squash is almost tender. Let stand for 5 minutes.

Transfer to a colander and gently press on the mixture with the back of a large spoon to extract excess liquid. Place the drained squash in a food processor. Process with on/off turns until the mixture is chunky.

Place the margarine or butter in the casserole dish. Microwave on high for 30 to 45 seconds, or until melted. Stir in the red peppers and scallions. Cover with wax paper and microwave on high for 3 to 4 minutes, or until crisp-tender.

Set aside 2 tablespoons of the breadcrumbs for a topping. Stir the eggs, Cheddar, parsley, and remaining breadcrumbs into the scallion mixture. Add the squash puree and mix well. Smooth the top and sprinkle with the reserved breadcrumbs.

Cover with a lid and microwave on high for 5 minutes. Rotate the dish a half turn.

Cover with wax paper and microwave on medium (50% power) for 4 to 5 minutes, or until the mixture is set around the edges. Replace the wax paper with a lid. Let stand for 5 minutes, or until the center is set.

MAKES 6 SERVINGS.

HERBED PEAS

Frozen peas are so handy. This easy recipe dresses them up nicely with fresh herbs. For variety, replace the tarragon with basil, parsley, mint, or marjoram.

1 box (10 ounces) frozen peas	1 tablespoon minced fresh tarragon	Lemon slices (garnish)
2 tablespoons water		

In a 3-cup casserole, combine the peas and water. Cover with wax paper and microwave on high for 2 minutes. Stir, cover, and microwave on high for 2 to 3 minutes, or until heated through.

Stir in the tarragon. Serve garnished with the lemon slices.

MAKES 4 SERVINGS.

DEALING WITH FROZEN VEGETABLES

Frozen vegetables can be a godsend at mealtime. They make easy side dishes with no washing, trimming, or peeling. With a microwave you can cook and serve them in the same dish, which will cut down on cleanup time. In addition, microwaving lets you warm these vegetables with just a tiny bit of water, so valuable nutrients won't leach out into the cooking liquid.

To cook a 10-ounce package of frozen vegetables, remove the wrapping and place the frozen block in a 1-quart casserole. Add 2 tablespoons water. Cover with a lid and microwave on high for 3 minutes. Stir or rearrange the vegetables, cover again, and microwave for another 3 minutes. Let stand, still covered, for 2 minutes to complete cooking.

Drain and serve with a little lemon juice or some minced fresh herbs.

CAULIFLOWER WITH HERBED PARMESAN SAUCE

Here's an impressive way to serve cauliflower.

1 head cauliflower (about 1½ pounds)
½ cup low-fat milk
¼ cup chicken stock
1 tablespoon cornstarch

1 clove garlic (optional)
2 tablespoons grated Parmesan cheese
2 tablespoons minced fresh parsley

1 tablespoon minced fresh basil or ¼ teaspoon dried basil
Pinch of grated nutmeg
Pinch of ground black pepper

Trim the leaves and tough stem from the cauliflower. Place the head upside down in a 1½-quart casserole. Cover with wax paper and microwave on high for 4 minutes. Turn the cauliflower right-side up. Cover with wax paper and microwave on high for 2 to 3 minutes, or until just tender. Place right-side up in a serving bowl or on a platter.

In a 1-quart saucepan, combine the milk, stock, and cornstarch. Add the garlic, if using. Stir over medium heat for 3 to 4 minutes, or until thickened. Stir in the Parmesan, parsley, basil, nutmeg, and pepper. Cook, stirring, for about 1 minute, or until the parsley wilts. Spoon over the cauliflower.

MAKES 6 TO 8 SERVINGS.

CHEESE 'N' CHIVE CAULIFLOWER

1 head cauliflower (about 1½ pounds)
2 tablespoons water
½ cup shredded reduced-fat Cheddar cheese

⅓ cup nonfat yogurt
¼ cup low-fat mayonnaise
1 tablespoon minced chives*

1 teaspoon coarse-grain mustard
¼ teaspoon paprika

Trim the leaves and tough stem from the cauliflower. Place the head right-side up in a 1½-quart casserole. Add the water. Cover with a lid and microwave on high for 3 minutes. Rotate the dish a quarter turn. Cover and microwave on high for 2 to 3 minutes, or until the cauliflower is just tender. Do not overcook. Drain off the water.

In a small bowl, combine the Cheddar, yogurt, mayonnaise, chives, mustard, and paprika. Using a knife or spatula, spread over the cauliflower. Cover the casserole with the lid and let stand for 3 to 4 minutes to heat the topping.

MAKES 6 TO 8 SERVINGS.

If you don't have fresh chives, omit them and increase the mustard to 2 teaspoons.

HONEY-BAKED ONIONS

2 large yellow onions 1 tablespoon honey	2 teaspoons margarine or butter	Minced fresh parsley

Peel the onions and cut in half crosswise. Place, cut-side up, in an 8″ × 8″ baking dish. Drizzle with the honey and dot with the margarine or butter.

Cover with wax paper. Microwave on high for 6 to 8 minutes, stopping every 2 minutes during this to baste the onions with pan juices and rotate the dish. Sprinkle with the parsley.

MAKES 4 SERVINGS.

Variation: For a more festive dish, combine 1 cup cooked peas and minced fresh mint. Place in a serving dish and serve the onions on top of the peas. Garnish the onions with mint in place of the parsley.

219

EASY POTATOES

Great with broiled chops and burgers.

3 medium baking potatoes, cut into 1" cubes
1 onion, chopped
1 tablespoon chopped celery

2 teaspoons olive oil
1 teaspoon paprika
½ teaspoon soy sauce

⅛ teaspoon ground black pepper

In a 2-quart casserole, combine the potatoes, onions, celery, oil, paprika, soy sauce, and pepper. Cover with a lid and microwave on high for 5 minutes. Stir, then cover and microwave on high for 5 to 7 minutes, or until tender.

MAKES 4 SERVINGS.

TWICE-BAKED STUFFED POTATOES

In addition to being a wonderful side dish, these potatoes make a satisfying light lunch. Just serve them with a green salad.

2 medium baking potatoes
¼ cup skim milk
2 tablespoons low-fat cottage cheese

1 tablespoon minced scallion tops or chives
⅛ teaspoon ground black pepper

2 tablespoons shredded reduced-fat Cheddar cheese

Scrub the potatoes and place them side by side on a paper towel. Microwave on high for 6 to 8 minutes, or until tender.

Cut a thin slice from the top of each potato (discard these slices). Scoop out the flesh, leaving a ¼″ sturdy shell, and place in a medium bowl. Add the milk, cottage cheese, scallions or chives, and pepper. Mash well. Spoon the mixture into the shells.

Place on a plate. Microwave on high for 3 to 4 minutes. Sprinkle with the Cheddar. Microwave on medium (50% power) for 2 minutes, or until the cheese is melted.

MAKES 2 SERVINGS.

Note: These potatoes freeze well. Stuff the shells, then wrap well and freeze. To thaw and reheat, unwrap and place one potato on a plate. Cover with wax paper and microwave on high for 5 to 7 minutes, or until hot. Sprinkle with Cheddar and microwave on medium (50% power) for 2 minutes.

POTATOES THE WAY YOU LIKE THEM

I am sure you already know that the microwave "bakes" potatoes in record time. But you might not realize that you can get the skins to turn out the way you like them—whether that's crisp or soft.

Either way, start with 8-ounce baking potatoes. Prick each twice with a fork. Place on a paper towel directly on the floor of the microwave. If you're doing just one, place it in the middle. If you're doing more, arrange them in a spoke formation.

For one potato, microwave on high for 3 to 5 minutes. For two potatoes, you'll need 5 to 7½ minutes; for three potatoes, 7 to 10 minutes. If you're using 9- or 10-ounce potatoes, add 1 minute to the cooking time.

For soft skin, wrap each cooked potato in foil and let stand for at least 5 minutes. Potatoes will stay hot for up to 30 minutes in foil.

For crisp skin, wrap each potato in a paper towel and let stand for 5 minutes. They will stay hot for up to 15 minutes. For even crispier skin, transfer the cooked potatoes from the microwave to a 450° to 500° oven for 10 to 15 minutes.

If you like a mealy texture to your potatoes, just before serving place each spud in a clean kitchen towel and knead it gently with your hands. Cut open and serve. If your potatoes cool too much for any reason, just pop them back into the microwave and heat on high for 2 minutes.

SCALLOPED POTATOES

Potatoes are a good source of vitamin C, so you'll do well to serve them often. This recipe is particularly nice when company comes.

2 tablespoons margarine or butter

2 tablespoons unbleached flour

¼ teaspoon paprika

¼ teaspoon ground black pepper

2 cups low-fat milk

3 baking potatoes, thinly sliced

1 onion, diced

1 tablespoon minced fresh parsley or chives

Place the margarine or butter in a 1½-quart bowl. Microwave on high for 30 to 45 seconds, or until melted. Stir in the flour, paprika, and pepper. Gradually whisk in the milk until smooth. Microwave on high for 3 minutes. Stir, then microwave on high for 4 to 5 minutes, or until boiling and slightly thickened.

Coat a shallow 2-quart casserole with no-stick spray. Arrange half of the potatoes in the casserole. Sprinkle with half of the onions. Spoon on half of the sauce. Repeat the layers to use all the potatoes, onions, and sauce.

Microwave on high for 8 minutes. Rotate the dish a half turn. Microwave on high for 8 to 10 minutes, or until the potatoes are tender. Cover with foil and let stand for 5 minutes. Sprinkle with the parsley or chives.

MAKES 4 SERVINGS.

Variations: For Scalloped Potatoes and Mushrooms, *drain a 4-ounce can of mushrooms and sprinkle them over the first layer of potatoes. If desired, mix some diced sweet red peppers with the onions.*

For Cheese Scalloped Potatoes, *sprinkle the casserole with ¼ cup shredded reduced-fat Cheddar cheese before covering with the foil.*

GARLIC POTATO WEDGES

1 clove garlic, minced

1 tablespoon olive oil

2 teaspoons soy sauce

½ teaspoon paprika

¼ teaspoon ground black pepper

4 medium baking potatoes

In a 7″ × 11″ baking dish, combine the garlic, oil, soy sauce, paprika, and pepper. Microwave on high for 30 seconds, or until the garlic softens.

Cut each potato lengthwise into six wedges. Add to the baking dish and toss with the garlic mixture to coat. Cover with wax paper. Microwave on high for a total of 15 to 18 minutes, rearranging the wedges twice during this time, until the potatoes are tender. Transfer the wedges to a plate lined with paper towels to soak up the excess oil.

MAKES 6 SERVINGS.

Variations: For Herbed Potato Wedges, *add 1 tablespoon minced fresh rosemary (or 1 teaspoon dried) to the garlic mixture.*

For Barbecue Potato Wedges, *drain the excess oil from the potatoes after microwaving, then return them to the casserole dish. Drizzle them with 3 tablespoons Barbecue Sauce (page 61). Cover with wax paper and microwave on high for 1 minute, or until the sauce is hot.*

For Deluxe Potato Wedges, *drain the excess oil from the potatoes after microwaving, then return them to the casserole. Sprinkle them with ½ cup shredded reduced-fat Cheddar cheese, ¼ cup minced red peppers, 2 tablespoons thinly sliced scallions, and 1 tablespoon chopped ripe olives. Microwave on medium (50% power) for 3 to 4 minutes, or until the cheese is melted.*

GLAZED SWEET POTATOES WITH PEARS

4–5 sweet potatoes (about 1½ pounds total), peeled and cut into 1″ cubes

1 tablespoon margarine or butter

½ cup orange juice

2 large pears, cut crosswise into ½″ slices

¼ cup chopped walnuts

¼ cup water

2 tablespoons maple syrup

1 tablespoon cornstarch

½ teaspoon ground cinnamon

In a 2-quart casserole, combine the sweet potatoes, margarine or butter, and ¼ cup of the juice. Cover with a lid and microwave on high for 6 minutes. Stir, cover, and microwave on high for 4 to 6 minutes, or until crisp-tender.

Add the pears. Cover with a lid and microwave on high for 2 to 4 minutes, or until the fruit is tender but still holds its shape. Stir in the walnuts. Cover and let stand.

In a 1-cup glass measure, combine the water, maple syrup, cornstarch, cinnamon, and remaining ¼ cup orange juice. Microwave on high for 1 minute. Stir and microwave on high for 1 to 2 minutes, or until the mixture comes to a boil and thickens. Pour over the sweet potato mixture and toss gently to coat.

MAKES 6 SERVINGS.

ACORN-SQUASH PANCAKES

These light pancakes contain vitamin-rich acorn squash. Microwaving considerably cuts the time needed to cook the squash. I like to serve these pancakes with a bowl of soup for an informal luncheon.

1 acorn squash
2 eggs or ½ cup fat-free egg substitute
2 tablespoons unbleached flour

2 tablespoons canola oil
1 tablespoon maple syrup
  Pinch of grated nutmeg

Chunky Raisin Applesauce (page 259)

Fold a paper towel in half and place it directly on the floor of the microwave. Pierce the squash several times with a sharp knife. Place the squash on the towel and microwave on high for 4 minutes. Flip the squash and microwave on high for 4 to 5 minutes, or until tender when pierced with a fork. Set aside until cool enough to handle.

In a medium bowl, beat the eggs with a whisk or an electric mixer until foamy. Beat in the flour, then add the oil, maple syrup, and nutmeg.

Halve the squash. Scoop out and discard the seeds and strings. Spoon the pulp into a bowl and mash well. Stir 1 cup of the squash into the pancake batter. Reserve the remaining squash for another use.

Coat a griddle or large frying pan with no-stick spray. Place over medium heat until hot. Drop in batter by scant ¼ cupfuls. Cook until browned underneath. Flip and brown the remaining side. Serve with the applesauce.

MAKES 4 SERVINGS.

MAGICAL MINI-PUMPKINS

Each autumn, new and different types of pumpkins and squash make their way to market. Particularly attractive are the mini varieties, such as Jack-Be-Little pumpkins and Delicata, Golden Nugget, and Sweet Dumpling squashes. These tender, sweet vegetables are just the right size for single-serving side dishes.

Before microwaving, pierce with a sharp knife in several places. Place on a paper towel and microwave each on high for 3 to 5 minutes, or until tender. Cut off the top, scoop out the seeds, and serve plain or drizzled with maple syrup. For a more festive treat, fill these little wonders with cooked vegetables (try peas, corn, or a mixture of your favorites), pilaf, a spicy meat casserole, or fruit compote. You could even use them as tiny soup bowls.

GREEK VEGETABLE MEDLEY

This dish is equally good hot or cold. Served hot, it's a terrific side dish for chicken or lamb. Served cold, it's a nice luncheon salad.

1 small eggplant (about 1 pound), cut into 1″ cubes
1 cup chopped onions
1 cup diced green peppers
1 cup diced sweet red peppers
1 tablespoon minced garlic

2 teaspoons olive oil
1 cup halved cherry tomatoes
½ cup sliced mushrooms
2 tablespoons lemon juice
1 tablespoon tomato paste*

¼ teaspoon dried oregano
⅛ teaspoon ground black pepper
½ cup crumbled feta cheese

Place the eggplant in a deep 2-quart casserole. Cover with a lid and microwave on high for 2 minutes. Stir, then cover and microwave on high for 2 to 4 minutes, or until just crisp-tender. Transfer to a colander to drain; set aside.

In the same casserole, combine the onions, green peppers, red peppers, garlic, and oil. Cover and microwave on high for 2 minutes. Stir, then cover and microwave on high for 2 to 3 minutes, or until the vegetables are crisp-tender. Stir in the eggplant, tomatoes, mushrooms, lemon juice, tomato paste, oregano, and black pepper.

Cover and microwave on high for 3 minutes. Stir, cover, and microwave on high for 3 to 5 minutes, or until the vegetables are tender. Stir in the feta. Cover and let stand for 5 minutes.

MAKES 6 SERVINGS.

To keep leftover tomato paste fresh and in convenient-portion form, drop tablespoonfuls onto a baking sheet lined with wax paper. Freeze until solid. Then remove the dollops from the sheet and store in a freezer bag.

RATATOUILLE

This traditionally Mediterranean mélange, delicately flavored with garlic and herbs, is magic in your microwave.

- 2 onions, thinly sliced
- 1 tablespoon olive oil
- 1 teaspoon minced garlic
- 1 small eggplant (about 1 pound), cubed
- 2 medium zucchini, thinly sliced on the diagonal

- 1 green pepper, thinly sliced
- 2 cans (14½ ounces each) chopped tomatoes, drained
- ¼ cup minced fresh parsley
- 1 teaspoon dried basil

- ¼ teaspoon dried marjoram
- ¼ teaspoon dried tarragon
- ¼ teaspoon ground black pepper

In a 4-quart casserole, combine the onions, oil, and garlic. Cover with a lid and microwave on high for 5 minutes, or until the onions are translucent.

Add the eggplant, zucchini, and green peppers. Cover with a lid. Microwave on high for a total of 8 to 10 minutes, stirring twice during this time, until the vegetables are tender. Add the tomatoes, parsley, basil, marjoram, tarragon, and pepper.

Cover with a lid and microwave on high for 4 to 5 minutes, or until heated through. Stir, cover, and let stand for 2 to 3 minutes.

MAKES 8 SERVINGS.

HERBED OVEN POTATOES

2 large baking potatoes
1 teaspoon melted margarine
  or butter
1 teaspoon lemon juice

¼ teaspoon soy sauce
¼ cup grated Parmesan cheese
¼ teaspoon dried basil

¼ teaspoon dried thyme
¼ teaspoon dried marjoram
¼ teaspoon ground black
  pepper

Scrub the potatoes and halve them lengthwise.

In a cup, combine the margarine or butter, lemon juice, and soy sauce. Brush the cut side of the potatoes with the mixture.

In another cup, combine the Parmesan, basil, thyme, marjoram, and pepper. Sprinkle on the cut side of each potato and pat into place.

Arrange the potatoes, coated-side down, in a spoke pattern in a 10″ glass pie plate. Microwave on high for 7 minutes. Rotate the dish a half turn. Microwave on high for 7 to 9 minutes, or until the potatoes are tender and the edges are lightly browned. Let stand for 2 minutes.

MAKES 4 SERVINGS.

RICE PILAF

You can cook and serve this dish in the same container. And if you have leftovers, you can even store and reheat them in the same dish.

1 onion, chopped
1 celery stalk, chopped
1 clove garlic, minced
1 teaspoon margarine or butter

2 cups sliced mushrooms
1¾ cups chicken stock
1 cup long-grain white rice

¼ teaspoon dried marjoram
1 tablespoon chopped fresh
  parsley

In a deep 2-quart casserole, combine the onions, celery, garlic, and margarine or butter. Cover with a lid and microwave on high for 3 to 4 minutes, or until the onions are translucent.

Stir in the mushrooms, stock, rice, and marjoram. Cover with a lid and microwave on high for 4 to 6 minutes, or until boiling. Stir, cover, and microwave on medium (50% power) for 15 to 20 minutes, or until all the liquid has been absorbed. Let stand for 5 minutes. Stir in the parsley.

MAKES 4 SERVINGS.

EASY PEELING

Garlic and pearl onions have lots of health benefits. They may help lower cholesterol and fight heart disease. They're also wonderful flavoring agents that can reduce the need for salt and extra fat in recipes. But these foods can try your patience when it comes time to peel them. Fortunately, this is another case where the microwave can lend a helping hand.

Garlic. To quickly peel, just place one to three whole cloves in the microwave and heat on high for 15 to 30 seconds. Using a paper towel, pick up one clove at a time and squeeze an end to pop the clove from its skin. Mince as usual.

If you like to use a garlic press, remove the heated garlic from the microwave and place in the press. Squeeze as usual—the peel will pull free of the holes in the press, leaving the garlic press easier to clean.

To do a whole garlic bulb, microwave it on high for about 20 seconds. Then turn the bulb over and microwave another 15 to 30 seconds, depending on the size. Break the head apart and pop the cloves from their skin or put them through a press.

A bonus to this method is that the slight heating mellows the garlic and gives it a more pleasant flavor. That's especially nice for those times when you'll use it raw, as in salad dressings.

Pearl onions. Cut the root end from each onion. Place ½ cup of the onions in a pie plate and microwave on high for 45 seconds. As with the garlic, use a paper towel to protect your fingers if the onions are hot. Squeeze gently from the stem end to pop each onion from its skin. If any onions are stubborn, return them to the microwave for a few seconds.

CRANBERRY-APPLE RELISH

This tangy relish is perfect for special meals, such as holiday feasts. You may use fresh or frozen cranberries.

1 pound cranberries
2 tart apples, chopped
1/3–1/2 cup honey

1/4 cup apple juice or cider
1/4 teaspoon ground allspice
1/4 teaspoon ground cinnamon

1/4 teaspoon ground cloves
1–2 tablespoons chopped walnuts

In a 1 1/2-quart casserole, combine the cranberries, apples, honey, juice or cider, allspice, cinnamon, and cloves. Cover with wax paper and microwave on high for a total of 8 to 10 minutes, stirring twice during this time, until the cranberries pop.

Microwave on high for 3 to 4 minutes, or until slightly thickened. Stir in the walnuts. Chill before serving.

MAKES 8 TO 10 SERVINGS.

CARROT-CAULIFLOWER SALAD

Adding the dressing while the salad is hot heightens the flavor of the dried mint and mellows the garlic.

3 carrots, thinly sliced on the diagonal
2 tablespoons water
4 cups bite-size cauliflower florets
1 tablespoon olive oil

1 tablespoon nonfat yogurt
2 teaspoons lemon juice
1 teaspoon dried mint
1 clove garlic, minced

1/4 teaspoon ground black pepper
2 scallions, thinly sliced on the diagonal
Spinach leaves

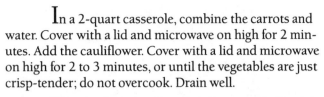

In a 2-quart casserole, combine the carrots and water. Cover with a lid and microwave on high for 2 minutes. Add the cauliflower. Cover with a lid and microwave on high for 2 to 3 minutes, or until the vegetables are just crisp-tender; do not overcook. Drain well.

In a small bowl, whisk together the oil, yogurt, lemon juice, mint, garlic, and pepper. Pour over the vegetables and toss well. Set aside to cool. Stir in the scallions. Chill.

Serve on a bed of spinach.

MAKES 4 SERVINGS.

HOMEMADE HERB VINEGAR—IN MINUTES

Whether you make herb vinegar for your own use or as a special gift, you'll be amazed at how simple it is to create this gourmet treat using a microwave. You save more than time—homemade herb vinegar costs a fraction of what you'd pay in a fancy shop. And you can make any flavor or combination of flavors you like. Dill, marjoram, basil, tarragon, and thyme are just a few of the fresh herbs that make terrific vinegar.

To make, place ¼ to ½ cup of fresh herb sprigs in a 4-cup glass measure. Add 1 pint white vinegar or apple cider vinegar. Microwave on high for 1 to 1½ minutes, or until warm. Pour into a pint bottle. Let cool, then cap the bottle. Store in a cool place for two weeks so the flavors have a chance to blend.

At that point, if you like, you can strain the vinegar into another container and add just a single sprig of fresh herb to identify the flavor.

If you want to add a hint of garlic to your herb vinegar, choose one or more small garlic cloves that will fit through the top of the bottle. Peel and thread on a stainless steel or wooden skewer. Place in an empty bottle. Add heated vinegar and herbs as described above. Cool and let stand overnight. Remove the garlic, cap, and then let the vinegar age as above.

For gift-giving, tie a ribbon around the neck of the bottle or tie a small, brightly colored square of fabric over the lid. If you'd like, add a pretty label.

CURRIED MIXED FRUIT

This side dish also makes a good dessert.

1 cup dried apple slices
1 cup chopped prunes
1 cup apple juice

⅓ cup raisins
1 teaspoon honey
⅛–¼ teaspoon curry powder

Pinch of grated nutmeg
2 large oranges, peeled and sectioned

In a 1½-quart casserole, combine the apples, prunes, juice, raisins, honey, curry powder, and nutmeg. Cover with a lid and microwave on high for 3 minutes. Stir, cover, and microwave on high for 1 to 3 minutes, or until the fruit is plump and tender.

Add the oranges and mix well. Cover with a lid and let stand for 5 minutes before serving.

MAKES 6 SERVINGS.

HOT GERMAN-STYLE POTATO SALAD

Here's an easy variation on a classic ethnic dish.

1½ pounds small red potatoes
¼ cup water
½ cup chopped onions
½ cup sliced celery
2 teaspoons unbleached flour

¼ teaspoon ground black pepper
½ cup chicken stock
2 tablespoons apple cider vinegar

1 tablespoon soy sauce
1 teaspoon maple syrup
1 tablespoon minced fresh parsley

Pierce the potatoes all over with a fork. Arrange them in a circle, without crowding, in a 9″ pie plate. Sprinkle with the water and invert another pie plate over the top as a lid.

Microwave on high for 5 minutes. Flip the potatoes, cover, and microwave on high for 3 to 5 minutes, or until almost tender. Let stand, covered, for 10 minutes.

In a 2-quart casserole, combine the onions and celery. Cover with a lid and microwave on high for 2 minutes, or until crisp-tender. Stir in the flour and pepper. Cover and microwave on high for 1 minute.

Add the stock, vinegar, soy sauce, and maple syrup. Microwave on high for 2 minutes. Stir, then microwave on high for 2 to 3 minutes, or until the mixture thickens.

Drain the potatoes and cut into ½" slices. Add to the casserole and stir gently to combine. Cover with a lid and microwave on high for 1 to 2 minutes, or until heated through. Sprinkle with the parsley.

MAKES 6 SERVINGS.

CLASSIC POTATO SALAD

1½ pounds boiling potatoes, cut into ¾" cubes

¼ cup water

¼ cup low-fat mayonnaise

2 tablespoons nonfat yogurt

¼ teaspoon ground black pepper

1 celery stalk, thinly sliced on the diagonal

1 hard-cooked egg, finely chopped

In a 2-quart casserole, combine the potatoes and water. Cover with a lid and microwave on high for 7 to 9 minutes, stirring twice during this time, until the potatoes are tender. Drain and cool slightly.

In a medium bowl, whisk together the mayonnaise, yogurt, and pepper. Add the potatoes, celery, and egg. Toss lightly to coat with dressing. Chill.

MAKES 6 SERVINGS.

Note: If doubling the recipe for a picnic or other occasion, cook the potatoes in ⅓ cup water for 13 to 15 minutes.

ANTIPASTO SALAD

A colorful, healthy combination for hot days.

1 small head cauliflower, separated into florets

2 tablespoons water

3 medium carrots, cut into thin sticks

Red-leaf lettuce

3 small zucchini, thickly sliced on the diagonal

1 package (9 ounces) frozen artichoke hearts

8 ounces reduced-fat Gouda cheese, cubed

2 medium tomatoes, cut into wedges

¼ cup olive oil

¼ cup red wine vinegar

1 teaspoon soy sauce

¼ teaspoon dried oregano

¼ teaspoon dried marjoram

⅛ teaspoon ground black pepper

1 small red onion, minced

In a shallow 9″ × 9″ casserole, combine the cauliflower and water. Cover and microwave on high for 2 minutes. Stir, then cover and microwave on high for 3 minutes. Add the carrots. Cover and microwave on high for 3 to 5 minutes, or until crisp-tender. Remove with a slotted spoon and place in a colander. Rinse with cold water and drain well.

Place the lettuce on a serving platter. Arrange the cauliflower and carrots on the lettuce.

Add the zucchini to the water remaining in the casserole. Cover and microwave on high for 1 minute. Stir, cover, and microwave on high for 1 to 2 minutes, or until crisp-tender. Transfer to a colander, rinse with cold water, and drain well. Add to the platter.

Place the artichoke hearts in the casserole. Cover and microwave on high for 2 minutes. Stir, cover, and microwave on high for 1 to 3 minutes, or until thawed. Transfer to a colander, rinse with cold water, and drain well. Add to the platter, along with the Gouda and tomatoes.

In a small bowl, whisk together the oil, vinegar, soy sauce, oregano, marjoram, and pepper. Stir in the onions. Spoon over the vegetables. Serve at room temperature.

MAKES 6 TO 8 SERVINGS.

Variations: You may replace the Gouda with part-skim mozzarella or Armenian string cheese. Cherry tomatoes are also nice in place of tomato wedges.

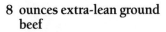

TACO SALAD

The warm lean beef mixture in this salad contrasts nicely with cool, crisp lettuce and a creamy low-fat topping.

8 ounces extra-lean ground beef
¼ cup finely chopped onions
1 teaspoon soy sauce
1 teaspoon chili powder
¼ teaspoon ground cumin

¼ teaspoon dried oregano
1½ cups cooked kidney beans
1 large tomato, seeded and chopped
1 tablespoon minced fresh coriander (optional)

¼ cup low-fat cottage cheese
¼ cup nonfat yogurt
4 cups shredded lettuce
½ cup Super Salsa (page 59)

In a 1½-quart casserole, combine the beef, onions, soy sauce, chili powder, cumin, and oregano. Microwave on high for 1 minute. Stir to break the meat into pieces, then microwave on high for 1 to 2 minutes, until the meat is no longer pink.

Add the beans and tomatoes. Microwave on high for 2 minutes, or until heated through. Stir in the coriander (if using).

In a blender, puree the cottage cheese and yogurt until smooth.

Divide the lettuce among four dinner plates. Top each with one-fourth of the meat mixture. Spoon some salsa over each serving and top with the yogurt mixture.

MAKES 4 SERVINGS.

TABBOULEH

Parsley is just jam-packed with vitamin A. Here's a refreshing way to work a good amount of it into your diet. This refreshing Middle Eastern salad pairs parsley with bulgur, scallions, and tomatoes.

½ cup fine bulgur

½ cup water

¼ cup lemon juice

2 large tomatoes, seeded and diced

½ cup tightly packed fresh parsley leaves, minced

6 scallions, thinly sliced on the diagonal

1 tablespoon olive oil

1 teaspoon minced fresh mint (optional)

In a 4-cup glass measure, combine the bulgur, water, and lemon juice. Microwave on high for 3 minutes, or until the water is hot but not necessarily boiling. Cover and let stand for 10 minutes.

Transfer the bulgur to a large bowl. Add the tomatoes, parsley, scallions, oil, and mint (if using).

MAKES 4 SERVINGS.

Variations: For Shrimp Tabbouleh, *stir 8 ounces cooked and chopped shrimp into the finished salad. For* Tuna Tabbouleh, *drain and flake a 6 ½-ounce can of water-packed tuna; add it to the finished salad.*

For Tabbouleh-Stuffed Tomatoes, *hollow out 4 large tomatoes and stuff them with the tabbouleh mixture; serve on a bed of lettuce.*

THE MICROWAVE BAKERY

Bread has, for centuries, been considered the staff of life. Whole-grain baked goods can still be a vitally important part of your diet. Whole wheat and other grains contain hunger-appeasing complex carbohydrates and plenty of dietary fiber to help prevent digestive disorders and high cholesterol. With the help of your microwave, you can have healthy piping-hot muffins, flavorful whole-grain quick breads, and fresh-baked yeast loaves in a fraction of the time usually required. Here's how:

 By whipping up a batch of whole-grain muffin batter and storing it in the refrigerator,

you can serve up fresh muffins in as little as 30 seconds. And you won't even have to wash a muffin tin.

- You can prepare a steaming-hot Boston brown bread in about 15 minutes, rather than the 3 hours that a stove-top version requires.
- "Quick breads," which need an hour in a conventional oven, really live up to their name in the microwave. A scant 10 or 15 minutes is all they take.
- Even yeast breads, which don't bake all that well in the microwave, can get an assist from this appliance. The microwave is an ideal warm, draft-free place for dough to rise—and the rising can be accomplished in minutes rather than hours. (See Whole Wheat Bread on page 242 for complete details.)

KEEP IN MIND

For best results when "baking" in the microwave, you'll need to make a few changes in your usual procedures. Here are some of the secrets I use to guarantee success. First, breads and muffins generally need a few minutes of standing time to finish cooking outside the microwave. To keep the bottom from turning soggy during this time, unmold the product from its baking dish and place it on a wire rack.

To make this unmolding easier when doing muffins, line the muffin pan or custard cup with a single or double paper cupcake liner. Then simply lift the muffin from its pan. If using a double liner, discard the outer paper. If you're preparing a larger product, such as a quick bread, line the baking dish with wax paper. (Cut a piece just big enough to fit in the bottom of the dish.) To keep the wax paper from slipping around when you add the batter, coat the bottom of the dish with no-stick spray, then insert the paper.

With all baked goods, always check for doneness after the minimum amount of time specified in the recipe. Overcooking toughens bread and muffins. When properly done, both should spring back when lightly pressed in the center. Don't worry about small moist spots on top. They'll evaporate during the standing time. Remember that you can always return an underdone bread or muffin to the microwave for a little extra cooking time, but you can't rescue an overcooked product.

Whole wheat pastry flour, which contains less gluten than regular whole wheat flour, produces especially tender muffins and quick breads. It's available in health-food stores and large supermarkets. If you substitute standard whole wheat flour, be careful not to overbeat the batter. Otherwise you'll activate the gluten and end up with tough baked goods. Buttermilk also helps keep bakery products tender. If you don't have any, you can make an acceptable substitute: Either add 1 tablespoon lemon juice (or mild vinegar) to 1 cup skim milk or mix ¾ cup nonfat yogurt with ¼ cup skim milk.

Adding fruit to low-fat breads and muffins serves a double purpose. First, it adds extra fiber and valuable nutrients to the products. Second, it helps keep them moist in the absence of fat. Even so, low-fat breads may dry out if not stored properly. Always let them cool completely, then wrap tightly in plastic bags or foil.

So by all means, use your microwave to enjoy robust, healthy breads—at your own convenience.

CRANBERRY BREAD

Studded with fruit—cranberries, pineapple, and raisins—this quick and easy bread is a nice addition to breakfasts or luncheons.

½ cup whole wheat pastry flour
½ cup yellow cornmeal
⅓ cup unbleached flour
1 teaspoon baking soda
¼ teaspoon ground allspice
⅛ teaspoon ground mace

⅛ teaspoon grated nutmeg
½ cup crushed pineapple, with juice
½ cup chopped fresh cranberries
¼ cup molasses

¼ cup margarine or butter, softened
1 egg or ¼ cup fat-free egg substitute
3 tablespoons chopped raisins

In a medium bowl, combine the whole wheat flour, cornmeal, unbleached flour, baking soda, allspice, mace, and nutmeg. Using a wooden spoon, beat in the pineapple, cranberries, molasses, margarine or butter, egg, and raisins until well mixed.

Coat a 2-cup glass measure with no-stick spray. Pour in half of the batter (just under 1¼ cups).

Microwave on medium (50% power) for 6 to 9 minutes, rotating the container a quarter turn every 3 minutes during this time, until the center of the bread springs back when touched lightly and no uncooked batter is visible on the sides.

Let stand for 5 minutes. Run a knife around the edges and invert the bread onto a wire rack.

Repeat with the remaining batter. Let the loaves cool before slicing.

MAKES 2 SMALL LOAVES.

ZUCCHINI-NUT BREAD

Here's a fast and easy way to use up your garden's abundance of zucchini.

1½ cups whole wheat pastry flour

2 teaspoons ground cinnamon

1 teaspoon baking powder

1 teaspoon baking soda

½ teaspoon grated nutmeg

3 eggs or ¾ cup fat-free egg substitute

½ cup canola oil

½ cup honey

2 teaspoons minced fresh ginger

1 teaspoon vanilla

3 cups shredded zucchini

1 cup chopped walnuts

⅓ cup raisins

2 tablespoons unbleached flour

In a medium bowl, combine the whole wheat flour, cinnamon, baking powder, baking soda, and nutmeg.

In a large bowl, whisk together the eggs, oil, honey, ginger, and vanilla until smooth. Stir in the zucchini and ⅔ cup of the walnuts.

Add the dry ingredients and stir just until moistened; do not overmix.

Coat a 10″ Bundt pan with no-stick spray.

In a cup, combine the raisins, unbleached flour, and remaining ⅓ cup walnuts. Sprinkle the mixture in the bottom of the pan. Add the batter to the pan.

Place the pan in the microwave on an inverted glass pie plate. Microwave on high for 13 to 15 minutes, rotating the pan a quarter turn every 3 minutes during this time, until the bread begins to shrink away from the sides of the pan. Let stand for 5 minutes.

MAKES 1 LOAF

Note: If you don't have a Bundt pan, use a deep, round 2-quart casserole. Coat it with no-stick spray. Also spray the outside of a straight-sided glass jar or bottle (at least 4″ high and 2″ in diameter). Place the jar, open-end up, in the center of the casserole. Spread the batter evenly around the jar.

ENGLISH-MUFFIN BREAD

Easy to make, this bread is especially delicious sliced and toasted for breakfast.

¾ cup skim milk

½ cup water

1 tablespoon honey

1 package active dry yeast

2 tablespoons mashed potatoes

¼ teaspoon baking soda

2½ cups unbleached flour

⅓–½ cup whole wheat pastry flour

1 tablespoon yellow cornmeal

In a large bowl, combine the milk, water, and honey. Microwave on high for 1 to 1½ minutes, or until quite warm (about 110°). Stir in the yeast and let stand for 3 minutes, or until the mixture starts to bubble.

Stir in the potatoes, baking soda, and 1 cup of the unbleached flour. Mix well. Stir in the remaining 1½ cups unbleached flour and enough of the whole wheat flour to make a soft dough.

Coat a 9″ × 5″ loaf pan with no-stick spray. Coat with 2 teaspoons of the cornmeal. Add the dough and sprinkle with the remaining 1 teaspoon cornmeal. Cover with wax paper.

Place the pan in 7″ × 11″ baking dish. Add 1″ of hot water to the outer dish. Microwave on low (10% power) for 5 minutes. Let stand for 10 minutes. Repeat, if necessary, until the dough has doubled in bulk. Remove the wax paper.

Remove the baking dish from the microwave. Place an inverted pie plate in the microwave and top with the loaf pan. Microwave on high for 3 minutes. Rotate the dish a half turn. Microwave on high for 3 to 4 minutes, or until the surface appears dry. Let stand for 5 minutes.

MAKES 1 LOAF.

WHOLE WHEAT BREAD

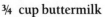

Here's an example of how your microwave can help you make yeast bread. Although the loaf is baked in a conventional oven, the microwave speeds rising time.

¾ cup buttermilk

¾ cup water

2 tablespoons margarine or butter

2 tablespoons honey

4 cups whole wheat flour

1 package active dry yeast

1 teaspoon caraway seeds (optional)

In a 2-cup glass measure, combine the buttermilk, water, margarine or butter, and honey. Microwave on high for 2 to 2½ minutes, or until the margarine or butter is melted. Stir well. Let cool to 120° to 130° (until quite warm but not too hot to touch).

In a large bowl, combine 2 cups of the flour with the yeast and caraway seeds (if using). Stir in the milk mixture. Using an electric mixer, beat the dough on medium speed for 2 minutes. Stir in enough of the remaining flour to make a stiff dough.

Turn the dough out onto a lightly floured surface. Knead until smooth and elastic, about 8 minutes.

Wash and dry the bowl. Coat it with no-stick spray. Add the dough, turning to coat all sides with the spray.

If you have a removable turntable in your microwave, take it out so you'll have plenty of floor space. Place 3 cups hot tap water in a 4-cup glass measure. Microwave on high for 5 to 6 minutes, or until the water boils. Move the glass to one side of the oven. Add the dough bowl.

Microwave the dough, covered with a plate, on low (10% power) for 5 minutes. Let stand for 5 minutes. Repeat once or twice, or until the dough has doubled in bulk.

With your fist, punch down the dough. Let stand for 5 minutes. Shape into a loaf. Coat a glass 9″ × 5″ loaf pan with

no-stick spray. Add the dough. Place in the microwave next to the hot water. Microwave on low (10% power) for 5 minutes. Let stand for 5 minutes. Repeat once or twice, or until the dough has doubled in bulk.

Transfer to an oven. Bake at 375° for 30 to 35 minutes, or until the loaf sounds hollow when tapped. Remove from the pan and cool on a wire rack.

MAKES 1 LOAF

RYE, WHEAT, AND WALNUT BREAD

A dark, delicious loaf ready in minutes!

½ cup whole wheat flour

½ cup rye flour

2 tablespoons bran

2 tablespoons finely chopped walnuts

½ teaspoon baking soda

½ cup buttermilk

1 egg or ¼ cup fat-free egg substitute

2 teaspoons blackstrap or other molasses

1 teaspoon honey

1 tablespoon wheat germ

In a large bowl, combine the whole wheat flour, rye flour, bran, walnuts, and baking soda.

In a small bowl, combine the buttermilk, egg, molasses, and honey. Pour over the dry ingredients and stir until blended.

Coat a round 1-quart casserole with no-stick spray. Sprinkle with 1½ teaspoons of the wheat germ. Add the batter, mounding it slightly in the center to form a loaf. Sprinkle the top with the remaining wheat germ.

Microwave on medium (50% power) for 6 to 10 minutes, rotating the dish a quarter turn every 3 minutes during this time, until the center springs back when touched. Let stand for 5 minutes.

MAKES 1 LOAF

STRAWBERRY-BANANA BREAD

- 2 eggs or ½ cup fat-free egg substitute
- ¼ cup maple syrup
- ¼ cup canola oil
- ¼ cup buttermilk

- ½ cup mashed bananas
- ¼ cup finely chopped walnuts
- 1 teaspoon baking soda
- ¼ teaspoon ground cinnamon

- ⅛ teaspoon grated nutmeg
- 1 cup sliced strawberries
- 1½ cups whole wheat pastry flour

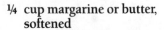

In a large bowl, combine the eggs, maple syrup, oil, buttermilk, bananas, walnuts, baking soda, cinnamon, and nutmeg. Add the strawberries. Stir in the flour and beat with a wooden spoon until well combined.

Coat a 7″ soufflé dish with no-stick spray. Spoon the batter into the dish and smooth the top.

Place in the microwave on an inverted saucer. Microwave on medium (50% power) for 9 minutes, rotating the dish a quarter turn every 3 minutes during this time.

Microwave on high for 3 to 4 minutes, or until the center springs back when lightly touched. Let stand for 5 minutes.

Run a knife around the sides of the dish to loosen the bread. Invert onto a wire rack. Cool slightly before cutting.

MAKES 1 LOAF

HERBED GARLIC BREAD

- ¼ cup margarine or butter, softened
- 3 cloves garlic, minced
- 2 tablespoons olive oil
- 2 tablespoons grated Parmesan cheese

- 2 tablespoons minced fresh parsley
- ½ teaspoon dried marjoram
- ⅛ teaspoon dried basil

- ⅛ teaspoon ground black pepper
- 1 large loaf Italian or French bread

In a small bowl, mix together the margarine or butter and garlic. Microwave on high for 1½ to 2½ minutes, or until the margarine or butter is melted. Stir in the oil, Parmesan, parsley, marjoram, basil, and pepper.

Without cutting all the way through, slice the bread into 2″ sections. Brush one side of each slice with the herb mixture.

Place the loaf on a double layer of paper towels. Microwave on medium (50% power) for 1 to 1½ minutes, or until heated through.

MAKES 8 SERVINGS.

BOSTON BROWN BREAD

½ cup whole wheat pastry flour

½ cup cornmeal

¼ cup rye flour

¼ cup unbleached flour

1 teaspoon baking soda

¾ cup buttermilk

½ cup molasses

¾ cup raisins

In a medium bowl, combine the whole wheat flour, cornmeal, rye flour, unbleached flour, and baking soda. Stir in the buttermilk and molasses until well combined. Stir in the raisins.

Coat a 2-cup glass measure with no-stick spray. Spoon half of the batter into the measure. Cover with wax paper.

Microwave on medium (50% power) for 3 minutes. Rotate the dish a half turn. Microwave on medium (50% power) for 4 minutes, or until the surface is only slightly wet. Uncover and let stand for 5 minutes.

Unmold the loaf and wrap it in foil or a plastic bag to keep it from drying out.

Repeat with the remaining batter.

MAKES 2 LOAVES.

APRICOT-PECAN RING

*Apricots are high in cancer-fighting beta-carotene,
so I like to use them in various recipes. This
delicious ring is good for brunches.*

1½ cups chopped dried
   apricots
1 cup water
1½ cups whole wheat pastry
   flour

1 cup unbleached flour
1 tablespoon baking soda
1 cup buttermilk
¼ cup honey

3 tablespoons canola oil
1 egg or ¼ cup fat-free egg
   substitute
½ cup coarsely chopped pecans

In a 4-cup glass measure, combine the apricots
and water. Microwave on high for 3 to 4 minutes, or until
the apricots are soft. Let stand for 2 minutes. Drain and set
aside.

In a large bowl, mix the whole wheat flour, unbleached
flour, and baking soda. Stir in the buttermilk, honey, oil,
and egg until just blended. Fold in the pecans and apricots.

Coat a 10″ Bundt pan with no-stick spray. Add the batter.

Place in the microwave on top of an inverted saucer.
Microwave on high for 8 to 9 minutes, rotating the dish a
quarter turn twice during this time, until a toothpick
inserted into the bread comes out clean. Let stand for
10 minutes.

Unmold the bread onto a wire rack. Cool before cutting.

MAKES 1 LOAF

*Note: If you don't have a Bundt pan, use a deep, round 2-quart
casserole. Coat it with no-stick spray. Also spray the outside of
a straight-sided glass jar or bottle (at least 4″ high and 2″ in
diameter). Place the jar, open-end up, in the center of the
casserole. Spread the batter evenly around the jar.*

HONEY-RAISIN TEA SCONES

Serve these scones warm or at room temperature. They go great with all-fruit preserves and herb tea.

1½ cups whole wheat pastry flour

1 cup unbleached flour

1 tablespoon baking powder

1 teaspoon ground cinnamon

¼ teaspoon grated nutmeg

¼ teaspoon baking soda

½ cup cold margarine or butter

½ cup skim milk

⅓ cup nonfat yogurt or buttermilk

1 egg or ¼ cup fat-free egg substitute

½ cup raisins

3 tablespoons honey or maple syrup

In a large bowl, combine the whole wheat flour, unbleached flour, baking powder, cinnamon, nutmeg, and baking soda. With a pastry blender or two knives, cut in the margarine or butter until the mixture resembles coarse crumbs.

Stir in the milk, yogurt or buttermilk, egg, raisins, and honey or maple syrup. You should have a soft dough. Divide the dough in half.

Coat two large (10″ or 12″) plates with no-stick spray. Form each portion of dough into a flattened round. Place on a plate. With lightly floured fingertips, pat each into an 8″ round. Cut each into eight wedges but don't separate the pieces.

Place one plate in the microwave on top of an inverted saucer. Microwave on high for 2 minutes. Rotate the plate a half turn. Microwave on high for 1 to 2 minutes, or until the top is almost dry. (The few remaining moist spots will dry upon standing.)

Cool on a wire rack.

Microwave the remaining scones.

MAKES 16 SCONES.

SOUTHERN CORN MUFFINS

¾ cup yellow cornmeal

¾ cup unbleached flour

¼ cup whole wheat pastry
  flour

1 tablespoon baking powder

1 cup buttermilk

¼ cup honey

¼ cup canola oil

1 egg or ¼ cup fat-free egg
  substitute

In a medium bowl, combine the cornmeal, unbleached flour, whole wheat flour, and baking powder.

In a small bowl, mix the buttermilk, honey, oil, and egg. Pour over the dry ingredients and stir until just combined.

Line six muffin cups or 6-ounce custard cups with two paper cupcake liners. Spoon about 3 tablespoons of batter into each cup. Arrange the cups in a circle in the microwave.

Microwave on medium (50% power) for 3 minutes. Rotate the pan a half turn or rearrange the cups. Microwave on high for 2 to 3 minutes, or until a toothpick comes out clean when inserted in the center of each muffin.

Remove and discard the outer paper liners. Let stand on a wire rack for 3 minutes, or until the tops are dry and spring back when lightly touched. Repeat with the remaining batter.

MAKES 12 MUFFINS.

MUFFINS FOR ONE . . . OR MORE

You have several options when it comes to making muffins. With some types of batter, especially those containing baking powder instead of just baking soda, you can mix a batch, microwave a few, and refrigerate the remaining batter for another time.

As with any other food done in the microwave, cooking times vary according to how many items you're doing at a time. Two muffins require more time than just one; four take longer than two. I use the time guidelines below to get perfect muffins every time, whether I'm microwaving one or six. In all cases I use either a microwave muffin pan or 6-ounce custard cups. I line them with two paper cupcake liners and add about 2 tablespoons of batter to each cup.

A single muffin should be positioned in the center of the microwave, two go side by side, and three or more should be arranged in a circle. To compensate for any hot spots your microwave might have, rearrange the cups halfway through the cooking time.

For times when you bake a whole batch of muffins at a time—perhaps a dozen or so in your regular oven—the microwave makes reheating them quick and easy. They turn out so soft and moist you'd say they were freshly baked. Wrap each muffin in a microwave-safe paper towel. Microwave one muffin on high for 15 to 35 seconds; do two on high for 30 to 60 seconds.

You can also freshen slightly stale bread slices or rolls in the microwave. Wrap each piece in a paper towel. Microwave each roll or bread slice on high for 15 seconds. Bread will turn rubbery if it's microwaved too long.

To defrost a 1-pound loaf of bread, remove any twist-ties from the wrapper and leave the wrapper open. Microwave the loaf on high for 1 minute, or until the loaf feels cool but not icy. Let it stand for 5 minutes.

BAKING TIMES FOR MUFFINS

NUMBER	TIME (on high)	NUMBER	TIME (on high)
1 muffin	30–35 sec.	4 muffins	2–2½ min.
2 muffins	55–60 sec.	5 muffins	2½–3 min.
3 muffins	1½–2 min.	6 muffins	3–4 min.

PUMPKIN MUFFINS

Autumn is an excellent time to serve these spicy muffins. This batter will keep in the refrigerator for up to three days, so you can bake the muffins as you need them.

1 cup whole wheat pastry flour
1 cup unbleached flour
2 teaspoons baking powder
¾ teaspoon ground cinnamon
½ teaspoon ground ginger
¼ teaspoon ground cloves

½ cup honey
2 eggs or ½ cup fat-free egg substitute
¼ cup margarine or butter, softened

1 cup canned pumpkin
⅓ cup buttermilk
⅓ cup chopped walnuts or pecans

In a small bowl, mix the whole wheat flour, unbleached flour, baking powder, cinnamon, ginger, and cloves.

In a large bowl, blend the honey, eggs, and margarine or butter with an electric mixer. Stir in the pumpkin and buttermilk. Beat on high speed for 2 to 3 minutes. Stir in the flour mixture and walnuts or pecans.

Line six muffin cups or 6-ounce custard cups with two paper cupcake liners. Spoon about 3 tablespoons of batter into each cup. Arrange the cups in a circle in the microwave.

Microwave on high for 2 minutes. Rotate the pan a half turn or rearrange the cups. Microwave on high for 2 to 3 minutes, or until the tops spring back when lightly touched.

Remove and discard the outer paper liners. Let stand on wire racks for 3 minutes.

Refrigerate the remaining batter until needed (up to 3 days). Then repeat the microwaving procedure.

MAKES 15 TO 18 MUFFINS.

250

DATE MUFFINS

High in fiber, these moist and scrumptious muffins are a snap to make.

¾ cup bran-flake cereal
⅔ cup whole wheat pastry flour
½ cup unbleached flour
2 teaspoons baking powder
1 cup skim milk

2 eggs or ½ cup fat-free egg substitute
⅓ cup chopped dates
¼ cup canola oil
3 tablespoons honey

½ teaspoon grated lemon rind
1 tablespoon finely chopped walnuts
1 tablespoon wheat germ

In a large bowl, combine the cereal, whole wheat flour, unbleached flour, and baking powder. Stir in the milk, eggs, dates, oil, honey, and lemon rind.

In a cup, combine the walnuts and wheat germ.

Line six muffin cups or 6-ounce custard cups with two paper cupcake liners. Spoon a scant 2 tablespoons of batter into each cup. Sprinkle each muffin with a rounded ¼ teaspoon of the walnut mixture. Arrange the cups in a circle in the microwave.

Microwave on high for 2 minutes. Rotate the pan a half turn or rearrange the cups. Microwave on high for 1 to 3 minutes, or until the tops spring back when lightly touched.

Remove and discard the outer paper liners. Let stand on a wire rack for 3 minutes.

Refrigerate the remaining batter until needed (up to 3 days). Then repeat the microwaving procedure.

MAKES 18 MUFFINS.

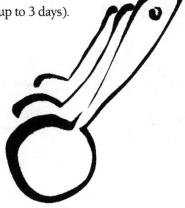

BRAN MUFFINS

Makes a small batch—just right for small families, couples, or singles. Freeze and reheat extras for extra-fast breakfasts.

¾ cup All-Bran cereal

¾ cup whole wheat pastry flour

1½ teaspoons baking powder

½ teaspoon ground cinnamon

⅔ cup skim milk

½ cup honey

¼ cup canola oil

1 egg or ¼ cup fat-free egg substitute

¼ cup raisins

In a medium bowl, combine the cereal, flour, baking powder, and cinnamon.

In a small bowl, combine the milk, honey, oil, and egg. Pour over the dry ingredients and mix until just combined. Stir in the raisins. Let stand for 5 minutes to let the cereal absorb the liquid, then stir thoroughly.

Line six to eight muffin cups or 6-ounce custard cups with two paper cupcake liners. Spoon about ¼ cup of batter into each cup. Arrange the cups in a circle in the microwave.

Microwave on high for 2½ minutes. Rotate the pan a half turn or rearrange the cups. Microwave on high for 2½ to 3½ minutes, or until the tops spring back when lightly touched.

Remove and discard the outer paper liners. Let stand on a wire rack for 5 minutes.

MAKES 6 TO 8 MUFFINS.

BLENDER OAT-BRAN MUFFINS

With the help of your blender, you can whip up this batter in a minute.

1 cup whole wheat flour
½ cup unbleached flour
⅓ cup oat bran
1 teaspoon baking soda
½ teaspoon ground cinnamon

¼ teaspoon ground ginger
¾ cup nonfat yogurt
¼ cup canola oil
1 egg or ¼ cup fat-free egg substitute

¼ cup maple syrup or honey
¼ cup chopped walnuts
¼ cup currants or chopped raisins

In a medium bowl, combine the whole wheat flour, unbleached flour, oat bran, baking soda, cinnamon, and ginger.

In a blender container, place the yogurt, oil, egg, and maple syrup or honey. Process on medium speed until smooth.

Add half of the flour mixture; process until combined. Scrape down the sides of the container. Add the remaining flour mixture and process until smooth.

Stir in the walnuts and currants or raisins.

Line six muffin cups or 6-ounce custard cups with two paper cupcake liners. Spoon about 2 tablespoons of batter into each cup. Arrange the cups in a circle in the microwave.

Microwave on high for 2 minutes. Rotate the pan a half turn or rearrange the cups. Microwave on high for 1 to 2 minutes, or until the tops spring back when lightly touched.

Remove and discard the outer paper liners. Let stand on a wire rack for 3 minutes.

Refrigerate the remaining batter until needed (up to 3 days). Then repeat the microwaving procedure.

MAKES 12 MUFFINS.

BLUEBERRY-CORNMEAL MUFFINS

¾ cup yellow cornmeal

⅔ cup whole wheat pastry flour

2 teaspoons baking powder

¾ cup skim milk

¼ cup maple syrup

¼ cup canola oil

1 egg or ¼ cup fat-free egg substitute

½ cup blueberries

In a medium bowl, combine the cornmeal, flour, and baking powder.

In a small bowl, mix the milk, maple syrup, oil, and egg. Pour over the dry ingredients and stir until just combined. Fold in the blueberries.

Line six muffin cups or 6-ounce custard cups with two paper cupcake liners. Divide the batter among the cups. Arrange the cups in a circle in the microwave.

Microwave on high for 3½ to 6 minutes, or until the tops spring back when lightly touched.

Remove and discard the outer paper liners. Let stand on a wire rack for 5 minutes.

MAKES 6 MUFFINS.

C H A P T E R 11

FOR THE SWEET TOOTH

Fresh fruit is the ultimate healthy dessert. But when you want a change from plain raw fruit, let your microwave help you create delicious low-fat treats. Here are just a few of the goodies you can prepare at a moment's notice:

- *Homemade applesauce, which is a delicious dessert in its own right but which can also add fiber, moisture, and texture to low-fat cakes and sweet breads.*

- *Date and nut bars that are extra-moist and delicious.*

- *Quick baked apples that really satisfy a sweet tooth.*

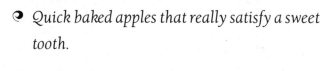

Steamed puddings brimming with vitamin-rich dried fruit—ready in a fraction of the time traditionally required.

The microwave also lets you cook and serve many desserts in the same dish, which simplifies cleanup and saves you valuable kitchen time. Lots of desserts can also be cooked in such a short time that you can prepare them at the last minute. That lets you enjoy them while they're piping hot and at their flavor peak.

SIMPLY WONDERFUL CAKES

You *can* make great cakes and other baked goods in the microwave. But choose your recipes carefully. Not all conventional recipes make the transition to the microwave successfully. And many rely on a hefty amount of fat to achieve a tender finished product. Some microwave carrot cakes, for instance, call for a full cup of oil. You don't need all that fat in your diet! You'll find the recipes in this chapter, including Carrot Cake

on page 265, are nicely slimmed down for you.

One tip: When making microwave cakes, don't flour the pans. You'll end up with an unattractive white film on the finished product. Instead, coat pans with no-stick spray. For a more decorative touch, especially on cakes that won't be frosted, dust the baking dish with ground nuts before adding the batter.

The microwave lets you do other dessert-oriented things. You can, for instance, recapture the taste and texture of just-baked cookies. To do this, wrap two to four cookies in a paper towel and microwave on high for 30 to 45 seconds. The cookies come out warm and soft. That's particularly nice with low-fat cookies, which can turn hard quickly.

The microwave is an essential tool for the health-conscious cook. It lets you prepare satisfying desserts that are high in fiber and low in fat and calories. Look at it this way: With a microwave on hand, you'll always get your just desserts!

QUICK STUFFED APPLE

Perfect as either a dessert or a quick and healthy snack. If you're using a sweet apple, add a few drops of lemon juice to the filling to zip up the flavor.

1 large tart green apple	½ teaspoon maple syrup	Low-fat milk (optional)
1 tablespoon raisins	1 tablespoon granola	

Using a sharp knife and working from the stem end, remove most of the core from the apple (leave about ½″ at the bottom intact). Fill the cavity with the raisins. Drizzle the maple syrup over the raisins.

Place in a small bowl. Cover with wax paper, tucking the ends under the apple. Microwave on high for 4 to 5 minutes, or until tender. Sprinkle with the granola. Add milk (if using) and serve warm.

MAKES 1 SERVING.

Variations: Substitute chopped dates for the raisins, or use a mixture of raisins and chopped walnuts.

APPLE CRUNCH

6 cups thinly sliced tart green apples
1 tablespoon lemon juice
½ cup maple syrup

½ cup whole wheat pastry flour
¼ cup cold margarine or butter

⅔ cup rolled oats
¼ cup chopped pecans or walnuts
½ teaspoon ground cinnamon

Place the apples in an 8″ × 8″ baking dish. Drizzle with the lemon juice and 6 tablespoons of the maple syrup. Mix well and set aside.

Place the flour in a medium bowl. Use a pastry blender to cut in the margarine or butter until the mixture resembles coarse meal. Stir in the oats, pecans or walnuts, cinnamon, and the remaining 2 tablespoons maple syrup. Spoon this mixture over the apples.

Microwave on high for 6 minutes. Rotate the dish a half turn. Microwave on high for 6 to 7 minutes, or until the apples are tender.

MAKES 8 SERVINGS.

MAPLE-CINNAMON APPLE SLICES

Simple and delicious.

1 tablespoon margarine or butter

1 tablespoon maple syrup

1 tablespoon orange juice

¼ teaspoon ground cinnamon

3 large tart green apples, thinly sliced

Place the margarine or butter in a 7″ × 11″ baking dish. Microwave on high for 1 minute, or until the margarine or butter is melted. Stir in the maple syrup, orange juice, and cinnamon.

Add the apples and stir to coat with the cinnamon mixture. Cover with wax paper. Microwave on high for 2 minutes. Stir, cover with wax paper, and microwave on high for 3 to 4 minutes, or until the apples are tender. Serve warm.

MAKES 6 SERVINGS.

BRING OUT THE FLAVOR OF FRESH CITRUS

Many recipes call for fresh lemon, lime, or orange juice. Your microwave can help you get the most flavor and the maximum amount of juice from these citrus fruits.

To make squeezing juice from citrus fruit easier, microwave one lemon, orange, or lime on high for 30 seconds to 1 minute, until just warm. Cut in half and squeeze as usual. You'll actually get more juice than you would from cold fruit.

If your recipe calls for grated citrus rind, grate the peel before microwaving and juicing the fruit. Save extra grated rind for future use by drying it in the microwave. Spread the rind in a thin layer on a paper towel. Microwave on high for 30 seconds. Stir lightly and microwave for another 30 seconds to 1½ minutes, or until the rind is dry to the touch. Let cool. Store in an airtight container. One-half teaspoon dried peel equals 1 teaspoon fresh.

JEWELED MINTED FRUIT

2 peaches, sliced

2 plums, quartered

1 cup red or green grapes, halved

1 cup apple juice

2 tablespoons quick-cooking tapioca

1 tablespoon minced fresh mint or ½ teaspoon dried mint

1 teaspoon maple syrup

In a 1½-quart casserole, combine the peaches, plums, grapes, juice, tapioca, mint, and maple syrup. Cover with a lid and microwave on high for a total of 15 to 20 minutes, stirring twice during this time, until the tapioca is translucent and the fruit is tender. Chill for at least 3 hours.

MAKES 8 SERVINGS.

CHUNKY RAISIN APPLESAUCE

This sweet-tart dessert can double as a wonderful side dish or a topping for pancakes and waffles.

3 large tart green apples, cubed

¼ cup apple juice or cider

1 tablespoon maple syrup

2 tablespoons raisins

Pinch of ground cinnamon

In a medium bowl, toss together the apples, juice or cider, and maple syrup. Cover with a lid or large plate. Microwave on high for 3 minutes. Stir, cover, and microwave on high for 3 minutes.

Add the raisins and cinnamon. Stir briskly to break up the apples. Microwave on high for 2 minutes, or until the apples are soft. Serve warm or chilled.

MAKES 4 TO 6 SERVINGS.

SPICY PINEAPPLE SPEARS

Here's a slightly exotic way to serve pineapple.

1 small pineapple	¼ teaspoon ground ginger	⅛ teaspoon grated lime rind
1½ tablespoons maple syrup	⅛ teaspoon ground cinnamon	

Remove the top and bottom ends from the pineapple. Cut the center section lengthwise into quarters. Remove and discard the tough inner core and the rind. Slice each quarter in half crosswise, then into long thin spears.

Place in a 10″ round baking dish. Cover with a lid and microwave on high for 3 to 4 minutes, or until hot.

In a cup, combine the maple syrup, ginger, cinnamon, and lime rind. Drizzle over the pineapple and stir to coat. Cover with a lid and microwave on high for 1 to 2 minutes. Serve warm.

MAKES 4 SERVINGS.

GINGER-POACHED PEARS

¾ cup water	1 tablespoon grated lemon rind	6 firm pears
¼ cup maple syrup or honey	1 tablespoon grated fresh ginger	Mint sprigs (garnish)
1 tablespoon lemon juice		

In an 8″ × 8″ baking dish, combine the water, maple syrup or honey, lemon juice, lemon rind, and ginger. Microwave on high for 3 minutes, or until boiling.

Using a vegetable peeler, remove a thin slice of skin from the upper end of each pear; keep the stems intact. Stand the pears in the dish. Cover with wax paper, allowing the stems to poke through.

Microwave on high for a total of 7 to 9 minutes, rotating the dish a quarter turn twice during this time, until the pears are tender. Transfer the pears to a serving plate.

Microwave the cooking liquid on high for 10 minutes, or until reduced by half. Pour over the pears and let cool. Chill. Serve garnished with the mint.

MAKES 6 SERVINGS.

NEWPORT FRUIT COMPOTE

Here's a classy way to end a meal. In cool weather, serve the compote hot; in summer, serve it chilled.

1 cup orange juice	1 tablespoon grated orange rind	1 cinnamon stick
¼ cup water	⅔ cup prunes, quartered	2 tart green apples, thinly sliced
2 tablespoons honey	⅓ cup dried apricots, halved	Orange slices (garnish)

In a 2-quart casserole, combine the juice, water, honey, and orange rind. Microwave on high for 5 minutes. Add the prunes, apricots, and cinnamon stick. Microwave on high for 5 minutes.

Add the apples. Microwave on high for 5 minutes, or until the apples are crisp-tender. Cover with a lid and let stand for 5 minutes. Remove and discard the cinnamon stick. Serve garnished with the oranges.

MAKES 4 SERVINGS.

EASY CUSTARD

Serve with Raspberry Sauce (page 264) for a simple, elegant dessert.

1¼ cups low-fat milk
4 eggs or 1 cup fat-free egg substitute

¼ cup maple syrup

2 teaspoons vanilla

Place the milk in a 4-cup glass measure and microwave on high for 2 minutes, or until hot but not boiling.

In a medium bowl, whisk the eggs, maple syrup, and vanilla until frothy. Slowly whisk in the milk.

Pour into four 6-ounce custard cups. Place the cups in a circle on a plate, leaving about 1″ between them. Lay a piece of wax paper over the cups. Microwave on medium (50% power) for 3 minutes. Rotate the dish a half turn. Microwave on medium (50% power) for 3 to 5 minutes, or until the custards are just set and the centers are still slightly loose. Do not overcook. Let stand for 10 minutes.

Unmold onto serving plates. Serve warm or chilled.

MAKES 4 SERVINGS.

DATE-NUT BARS

2 eggs or ½ cup fat-free egg substitute
⅓ cup maple syrup
2 tablespoons margarine or butter, melted

½ teaspoon vanilla
⅔ cup whole wheat pastry flour
½ teaspoon baking powder

½ teaspoon grated orange rind
2 cups finely chopped dates
1 cup finely chopped walnuts

Place the eggs in a medium bowl. Using an electric mixer, beat until foamy. Beat in the maple syrup, margarine or butter, and vanilla.

Add the flour, baking powder, and orange rind. Stir just until combined. Fold in the dates and walnuts.

Spread in an 8″ × 8″ baking dish. Microwave on medium (50% power) for 3 minutes. Rotate the dish a quarter turn. Microwave on medium (50% power) for 3 minutes. Rotate the dish a quarter turn.

Microwave on high for a total of 4 to 6 minutes, rotating the dish a quarter turn every 2 minutes during this time, until the bars spring back when lightly pressed in the center.

Cover with wax paper and let stand for 15 minutes. Cut into bars while warm.

MAKES 32 BARS.

Variation: To make Mixed Fruit Bars, *replace 1 cup of the dates with ½ cup raisins and ½ cup finely chopped dried apricots.*

DRIED FRUIT: PLUMP IT UP

It's so simple to plump up dried peaches, prunes, and other fruit in the microwave. Once softened, these fruits make delicious fiber-rich desserts. You can serve them plain or top them with a spoonful of crunchy granola. For variety, replace the granola with a little maple syrup, grated lemon rind, or grated nutmeg. On special occasions, spoon the fruit over low-fat frozen yogurt.

To plump fruits, place 1 cup dried fruit in a 2-cup glass measure. Sprinkle with 2 table-spoons water or a mixture of 1 tablespoon water and 1 tablespoon lemon juice. Cover with wax paper. Microwave on high for 30 seconds. Stir, then cover again and microwave on high for another 30 seconds. Cover tightly with foil and let stand for 2 to 3 minutes. If using the fruit in a recipe, drain off any excess liquid.

To soften raisins, place ½ cup in a 1-cup glass measure. Microwave on high for 15 to 20 seconds.

NO-FUSS PEACH CRISP

This fast dessert uses fresh fruit and a cookie to make a low-fat treat. Nothing could be simpler. If fresh peaches are out of season, use ½ cup of canned fruit.

1 peach, diced   ⅛ teaspoon lemon juice   1 oatmeal-raisin cookie
½ teaspoon maple syrup or
   honey

Place the peaches in a 6-ounce custard cup. Drizzle with the maple syrup or honey and lemon juice. Cover with wax paper and microwave on high for 1 minute. Crumble the cookie over the peaches. Let stand for 3 minutes.

MAKES 1 SERVING.

RASPBERRY SAUCE

Serve with fresh fruit and sherbet.

2 cups raspberries   ¼ cup maple syrup

In a 2-quart casserole, combine the raspberries and maple syrup. Cover with a lid and microwave on high for 3 minutes. Stir, then microwave on high for 1 minute.

Press the sauce through a sieve to remove the seeds. Store tightly covered in the refrigerator.

MAKES 1½ CUPS.

CARROT CAKE

Beware of microwave cakes that are high in fats. Some recipes for carrot cake, for example, call for a full cup of oil. This moist cake is far lower in fat. To keep it low, serve it plain or with low-fat frozen yogurt.

4 eggs or 1 cup fat-free egg substitute

¾ cup honey

⅓ cup canola oil

¼ cup buttermilk

1 teaspoon vanilla

1½ cups whole wheat pastry flour

1 tablespoon ground cinnamon

2 teaspoons baking powder

1½ teaspoons baking soda

¼ teaspoon grated nutmeg

2 cups lightly packed shredded carrots

In a large bowl, beat together the eggs, honey, oil, buttermilk, and vanilla. Stir in the flour, cinnamon, baking powder, baking soda, and nutmeg. Fold in the carrots.

Coat a Bundt pan with no-stick spray. Add the batter. Microwave on medium (50% power) for a total of 12 minutes, rotating the dish a quarter turn every 4 minutes during this time.

Microwave on high for 2 to 4 minutes, or until the cake starts to pull away from the sides of the pan.

Let stand for 15 minutes. Invert onto a serving platter. Cover loosely with wax paper and let cool.

MAKES 12 SERVINGS.

Note: If you don't have a Bundt pan, use a deep, round 2-quart casserole. Coat it with no-stick spray. Also spray the outside of a straight-sided glass jar or bottle (at least 4″ high and 2″ in diameter). Place the jar, open-end up, in the center of the casserole. Spread the batter evenly around the jar.

THE PERFECT MICROWAVE PIE SHELL

It's so easy to whip up fruit pie fillings in the microwave. And believe it or not, it's also easy to prepare a microwaved pie shell. I like to make mine whole wheat because crusts don't brown in the microwave and white ones turn out looking pale. Besides, whole wheat has more fiber. And whole wheat pastry flour gives the crust a nice texture.

WHOLE WHEAT PIE SHELL

1¼ cups whole wheat pastry flour

3 tablespoons cold margarine or butter

2 tablespoons canola oil

2–3 tablespoons ice water

Place the flour in a medium bowl. With a pastry blender, cut in the margarine or butter until the pieces are the size of peas. Slowly drizzle with the oil and continue blending until the mixture resembles coarse meal. Sprinkle with enough water to make a dough that can be gathered into a ball.

Sprinkle a large piece of wax paper with additional flour. Flatten the dough slightly with your hands and place on the paper. Sprinkle with a little more flour and cover with another piece of wax paper. Roll the dough into a 12″ circle. Remove the top piece of paper.

Coat a 9″ glass pie plate with no-stick spray. Flip the dough and ease it into the pan. Peel off the paper. Gently press the dough into place, being careful not to stretch it. Trim or flute the edges.

Prick the bottom and sides of the dough all over with a fork. Microwave on high for 3 minutes. Rotate the dish a half turn. Microwave on high for 3 to 5 minutes, or until the pastry is opaque and the bottom is dry.

MAKES 1 PIE SHELL.

NEW-FASHIONED APPLE PIE

1 can (12 ounces) apple juice concentrate

3 tablespoons cornstarch

1 tablespoon lemon juice

1 teaspoon ground cinnamon

¼ teaspoon grated nutmeg

¼ teaspoon grated lemon rind

⅛ teaspoon ground allspice

7 cups sliced tart green apples

1 tablespoon cold margarine or butter

1 (9″) Whole Wheat Pie Shell (opposite page), baked

In a 4-quart casserole, combine the apple juice concentrate, cornstarch, lemon juice, cinnamon, nutmeg, lemon rind, and allspice. Stir in the apples. Dot the surface with small pieces of the margarine or butter.

Cover with wax paper and microwave on high for a total of 16 to 20 minutes, stirring the mixture every 4 minutes during this time.

Cool, then spoon the filling into the baked pie shell.

MAKES 8 SERVINGS.

SO-QUICK BLUEBERRY PIE

½ cup water

¼ cup maple syrup

2 tablespoons cornstarch

2 pints blueberries

1 (9″) Whole Wheat Pie Shell (opposite page), baked

In a medium bowl, whisk together the water, maple syrup, and cornstarch. Stir in the blueberries.

Microwave on high for 5 minutes. Stir and microwave on high for 3 to 5 minutes, or until the mixture is thick. Cool slightly, then pour into the pie shell. Cool before serving.

MAKES 8 SERVINGS.

STEAMED PUDDING

A traditional yuletide dessert, this old-fashioned pudding can shine on other occasions as well. It cooks in about a third the amount of time usually needed—and you don't have to bother with the standard water bath.

1 cup applesauce

2 eggs or ½ cup fat-free egg substitute

½ cup honey

½ cup canola oil

2 tablespoons apple juice or orange juice

1 teaspoon vanilla

1 teaspoon lemon juice

¼ teaspoon grated lemon rind

1 cup whole wheat pastry flour

1 teaspoon ground cinnamon

2 teaspoons baking soda

¼ teaspoon ground allspice

1 cup finely chopped dates or raisins

½ cup chopped nuts

In a large bowl, combine the applesauce, eggs, honey, oil, apple juice or orange juice, vanilla, lemon juice, and lemon rind. Stir in the flour, cinnamon, soda, and allspice. Fold in the dates or raisins and nuts.

Coat a 6-cup ring mold with no-stick spray. Add the batter and cover with wax paper. Microwave on medium (50% power) for a total of 50 minutes, rotating the dish a quarter turn every 10 minutes during this time.

Cover with wax paper and microwave on high for 3 minutes. Cover tightly with foil and let stand for 15 minutes. Unmold onto a plate. Serve warm.

MAKES 8 TO 10 SERVINGS.

Note: If you don't have a microwave ring mold, use a 1½-quart casserole. Place a 6-ounce glass upright in the center and lightly coat it with no-stick spray. Pour the batter around it. Continue with the recipe as above. If you don't plan to serve the steamed pudding as soon as it's cooked, eliminate the final 3 minutes of microwaving. Cover the dish with foil and store for up to two days. To reheat, cover the pan with wax paper and microwave on medium (50% power) for 15 minutes.

PUMPKIN PUDDING

2 cups cooked pumpkin
¾ cup evaporated skim milk
2 eggs or ½ cup fat-free egg substitute

¼ cup maple syrup
1 tablespoon cornstarch
1 teaspoon ground cinnamon

¼ teaspoon grated nutmeg
⅛ teaspoon ground ginger

In a 3-quart casserole, whisk together the pumpkin, milk, eggs, maple syrup, cornstarch, cinnamon, nutmeg, and ginger. Cover with a lid and microwave on high for 5 minutes. Stir, cover with a lid, and microwave on high for 5 minutes.

Cover with a lid and microwave on medium (50% power) for a total of 15 minutes, stirring twice during this time. Let stand for 15 minutes.

MAKES 8 SERVINGS.

BREAD PUDDING

8 slices bread, cubed
½ cup raisins
2 cups low-fat milk

2 eggs or ½ cup egg substitute
¼ cup maple syrup

1 teaspoon vanilla
½ teaspoon ground cinnamon

In a 9″ round cake dish, combine the bread and raisins. Set aside.

Place the milk in a medium bowl and microwave on high for 5 minutes, or until the milk comes to a boil. Whisk in the eggs, maple syrup, vanilla, and cinnamon.

Pour the egg mixture over the bread. Microwave on high for 8 to 9 minutes, or until the pudding is set. Let stand for 15 minutes before serving.

MAKES 6 SERVINGS.

GINGERBREAD
WITH APPLESAUCE TOPPING

This moist gingerbread contains no added fat. The time-saver here is that you can make quick applesauce in the microwave. Then you bake the gingerbread in a conventional oven.

1 large tart green apple, peeled and chopped

1 large red apple, chopped

¼ cup apple juice or cider

2 cups whole wheat pastry flour

1½ teaspoons baking soda

2 teaspoons ground ginger

¼ teaspoon ground cinnamon

⅛ teaspoon ground cloves

¼ cup raisins

¾ cup skim milk

1 teaspoon apple cider vinegar

1 egg or ¼ cup fat-free egg substitute

1 cup molasses

In a 4-cup glass measure, combine the green apples, red apples, and apple juice or cider. Cover with wax paper and microwave on high for 3 minutes. Transfer to a blender or food processor and puree until smooth. Set aside.

In a large bowl, combine the flour, baking soda, ginger, cinnamon, and cloves. Stir in the raisins.

In a small bowl, combine the milk and vinegar. Whisk in the egg and molasses. Add ½ cup of the applesauce. Pour over the dry ingredients and stir until just combined.

Coat a 9″ × 9″ baking dish with no-stick spray. Add the batter. Bake at 325° for 35 to 40 minutes, or until a knife inserted in the center comes out clean.

If desired, serve topped with the remaining applesauce.

MAKES 9 SERVINGS.

TAPIOCA PUDDING

This maple-flavored pudding is old-fashioned comfort food—serve it warm on nippy days.

2 cups low-fat milk

2 eggs or ½ cup fat-free egg substitute

¼ cup quick-cooking tapioca

¼ cup maple syrup

¼ teaspoon vanilla

In a 1½-quart casserole, combine the milk, eggs, tapioca, and maple syrup. Let stand for 5 minutes, then stir well.

Microwave on high for 3 minutes; whisk until smooth. Microwave on high for 2 minutes; whisk until smooth.

Continue to microwave on high, stirring every 30 seconds, until the tapioca is thickened. Stir in the vanilla. Cover with a lid and let stand for 5 minutes.

MAKES 4 SERVINGS.

Variation: For Tapioca Parfaits, *chill the finished pudding, then layer it in parfait glasses with sliced fruit.*

BEVERAGES YOU CAN WARM UP TO

HOT CRANBERRY PUNCH

2 cups cranberry-juice cocktail

1 cup white grape juice

1 cup orange juice

1 tablespoon lemon juice

1 tablespoon maple syrup

1 cinnamon stick

1 teaspoon grated orange rind

4 whole cloves

In a 2-quart casserole or bowl, combine the cranberry juice, grape juice, orange juice, lemon juice, maple syrup, cinnamon, orange rind, and cloves. Microwave on high for 4 minutes. Stir and microwave on high for 4 to 6 minutes, or until the mixture comes to a boil. Strain into mugs.

MAKES 4 SERVINGS.

HOT MAPLE-CAROB TODDY

1 tablespoon carob powder

1 teaspoon maple syrup

1 drop vanilla

1 cup low-fat milk

Pinch of ground cinnamon

In a large mug, combine the carob, maple syrup, and vanilla. Stir in 1 tablespoon of the milk to make a smooth paste. Gradually stir in the remaining milk.

Microwave on high for 2 to 2½ minutes, or until the milk is hot with small bubbles on the surface. Dust with the cinnamon.

MAKES 1 SERVING.

MULLED APPLE PUNCH

½ cup apple juice or cider
½ cup water

1 rose-hip tea bag or apple-
herb tea bag

1 cinnamon stick
1 lemon slice

In a large mug, combine the juice or cider, water, tea bag, and cinnamon. Microwave on high for 3 to 4 minutes, or until boiling. Add the lemon. Let stand for 1 minute. Remove and discard the tea bag and cinnamon.

MAKES 1 SERVING.

Note: If your tea bag contains metal staples, remove them before microwaving. Otherwise, they may cause undesirable arcing.

MULLED CIDER

6 cups apple cider
1 tablespoon maple syrup

16 whole cloves
8 lemon slices

6 cinnamon sticks

In a 3-quart casserole or bowl, combine the cider and maple syrup. Stick two cloves into each lemon slice. Add the lemon slices and cinnamon sticks to the cider.

Microwave on high for 10 to 12 minutes, or until the cider comes to a boil. Remove and discard the lemon slices. Pour the liquid into six warmed cups. Add one of the cinnamon sticks to each cup.

MAKES 6 SERVINGS.

I N D E X

A

Acorn squash. *See also* Winter squash
  Acorn-Squash Pancakes, 224–25
  New-England Acorn-Squash Soup, 197
Aluminum foil, microwave cooking and, 13
Amount of food, timing in microwave and, 8
Angel hair pasta
  Chicken Breasts with Herbed Angel Hair Pasta, 87
  Garlic Shrimp with Capellini, 130
Antipasto. *See also* Appetizers
  Antipasto Salad, 234–35
Appetizers, 36–51
  Anne's Super-Bowl Shrimp, 42
  Baba Ganoush, 46
  Baby Potatoes Stuffed with Herbed Cheese, 49
  Basil Gazpacho with Shrimp, 45
  Chive Yogurt Cheese, 51
  Eggplant Caviar, 38–39
  Feta-Spinach Squares, 50
  Garlic Eggplant and Peppers, 42–43
  Herbed Yogurt Cheese, 51
  Honey-Gingered Shrimp, 40
  Hot Chicken Wings, 39
  Low-Fat Tortilla Chips, 41
  Marrakech Stuffed Mushrooms, 44
  Minted Yogurt Cheese, 51
  Mushroom Pâté, 47
  Parmesan Pita Triangles, 43
  Pimento-Cheese Spread, 51
  Scallop Coins with Dill Sauce, 40–41
  Taco Dip, 48
  Turkey-Stuffed Mushroom Caps, 46–47

Apple cider
  Apple-Cider Coffee Cake, 31
  Mulled Apple Punch, 273
  Mulled Cider, 273
Apples
  Apple-Cider Coffee Cake, 31
  Apple Crunch, 257
  Apple-Raisin Millet Cereal, 23
  Apple and Raisin Stuffing, 83
  Chunky Raisin Applesauce, 259
  Cranberry-Apple Relish, 230
  Gingerbread with Applesauce Topping, 270
  Honey-Apple Sauce, 29
  Maple-Cinnamon Apple Slices, 258
  New-Fashioned Apple Pie, 267
  Quick Stuffed Apple, 256–57
  Strawberry-Apple Sauce, 29
Apricots
  Apricot-Pecan Ring, 246
  Puffed Apricot Pancake, 27
Artichokes
  Artichokes with Curry Sauce, 211
Asparagus, 212
  cooking times, 185
Avocados
  California Avocado Turkey Melt, 105

B

Baba Ganoush, 46
Baby vegetables
  Baby Potatoes Stuffed with Herbed Cheese, 49
  stuffed, 39
Baked goods, 237–54. *See also* Desserts
Baking methods, 238
Bananas
  Strawberry-Banana Bread, 244

Barbecue Sauce, 61
Barbecuing
  Barbecued Ribs, 60–61
  chicken, 101
  Grilled Turkey Breast with Corn on the Cob, 100
Barley
  Chicken with Barley, 93
  Chicken-Barley Soup, 200
Basil
  Basil Gazpacho with Shrimp, 45
Basting poultry, 81
Bay scallops. *See* Scallops
Beans. *See also* Lentils; Split peas
  Bean Burritos Deluxe, 155
  Chicken 'n' Chili, 95
  Chili Bean Soup, 186
  cooking methods, 153
  Minestrone, 189
  Stacked Enchiladas, 58
  Taco Dip, 48
  Taco Salad, 235
Beef
  Barbecued Ribs, 60–61
  Beef Stew, 206
  Beef Stock, 182
  Cabbage Rolls with Poppy-Seed Noodles, 78
  Lean and Light Lasagna, 67
  Lew's Skinny Chili, 71
  Light Beef and Mushrooms Stroganoff, 72
  Mexican-Style Tacos with Salad Toppings, 57
  My Favorite Stuffed Peppers, 64
  Oriental Beef, 66
  Party Meat Loaf with Parsley Mashed Potatoes, 56
  Pot Roast with Vegetables, 65

selecting, 53
Shepherd's Pie, 55
Spaghetti and Meatballs, 77
Spaghetti Squash with Peppers and
    Meat Sauce, 76
Spinach Lasagna Roll-Ups, 73
Stacked Enchiladas, 58
Taco Dip, 48
Taco Salad, 235
testing for doneness, 14
Vegetable and Ground Beef Soup, 205
Beets
    Beets with Orange Sauce, 212–13
Beverages
    Hot Cranberry Punch, 272
    Hot Maple-Carob Toddy, 272
    Mulled Apple Punch, 273
    Mulled Cider, 273
Blueberries
    Blueberry-Cornmeal Muffins, 254
    Blueberry Sauce, 29
    So-Quick Blueberry Pie, 267
Bluefish
    Bluefish with Green Onions, 115
Boston Brown Bread, 245
Bran
    Blender Oat-Bran Muffins, 253
    Bran Muffins, 252
    Mixed-Grain Porridge, 24–25
Bread Pudding, 269
Breads
    Apricot-Pecan Ring, 246
    baking methods, 238
    Boston Brown Bread, 245
    Cranberry Bread, 239
    English-Muffin Bread, 241
    freshening in microwave, 249
    Herbed Garlic Bread, 244–45
    Rye, Wheat, and Walnut Bread, 243
    Strawberry-Banana Bread, 244
    Whole Wheat Bread, 242–43
    Zucchini-Nut Bread, 240
Breakfast, 16–35
    Apple-Cider Coffee Cake, 31
    Apple-Raisin Millet Cereal, 23
    Basic Granola, 19
    Breakfast Polenta, 24
    Bulgur Hot Cereal, 20
    Dilled Pita-Pocket Eggs, 32
    French Toast with Fruit Sauce, 26–27
    Fruit Pancakes, 29
    Inca Breakfast Bowl, 25
    Maple Oatmeal, 22–23
    Mixed-Grain Porridge, 24–25
    Moroccan Pilaf Porridge, 18

Nut Pancakes, 29
Pancake Mix, 28
Perfect Pancakes, 29
Puffed Apricot Pancake, 27
Puffed Nectarine Pancake, 27
Puffed Peach Pancake, 27
Raisin Quinoa, 25
Rice-Pudding Porridge, 21
Turkey Sausage with Home-Style
    Potatoes, 30–31
Vegetable Omelet, 32–33
waffles, 28–29
Warren Street Cheese Soufflé Omelet,
    35
Western Frittata, 34
Broccoli
    Broccoli with Cheddar Salsa, 213
    cooking instructions, 185
    Italian-Style Broccoli, 215
    Lemon-Broccoli Curry with Cashews,
        159
Brown bags, microwave cooking and, 13
Brown rice. See Rice
Bulgur
    Bulgur Hot Cereal, 20
    cooking methods, 177
    hot cereal, 21
    Mixed-Grain Porridge, 24–25
    Shrimp Tabbouleh, 236
    Tabbouleh, 236
    Tabbouleh-Stuffed Tomatoes, 236
    Tuna Tabbouleh, 236
Burritos
    Bean Burritos Deluxe, 155
    Garden-Style Burritos, 154
Buttermilk, substitutes for, 238
Butternut squash. See also Winter squash
    Winter-Squash Soup, 192

C

Cabbage
    Cabbage Rolls with Poppy-Seed
        Noodles, 78
    Cabbage Soup, 190
    Sweet-and-Sour Red Cabbage, 214
Cakes
    Apple-Cider Coffee Cake, 31
    baking methods, 256
    Carrot Cake, 265
Canning foods, 14
Capellini. See also Pasta
    Chicken Breasts with Herbed Angel
        Hair Pasta, 87
    Garlic Shrimp with Capellini, 130

Carob
    Hot Maple-Carob Toddy, 272
Carrots
    Carrot Cake, 265
    Carrot-Cauliflower Salad, 230–31
    cooking instructions, 185
    Cream of Carrot Soup, 208
    Glazed Carrots and Parsnips, 214–15
Cashews
    Lemon-Broccoli Curry with Cashews,
        159
    Spicy Cashew Chicken, 84–85
Cauliflower
    Carrot-Cauliflower Salad, 230–31
    Cauliflower with Herbed Parmesan
        Sauce, 218
    Cheese 'n' Chive Cauliflower, 218–19
    cooking instructions, 185
    Cream of Cauliflower Soup, 198
    Pleasant Peasant Pasta, 158
Ceramic cookware, microwave cooking
    and, 9
Cereals, 17
    Apple-Raisin Millet Cereal, 23
    Basic Granola, 19
    Breakfast Polenta, 24
    Bulgur Hot Cereal, 20
    cooking instructions, 21
    Inca Breakfast Bowl, 25
    Maple Oatmeal, 22–23
    Mixed-Grain Porridge, 24–25
    Moroccan Pilaf Porridge, 18
    Raisin Quinoa, 25
    Rice-Pudding Porridge, 21
Cheddar cheese. See also Cheese
    Broccoli with Cheddar Salsa, 213
    Cheddar Tomato Soup, 188
Cheese
    Baby Potatoes Stuffed with Herbed
        Cheese, 49
    Broccoli with Cheddar Salsa, 213
    Cauliflower with Herbed Parmesan
        Sauce, 218
    Cheddar Tomato Soup, 188
    Cheese 'n' Chive Cauliflower, 218–19
    Cheese Scalloped Potatoes, 222
    Cheese and Tofu Stuffed Shells, 166
    Chicken Cutlets with Tomato Sauce
        and Cheese, 89
    Chive Yogurt Cheese, 51
    Eggplant Parmigiana, 162
    Feta-Spinach Squares, 50
    Herbed Yogurt Cheese, 51
    Italian-Style Turkey Rigatoni with
        Mozzarella, 108

Cheese *(continued)*

Macaroni and Cheese, 173
Minted Yogurt Cheese, 51
Parmesan Pita Triangles, 43
Pimento-Cheese Spread, 51
Tomato Cheese Quiche, 147
Warren Street Cheese Soufflé Omelet, 35
Zucchini-Cheese Casserole, 148–49

Chicken
barbecuing, 101
Breaded Chicken Cutlets with Polenta, 88–89
Chicken with Barley, 93
Chicken-Barley Soup, 200
Chicken Breasts with Herbed Angel Hair Pasta, 87
Chicken 'n' Chili, 95
Chicken Cutlets with Tomato Sauce and Cheese, 89
Chicken Stock, 180
Chicken-Vegetable Soup, 181
Chicken and Vegetables with Tarragon, 96
cooking instructions, 91
Dijon Chicken with Scallions, 97
Fry-Style Chicken with Potato Dumplings, 92–93
Herb-Stuffed Chicken Breasts with Sweet-and-Sour Sauce, 82
Honey-Marinated Chicken with Penne and Vegetables, 94
Hot Chicken Wings, 39
Orange Chicken with Savory Pilaf, 99
Oriental Chicken Salad, 90–91
Pagoda Chicken Soup, 201
Roast Chicken with Vegetables, 103
Spicy Cashew Chicken, 84–85
Stir-Fried Chicken and Snow Peas, 86
Tortilla Casserole, 89
Wrapped Chicken and Vegetables, 85

Children, microwave cooking and, 12

Chili
Chicken 'n' Chili, 95
Chili Bean Soup, 186
Lew's Skinny Chili, 71
Quick Lentil Chili, 163

Chips
Low-Fat Tortilla Chips, 41

Chives
Cheese 'n' Chive Cauliflower, 218–19
Chive Yogurt Cheese, 51

Chowders. *See also* Soups
Creamy Clam Chowder, 198–99
Manhattan Clam Chowder, 200–201

Cider. *See* Apple cider

Cioppino, 203

Citrus fruit, preparation methods, 258

Clams
cooking methods, 131
Coquina-Fish Stew, 204
Creamy Clam Chowder, 198–99
Manhattan Clam Chowder, 200–201

Clay cookers, microwave cooking and, 9

Cleaning ovens, 15

Cod
Cancún Cod with Coriander Rice, 112

Coffee cake
Apple-Cider Coffee Cake, 31

Compotes
Jeweled Minted Fruit, 259
Newport Fruit Compote, 261

Convenience-food trays, microwave cooking and, 13

Converting recipes for microwave, 3

Cookies
Date-Nut Bars, 262–63
Mixed Fruit Bars, 263

Cooking methods. *See also* Microwave cooking
beans, 153
bulgur, 177
cakes, 256
cereals, 21
chicken, 91
clams, 131
corn, 219
couscous, 177
crêpes, 167
eggplant, 14
eggs, 33
fish, 117, 131
lobster, 131
muffins, 238
mussels, 131
potatoes, 221
pumpkins, 225
rice, 165
risotto, 165
scallops, 131
seafood, 131
shellfish, 131
shrimp, 131, 139
stock, 179
vegetables, 185, 210
winter squash, 210, 225

Cookware, 9–10

Coquinas
Coquina-Fish Stew, 204

Corn
cooking methods, 210
Grilled Turkey Breast with Corn on the Cob, 100
Savory Fish with Corn on the Cob, 128
Snappy Corn Soup, 191

Cornish hens
Raspberry-Glazed Cornish Hens with Pecan Wild Rice, 102

Cornmeal
Blueberry-Cornmeal Muffins, 254
Breaded Chicken Cutlets with Polenta, 88–89
Breakfast Polenta, 24
Southern Corn Muffins, 247

Corn muffins
Southern Corn Muffins, 247

Couscous
cooking methods, 177
hot cereal, 21
Marrakech Stuffed Mushrooms, 44
Mixed-Grain Porridge, 24–25
Moroccan Fish, 122
Moroccan Pilaf Porridge, 18
North African Couscous Pilaf, 176
Sunshine Fish Fillets with Couscous Pilaf, 123
Swordfish with Tomatoes and Couscous, 130–31
Tofu and Vegetables with Couscous, 145
Turkey Cutlets with Couscous Ratatouille, 98

Covering foods in microwave, 8, 10–11

Cracked wheat. *See also* Bulgur
Mixed-Grain Porridge, 24–25

Cranberries
Cranberry-Apple Relish, 230
Cranberry Bread, 239
Hot Cranberry Punch, 272

Cream soups, 184–85
Cream of Carrot Soup, 208
Cream of Cauliflower Soup, 198
Cream of Fresh Vegetable Soup, 184
Cream of Spinach Soup, 202
Creamy Clam Chowder, 198–99
Shrimp Bisque, 207
thickeners for, 199

Crêpes
cooking methods, 167
Florentine Crêpes, 167
Whole Wheat Crêpes, 169

Croutons, 188
Curry
Artichokes with Curry Sauce, 211
Curried Mixed Fruit, 232
Curried Shrimp and Vegetable Salad, 137
Curried Vegetables with Rice, 151
Fish Steaks with Curried Rice, 129
Indian Curried Casserole with Pine Nuts, 70
Lamb Curry with Yellow Rice, 68
Lemon-Broccoli Curry with Cashews, 159
Quick Curried Tomato Soup, 194
Singapore Lobster and Shrimp, 138–39

D

Dates
Date Muffins, 251
Date-Nut Bars, 262–63
Deep-frying, 14
Defrosting in microwave, 14
breads, 249
crêpes, 167
meat, 14
poultry, 14
Density of food, timing in microwave and, 8
Desserts, 255–73
Apple Crunch, 257
Bread Pudding, 269
Carrot Cake, 265
Chunky Raisin Applesauce, 259
Curried Mixed Fruit, 232
Date-Nut Bars, 262–63
Easy Custard, 262
Gingerbread with Applesauce Topping, 270
Ginger-Poached Pears, 260–61
Jeweled Minted Fruit, 259
Maple-Cinnamon Apple Slices, 258
Mixed Fruit Bars, 263
New-Fashioned Apple Pie, 267
Newport Fruit Compote, 261
No-Fuss Peach Crisp, 264
Pumpkin Pudding, 269
Quick Stuffed Apple, 256–57
Spicy Pineapple Spears, 260
Steamed Pudding, 268
Tapioca Parfaits, 271
Tapioca Pudding, 271
Dietary fat, microwave cooking and, 3–4

Dips. See also Spreads
Baba Ganoush, 46
Super Salsa, 59
Taco Dip, 48
Dried fruit, plumping, 263
Drinks. See Beverages
Dumplings
Fry-Style Chicken with Potato Dumplings, 92–93

E

Eggplant
Baba Ganoush, 46
cooking methods, 14
Eggplant Caviar, 38–39
Eggplant Parmigiana, 162
Garlic Eggplant and Peppers, 42–43
Greek Vegetable Medley, 226
Ratatouille, 227
Saucy Eggplant Casserole, 148
Turkey Cutlets with Couscous Ratatouille, 98
Eggs, 17
cooking methods, 14, 33
Dilled Pita-Pocket Eggs, 32
Mexican Turkey Scramble, 106
Middle Eastern Omelet, 157
Shrimp Frittata, 125
Vegetable Omelet, 32–33
Warren Street Cheese Soufflé Omelet, 35
Western Frittata, 34
Egg yolks, cooking in microwave, 14
Enchiladas
Stacked Enchiladas, 58
English-Muffin Bread, 241
Entertaining, 36–51

F

Fat content of food
poultry and, 80–81
timing in microwave and, 8
Fennel
Sole and Fennel with Orzo, 126
Feta Cheese
Feta-Spinach Squares, 50
Greek Vegetable Medley, 226
Fettuccine. See also Pasta
Creamy Herbed Fettuccine, 142–43
Herbed Salmon with Spinach Fettuccine, 132
Fiber, microwave cooking and, 4
Fillets, cooking times, 121

Fish
Bluefish with Green Onions, 115
Cancún Cod with Coriander Rice, 112
Cioppino, 203
cooking methods, 117, 131
cooking times, 121
Coquina-Fish Stew, 204
Fish Steaks with Curried Rice, 129
Fish Stock, 182–83
Haddock and Shrimp Stir-Fry, 113
Halibut with Vegetables, 127
Herbed Salmon with Spinach Fettuccine, 132
Mediterranean Fillets with Shells, 116–17
Moroccan Fish, 122
Savory Fish with Corn on the Cob, 128
Seafood Lasagna, 114–15
Sole and Fennel with Orzo, 126
Sombrero Red Snapper, 124
Stuffed Brook Trout, 118
Stuffed Sole with Parsleyed New Potatoes, 125
Sunshine Fish Fillets with Couscous Pilaf, 123
Swordfish with Tomatoes and Couscous, 130–31
Tilefish Provençale with Spaghetti Squash, 119
Tuna Salad Supreme, 137
Tuna Steaks with Dijon Sauce, 116
Tuna Tabbouleh, 236
Freezing
beans, 153
soups, 195
French toast
French Toast with Fruit Sauce, 26–27
Frittatas
Shrimp Frittata, 125
Western Frittata, 34
Frozen foods, microwaves and, 75
Fruit, 17–18. See also Fruit sauces; specific fruits
in breads and muffins, 238
Curried Mixed Fruit, 232
dried, plumping, 263
Fruit Pancakes, 29
Jeweled Minted Fruit, 259
Mixed Fruit Bars, 263
Newport Fruit Compote, 261
Tapioca Parfaits, 271
Fruit sauces
Blueberry Sauce, 29
French Toast with Fruit Sauce, 26–27

Fruit sauces *(continued)*
Honey-Apple Sauce, 29
Raspberry Sauce, 264
Strawberry-Apple Sauce, 29

G

Garlic
Garlic Eggplant and Peppers, 42–43
Garlic Potato Wedges, 223
Garlic Shrimp with Capellini, 130
Herbed Garlic Bread, 244–45
peeling tips, 229
Gazpacho
Basil Gazpacho with Shrimp, 45
German potato salad
Hot German-Style Potato Salad, 232–33
Ginger
Ginger-Poached Pears, 260–61
Honey-Gingered Shrimp, 40
Gingerbread with Applesauce Topping, 270
Glass cookware, microwave cooking and, 9
Glazes for poultry
Honey-Mustard Glaze, 81
Jelly Glaze, 81
Soy-Honey Glaze, 81
Terikayi Glaze, 81
Grains. *See also specific grains*
Basic Granola, 19
hot cereal, 21
Fruit Pancakes, 29
Mixed-Grain Porridge, 24–25
Nut Pancakes, 29
Pancake Mix, 28
Perfect Pancakes, 29
side dishes, 177
Green beans
cooking instructions, 185
Seafood Salad Supreme, 136–37
Grilling methods, 60

H

Haddock
Coquina-Fish Stew, 204
Haddock and Shrimp Stir-Fry, 113
Seafood Lasagna, 114–15
Halibut
Fish Steaks with Curried Rice, 129
Halibut with Vegetables, 127

Ham
Jambalaya, 133
Health advantages of microwave cooking, 2–5
Herb vinegar, 231
Honey
Honey-Apple Sauce, 29
Honey-Baked Onions, 219
Honey-Gingered Shrimp, 40
Honey-Marinated Chicken with Penne and Vegetables, 94
Honey-Mustard Glaze, 81
Honey-Raisin Tea Scones, 247
Soy-Honey Glaze, 81

J

Jambalaya, 133
Jelly Glaze, 81

K

Keeping foods warm, 9

L

Lamb
Indian Curried Casserole with Pine Nuts, 70
Lamb Curry with Yellow Rice, 68
Lamb Patties in Pita, 69
Shepherd's Pie, 55
Lasagna
Lazy Lasagna, 160
Lean and Light Lasagna, 67
Seafood Lasagna, 114–15
Spinach Lasagna Roll-Ups, 73
Leeks
cooking instructions, 185
Leek and Potato Soup, 193
Vichyssoise, 193
Lemons
Lemon-Broccoli Curry with Cashews, 159
preparation tips, 258
Lentils
Lentil Loaf Surprise, 152
Lentil Soup, 194–95
Quick Lentil Chili, 163
Limes, preparation tips, 258
Linguine. *See also* Pasta
Pasta Primavera, 156
Pleasant Peasant Pasta, 158

Turkey Bolognese Sauce and Linguine, 104
Lobster
cooking methods, 131
Singapore Lobster and Shrimp, 138–39

M

Macaroni. *See also* Pasta
Macaroni and Cheese, 173
Vegetarian Macaroni Casserole, 171
Main dishes, meat, 53–78
Barbecued Ribs, 60–61
Beef Stew, 206
Cabbage Rolls with Poppy-Seed Noodles, 78
Indian Curried Casserole with Pine Nuts, 70
Lamb Curry with Yellow Rice, 68
Lamb Patties in Pita, 69
Lean and Light Lasagna, 67
Lew's Skinny Chili, 71
Light Beef and Mushrooms Stroganoff, 72
Mexican-Style Tacos with Salad Toppings, 57
My Favorite Stuffed Peppers, 64
Oriental Beef, 66
Party Meat Loaf with Parsley Mashed Potatoes, 56
Pork Satay with Yellow Rice and Peanut Sauce, 74–75
Pot Roast with Vegetables, 65
Shepherd's Pie, 55
Spaghetti and Meatballs, 77
Spaghetti Squash with Peppers and Meat Sauce, 76
Spinach Lasagna Roll-Ups, 73
Stacked Enchiladas, 58
Sunday-Best Pork Stir-Fry, 62
Sweet-and-Sour Pork with Vegetables, 63
Tangy Pork Chops with Rosy Tomato Rice, 54
Main dishes, poultry, 79–109
Breaded Chicken Cutlets with Polenta, 88–89
California Avocado Turkey Melt, 105
Chicken with Barley, 93
Chicken Breasts with Herbed Angel Hair Pasta, 87
Chicken 'n' Chili, 95

Chicken Cutlets with Tomato Sauce and Cheese, 89
Chicken and Vegetables with Tarragon, 96
Dijon Chicken with Scallions, 97
Fry-Style Chicken with Potato Dumplings, 92–93
Grilled Turkey Breast with Corn on the Cob, 100
Herb-Stuffed Chicken Breasts with Sweet-and-Sour Sauce, 82
Honey-Marinated Chicken with Penne and Vegetables, 94
Italian-Style Turkey Rigatoni with Mozzarella, 108
Mexican Turkey Scramble, 106
Orange Chicken with Savory Pilaf, 99
Oriental Chicken Salad, 90–91
Raspberry-Glazed Cornish Hens with Pecan Wild Rice, 102
Roast Chicken with Vegetables, 103
Spicy Cashew Chicken, 84–85
Stir-Fried Chicken and Snow Peas, 86
Tortilla Casserole, 89
Turkey Bolognese Sauce and Linguine, 104
Turkey Cutlets with Couscous Ratatouille, 98
Turkey Meat Loaf with Saucy Scallion Noodles, 107
Turkey Picadillo, 104–5
Turkey Tostadas, 109
Wrapped Chicken and Vegetables, 85
Main dishes, seafood, 110–40
Bay Scallops and Peppers, 120–21
Bluefish with Green Onions, 115
Cancún Cod with Coriander Rice, 112
Cioppino, 203
Coquina-Fish Stew, 204
Fish Steaks with Curried Rice, 129
Garlic Shrimp with Capellini, 130
Haddock and Shrimp Stir-Fry, 113
Halibut with Vegetables, 127
Herbed Salmon with Spinach Fettuccine, 132
Mediterranean Fillets with Shells, 116–17
Moroccan Fish, 122
Savory Fish with Corn on the Cob, 128

Scallop Manicotti, 140
Seafood Lasagna, 114–15
Seafood Salad Supreme, 137
Seafood Tostadas, 134
Shrimp Frittata, 125
Singapore Lobster and Shrimp, 138–39
Sole and Fennel with Orzo, 126
Sombrero Red Snapper, 124
Stuffed Brook Trout, 118
Stuffed Sole with Parsleyed New Potatoes, 125
Sunshine Fish Fillets with Couscous Pilaf, 123
Swordfish with Tomatoes and Couscous, 130–31
Tilefish Provençale with Spaghetti Squash, 119
Tuna Salad Supreme, 137
Tuna Steaks with Dijon Sauce, 116
Main dishes, vegetarian, 141–77
Bean Burritos Deluxe, 155
Cheese and Tofu Stuffed Shells, 166
Creamy Herbed Fettuccine, 142–43
Curried Vegetables with Rice, 151
Eggplant Parmigiana, 162
Florentine Crêpes, 167
Garden-Style Burritos, 154
Garden-Style Pita Sandwiches, 154
Herbed Vegetable and Brown Rice Casserole, 164
Indonesian Tofu in Peanut Sauce, 144
Lazy Lasagna, 160
Lemon-Broccoli Curry with Cashews, 159
Lentil Loaf Surprise, 152
Macaroni and Cheese, 173
Middle Eastern Omelet, 157
North African Couscous Pilaf, 176
Pasta Primavera, 156
Pita Pizza, 170–71
Pleasant Peasant Pasta, 158
Quick Lentil Chili, 163
Rarebit Potatoes with Vegetables, 174
Saucy Eggplant Casserole, 148
Spaghetti Squash Riviera, 150
Spinach Pie, 146
Tofu Stir-Fry with Spinach, 172–73
Tofu and Vegetables with Couscous, 145
Tomato Cheese Quiche, 147
Vegetable Pizza, 170

Vegetarian Macaroni Casserole, 171
Zucchini-Cheese Casserole, 148–49
Manhattan Clam Chowder, 200–201
Manicotti
Scallop Manicotti, 140
Maple
Hot Maple-Carob Toddy, 272
Maple-Cinnamon Apple Slices, 258
Maple Oatmeal, 22–23
Meat, 53–78
defrosting in microwave, 14
testing for doneness, 14
Meatballs
Spaghetti and Meatballs, 77
Meat loaf
Party Meat Loaf with Parsley Mashed Potatoes, 56
Turkey Meat Loaf with Saucy Scallion Noodles, 107
Metal containers, microwave cooking and, 11, 12
Microwave cooking. See also Cooking methods; Microwave ovens
advantages of, 1–5
converting recipes for, 3
covering foods, 10–11
how it works, 5–6
Microwave ovens. See also Microwave cooking
cleaning, 15
power settings on, 7–8
safety considerations and, 13
selecting, 6–7
wattage, 7
Millet
Apple-Raisin Millet Cereal, 23
hot cereal, 21
Mixed-Grain Porridge, 24–25
Minestrone, 189
Mozzarella. See also Cheese
Italian-Style Turkey Rigatoni with Mozzarella, 108
Muffins
baking methods, 238
baking times, 249
Blender Oat-Bran Muffins, 253
Blueberry-Cornmeal Muffins, 254
Bran Muffins, 252
Date Muffins, 251
Pumpkin Muffins, 249
Southern Corn Muffins, 247
Mulled Apple Punch, 273
Mulled Cider, 273

Mushrooms
  Light Beef and Mushrooms Stroganoff, 72
  Marrakech Stuffed Mushrooms, 44
  Mushroom Pâté, 47
  Onion-Mushroom Stuffing, 83
  Scalloped Potatoes and Mushrooms, 222
  Turkey-Stuffed Mushroom Caps, 46–47
Mussels, cooking methods, 131

N

Nectarines
  Puffed Nectarine Pancake, 27
Newspapers, microwave cooking and, 13
Noodles. *See also* Pasta
  Cabbage Rolls with Poppy-Seed Noodles, 78
  Turkey Meat Loaf with Saucy Scallion Noodles, 107
Nuts
  Apricot-Pecan Ring, 246
  Date-Nut Bars, 262–63
  Lemon-Broccoli Curry with Cashews, 159
  Nut Pancakes, 29
  Raspberry-Glazed Cornish Hens with Pecan Wild Rice, 102
  Rye, Wheat, and Walnut Bread, 243
  Spicy Cashew Chicken, 84–85
  Walnut Stuffing, 83
  Zucchini-Nut Bread, 240

O

Oat bran
  Blender Oat-Bran Muffins, 253
  Mixed-Grain Porridge, 24–25
Oatmeal
  Maple Oatmeal, 22–23
Oats. *See also* Oatmeal
  Basic Granola, 19
  hot cereal, 21
  Pancake Mix, 28
Odors in oven, 15
Omelets. *See also* Frittatas
  Middle Eastern Omelet, 157
  Vegetable Omelet, 32–33
  Warren Street Cheese Soufflé Omelet, 35
Onions
  French-Style Onion Soup, 190–91
  Honey-Baked Onions, 219

Onion-Mushroom Stuffing, 83
  peeling tips, 229
Oranges
  Orange Chicken with Savory Pilaf, 99
  preparation tips, 258
Orzo
  Sole and Fennel with Orzo, 126

P

Pancake(s), 28–29
  Acorn-Squash Pancakes, 224–25
  Buckwheat Pancakes, 29
  Fruit Pancakes, 29
  Nut Pancakes, 29
  Pancake Mix, 28
  Perfect Pancakes, 29
  Puffed Apricot Pancake, 27
  Puffed Nectarine Pancake, 27
  Puffed Peach Pancake, 27
  toppings
    Blueberry Sauce, 29
    Honey-Apple Sauce, 29
    Strawberry-Apple Sauce, 29
Paper plates, microwave cooking and, 9
Paper towels
  for covering foods, 11
  microwave cooking and, 13
Parchment paper for covering foods, 11
Parmesan cheese. *See also* Cheese
  Cauliflower with Herbed Parmesan Sauce, 218
  Eggplant Parmigiana, 162
  Parmesan Pita Triangles, 43
Parsnips
  Glazed Carrots and Parsnips, 214–15
Party fare, 36–51
Pasta
  Cabbage Rolls with Poppy-Seed Noodles, 78
  Cheese and Tofu Stuffed Shells, 166
  Chicken Breasts with Herbed Angel Hair Pasta, 87
  Creamy Herbed Fettuccine, 142–43
  Garlic Shrimp with Capellini, 130
  Herbed Salmon with Spinach Fettuccine, 132
  Honey-Marinated Chicken with Penne and Vegetables, 94
  Italian-Style Turkey Rigatoni with Mozzarella, 108
  Lazy Lasagna, 160
  Lean and Light Lasagna, 67
  Macaroni and Cheese, 173

Mediterranean Fillets with Shells, 116–17
  Minestrone, 189
  Pasta Primavera, 156
  Pleasant Peasant Pasta, 158
  reheating, 143
  Scallop Manicotti, 140
  Seafood Lasagna, 114–15
  Sole and Fennel with Orzo, 126
  Spaghetti and Meatballs, 77
  Spinach Lasagna Roll-Ups, 73
  Tuna Steaks with Dijon Sauce, 116
  Turkey Bolognese Sauce and Linguine, 104
  Turkey Meat Loaf with Saucy Scallion Noodles, 107
  Vegetarian Macaroni Casserole, 171
Pâtés
  Mushroom Pâté, 47
Peaches
  No-Fuss Peach Crisp, 264
  Puffed Peach Pancake, 27
Peanuts
  Indonesian Tofu in Peanut Sauce, 144
  Pork Satay with Yellow Rice and Peanut Sauce, 74–75
Pearl onions, peeling tips, 229
Pears
  Ginger-Poached Pears, 260–61
  Glazed Sweet Potatoes with Pears, 224
Peas
  cooking instructions, 185
  Herbed Peas, 217
  Stir-Fried Chicken and Snow Peas, 86
Pecans
  Apricot-Pecan Ring, 246
  Raspberry-Glazed Cornish Hens with Pecan Wild Rice, 102
Peppers
  Bay Scallops and Peppers, 120–21
  Garlic Eggplant and Peppers, 42–43
  My Favorite Stuffed Peppers, 64
  Spaghetti Squash with Peppers and Meat Sauce, 76
Pies
  New-Fashioned Apple Pie, 267
  Shepherd's Pie, 55
  So-Quick Blueberry Pie, 267
  Spinach Pie, 146
  Whole Wheat Pie Shell, 266
Pimento
  Pimento-Cheese Spread, 51

Pineapple
  Spicy Pineapple Spears, 260
Pita pockets
  Dilled Pita-Pocket Eggs, 32
  Garden-Style Pita Sandwiches, 154
  Lamb Patties in Pita, 69
  Pita Pizza, 170–71
Pizza
  Pita Pizza, 170–71
  Vegetable Pizza, 170
Placement of food, timing in microwave and, 8
Plastic containers, microwave cooking and, 13
Plastic wrap for covering foods, 11
Polenta
  Breaded Chicken Cutlets with Polenta, 88–89
  Breakfast Polenta, 24
Pork
  Barbecued Ribs, 60–61
  Pork Satay with Yellow Rice and Peanut Sauce, 74–75
  selecting, 53
  Spaghetti and Meatballs, 77
  Sunday-Best Pork Stir-Fry, 62
  Sweet-and-Sour Pork with Vegetables, 63
  Tangy Pork Chops with Rosy Tomato Rice, 54
  testing for doneness, 14
Porridge. See also Cereals
  Mixed-Grain Porridge, 24–25
  Moroccan Pilaf Porridge, 18
  Rice-Pudding Porridge, 21
Potatoes
  Baby Potatoes Stuffed with Herbed Cheese, 49
  Barbecue Potato Wedges, 223
  Cheese Scalloped Potatoes, 222
  Classic Potato Salad, 233
  cooking methods, 14, 221
  Deluxe Potato Wedges, 223
  Easy Potatoes, 220
  Fry-Style Chicken with Potato Dumplings, 92–93
  Garlic Potato Wedges, 223
  Herbed Oven Potatoes, 228
  Herbed Potato Wedges, 223
  Hot German-Style Potato Salad, 232–33
  Leek and Potato Soup, 193
  Party Meat Loaf with Parsley Mashed Potatoes, 56

Rarebit Potatoes with Vegetables, 174
Scalloped Potatoes, 222
Scalloped Potatoes and Mushrooms, 222
Shepherd's Pie, 55
Stuffed Sole with Parsleyed New Potatoes, 125
for thickening soup, 199
Turkey Sausage with Home-Style Potatoes, 30–31
Twice-Baked Stuffed Potatoes, 220–21
Vichyssoise, 193
Pot roast
  Pot Roast with Vegetables, 65
Poultry, 79–109. See also Chicken; Cornish hens; Turkey
  basting, 81
  cooking in microwave, 14, 18
  defrosting in microwave, 14
  glazes for, 81
  standing time and, 9
  stuffings, 83
  testing for doneness, 14
Puddings
  Bread Pudding, 269
  Easy Custard, 262
  Pumpkin Pudding, 269
  Steamed Pudding, 268
  Tapioca Parfaits, 271
  Tapioca Pudding, 271
Pumpkins
  cooking methods, 225
  Pumpkin Muffins, 249
  Pumpkin Pudding, 269
Punch
  Hot Cranberry Punch, 272
  Mulled Apple Punch, 273

Q

Quiche
  Tomato Cheese Quiche, 147
Quinoa
  hot cereal, 21
  Inca Breakfast Bowl, 25
  Raisin Quinoa, 25

R

Raisins
  Apple-Raisin Millet Cereal, 23
  Apple and Raisin Stuffing, 83
  Chunky Raisin Applesauce, 259
  Honey-Raisin Tea Scones, 247

plumping, 263
  Raisin Quinoa, 25
Raspberries
  Raspberry-Glazed Cornish Hens with Pecan Wild Rice, 102
  Raspberry Sauce, 264
Ratatouille, 227
  Turkey Cutlets with Couscous Ratatouille, 98
Recipes, converting for microwave, 3
Red cabbage
  Sweet-and-Sour Red Cabbage, 214
Red snapper
  Sombrero Red Snapper, 124
Reheating foods, 14, 75, 149
  beans, 153
  pasta, 143
  soups, 195
Relish
  Cranberry-Apple Relish, 230
  Curried Mixed Fruit, 232
Rice
  Cancún Cod with Coriander Rice, 112
  Chicken 'n' Chili, 95
  Chicken and Vegetables with Tarragon, 96
  cooking methods, 165
  Curried Vegetables with Rice, 151
  Dijon Chicken with Scallions, 97
  Fish Steaks with Curried Rice, 129
  Herbed Vegetable and Brown Rice Casserole, 164
  Herb-Stuffed Chicken Breasts with Sweet-and-Sour Sauce, 82
  hot cereal, 21
  Indian Curried Casserole with Pine Nuts, 70
  Indonesian Tofu in Peanut Sauce, 144
  Jambalaya, 133
  Lamb Curry with Yellow Rice, 68
  Lemon-Broccoli Curry with Cashews, 159
  Lew's Skinny Chili, 71
  Orange Chicken with Savory Pilaf, 99
  Oriental Beef, 66
  Pork Satay with Yellow Rice and Peanut Sauce, 74–75
  Raspberry-Glazed Cornish Hens with Pecan Wild Rice, 102
  Rice Pilaf, 228–29
  Rice-Pudding Porridge, 21
  risotto, 165

Rice *(continued)*
>Singapore Lobster and Shrimp, 138–39
>Tangy Pork Chops with Rosy Tomato Rice, 54
>for thickening soup, 199
>Tofu Stir-Fry with Spinach, 172–73
>Turkey Picadillo, 104–5

Rigatoni
>Italian-Style Turkey Rigatoni with Mozzarella, 108

Risotto, cooking methods, 165

Roasts
>Pot Roast with Vegetables, 65
>Roast Chicken with Vegetables, 103

Rotation of foods in oven, *salmonella* and, 9

Rye
>Rye, Wheat, and Walnut Bread, 243

S

Safety
>children and microwave use, 12
>eggs cooked in microwave, 33
>microwave cooking and, 13–14
>*salmonella* and, 9, 80

Salads
>Antipasto Salad, 234–35
>Carrot-Cauliflower Salad, 230–31
>Classic Potato Salad, 233
>Curried Shrimp and Vegetable Salad, 137
>Hot German-Style Potato Salad, 232–33
>Oriental Chicken Salad, 90–91
>Seafood Salad Supreme, 136–37
>Shrimp Tabbouleh, 236
>Tabbouleh, 236
>Tabbouleh-Stuffed Tomatoes, 236
>Taco Salad, 235
>Tuna Salad Supreme, 137
>Tuna Tabbouleh, 236

Salmon
>Herbed Salmon with Spinach Fettuccine, 132
>Seafood Lasagna, 114–15

Salmonella
>poultry and, 80
>standing time and, 9

Salsa
>Super Salsa, 59

Sandwiches
>California Avocado Turkey Melt, 105
>Dilled Pita-Pocket Eggs, 32

Garden-Style Pita Sandwiches, 154
>Lamb Patties in Pita, 69

Sauces
>Barbecue Sauce, 61
>Basic Tomato Pasta Sauce, 161
>Blueberry Sauce, 29
>Honey-Apple Sauce, 29
>Raspberry Sauce, 264
>Strawberry-Apple Sauce, 29
>Turkey Bolognese Sauce and Linguine, 104

Sausage
>cooking in microwave, 14
>Sausage Stuffing, 83
>Turkey Sausage with Home-Style Potatoes, 30–31

Scalloped Potatoes, 222
>Scalloped Potatoes and Mushrooms, 222

Scallops
>Bay Scallops and Peppers, 120–21
>cooking methods, 131
>cooking times, 121
>Scallop Coins with Dill Sauce, 40–41
>Scallop Manicotti, 140

Scones
>Honey-Raisin Tea Scones, 247

Seafood, 110–40. *See also* Fish; Shellfish
>Cioppino, 203
>cooking methods, 131
>Coquina-Fish Stew, 204
>diet and, 111
>Seafood Lasagna, 114–15
>Seafood Salad Supreme, 136–37
>Seafood Stock, 183
>Seafood Tostadas, 134
>Singapore Lobster and Shrimp, 138–39

Shape of food, timing in microwave and, 8

Shellfish
>Anne's Super-Bowl Shrimp, 42
>Basil Gazpacho with Shrimp, 45
>Bay Scallops and Peppers, 120–21
>Cioppino, 203
>cooking methods, 131
>Coquina-Fish Stew, 204
>Creamy Clam Chowder, 198–99
>Curried Shrimp and Vegetable Salad, 137
>Garlic Shrimp with Capellini, 130
>Haddock and Shrimp Stir-Fry, 113
>Honey-Gingered Shrimp, 40
>Jambalaya, 133
>Manhattan Clam Chowder, 200–201
>Scallop Manicotti, 140

Seafood Lasagna, 114–15
Seafood Salad Supreme, 136–37
Seafood Stock, 183
Seafood Tostadas, 134
Shrimp Bisque, 207
Shrimp Frittata, 125
Shrimp Tabbouleh, 236
Singapore Lobster and Shrimp, 138–39

Shepherd's Pie, 55

Shrimp
>Anne's Super-Bowl Shrimp, 42
>Basil Gazpacho with Shrimp, 45
>Cioppino, 203
>cooking methods, 131, 139
>cooking times, 121
>Coquina-Fish Stew, 204
>Curried Shrimp and Vegetable Salad, 137
>Garlic Shrimp with Capellini, 130
>Haddock and Shrimp Stir-Fry, 113
>Honey-Gingered Shrimp, 40
>Jambalaya, 133
>Seafood Lasagna, 114–15
>Seafood Salad Supreme, 136–37
>Seafood Stock, 183
>Seafood Tostadas, 134
>Shrimp Bisque, 207
>Shrimp Frittata, 125
>Shrimp Tabbouleh, 236
>Singapore Lobster and Shrimp, 138–39

Side dishes, 177

Size of food, timing in microwave and, 8

Snow peas
>Stir-Fried Chicken and Snow Peas, 86

Sodium, microwave cooking and, 4–5

Sole
>Mediterranean Fillets with Shells, 116–17
>Moroccan Fish, 122
>Sole and Fennel with Orzo, 126
>Stuffed Sole with Parsleyed New Potatoes, 125

Soups, 178–208
>Basil Gazpacho with Shrimp, 45
>Cabbage Soup, 190
>Cheddar Tomato Soup, 188
>Chicken-Barley Soup, 200
>Chicken-Vegetable Soup, 181
>Chili Bean Soup, 186
>cream, 184–85
>Cream of Carrot Soup, 208
>Cream of Cauliflower Soup, 198

Cream of Fresh Vegetable Soup, 184
Cream of Spinach Soup, 202
Creamy Clam Chowder, 198–99
Dutch Split-Pea Soup, 187
French-Style Onion Soup, 190–91
Holiday Sweet-Potato Soup, 196
Leek and Potato Soup, 193
Lentil Soup, 194–95
Manhattan Clam Chowder, 200–201
Minestrone, 189
New-England Acorn-Squash Soup, 197
Pagoda Chicken Soup, 201
Quick Curried Tomato Soup, 194
reheating, 195
Shrimp Bisque, 207
Simple Tomato Soup, 188
Snappy Corn Soup, 191
thickeners for, 199
Vegetable and Ground Beef Soup, 205
Vichyssoise, 193
Winter-Squash Soup, 192
Soy-Honey Glaze, 81
Spaghetti. See also Pasta
Spaghetti and Meatballs, 77
Spaghetti squash
Spaghetti Squash with Peppers and Meat Sauce, 76
Spaghetti Squash Riviera, 150
Tilefish Provençale with Spaghetti Squash, 119
Spinach
Cream of Spinach Soup, 202
Feta-Spinach Squares, 50
Florentine Crêpes, 167
Mexican Turkey Scramble, 106
Party Meat Loaf with Parsley Mashed Potatoes, 56
Sombrero Red Snapper, 124
Spinach Lasagna Roll-Ups, 73
Spinach Pie, 146
Tofu Stir-Fry with Spinach, 172–73
washing tip, 50
Split peas
Dutch Split-Pea Soup, 187
Spreads. See also Dips
Chive Yogurt Cheese, 51
Eggplant Caviar, 38–39
Herbed Yogurt Cheese, 51
Minted Yogurt Cheese, 51
Mushroom Pâté, 47
Pimento-Cheese Spread, 51
Yogurt-cheese spreads, 51
Squash. See Summer squash; Winter squash; specific types of squash

Stacked Enchiladas, 58
Standing time, 8–9
Steamed Pudding, 268
Stews, 178–208
Beef Stew, 206
Cioppino, 203
Coquina-Fish Stew, 204
Stir-frying in microwave, 53
Haddock and Shrimp Stir-Fry, 113
Stir-Fried Chicken and Snow Peas, 86
Sunday-Best Pork Stir-Fry, 62
Tofu Stir-Fry with Spinach, 172–73
Stock
Beef Stock, 182
Chicken Stock, 180
cooking methods, 179
Fish Stock, 182–83
Seafood Stock, 183
Straw baskets, microwave cooking and, 10
Strawberries
Strawberry-Apple Sauce, 29
Strawberry-Banana Bread, 244
Stuffed baby vegetables, 39
Stuffing for poultry, 83
Apple and Raisin Stuffing, 83
Basic Poultry Stuffing, 83
Onion-Mushroom Stuffing, 83
Sausage Stuffing, 83
Walnut Stuffing, 83
Sugar content of food, timing in microwave and, 8
Summer squash. See also Zucchini
Summer-Squash Casserole, 216
Sweet-and-sour dishes
Herb-Stuffed Chicken Breasts with Sweet-and-Sour Sauce, 82
Sweet-and-Sour Pork with Vegetables, 63
Sweet-and-Sour Red Cabbage, 214
Sweet potatoes
cooking methods, 14
Glazed Sweet Potatoes with Pears, 224
Holiday Sweet-Potato Soup, 196
Swordfish
Swordfish with Tomatoes and Couscous, 130–31

T
Tabbouleh, 236
Shrimp Tabbouleh, 236
Tabbouleh-Stuffed Tomatoes, 236
Tuna Tabbouleh, 236

Tacos
Mexican-Style Tacos with Salad Toppings, 57
Taco Dip, 48
Taco Salad, 235
Tapioca
Tapioca Parfaits, 271
Tapioca Pudding, 271
Temperature of foods, 9
timing in microwave and, 8
Temperature probes, 149
Terikayi Glaze, 81
Thawing in microwave, 14
breads, 249
crêpes, 167
meat, 14
poultry, 14
Tilefish
Tilefish Provençale with Spaghetti Squash, 119
Timing
factors affecting, 8
standing time and, 8–9
Toddy
Hot Maple-Carob Toddy, 272
Tofu
Cheese and Tofu Stuffed Shells, 166
Indonesian Tofu in Peanut Sauce, 144
Tofu Stir-Fry with Spinach, 172–73
Tofu and Vegetables with Couscous, 145
Tomatoes
Basic Tomato Pasta Sauce, 161
Basil Gazpacho with Shrimp, 45
Cheddar Tomato Soup, 188
Chicken Breasts with Herbed Angel Hair Pasta, 87
Chicken 'n' Chili, 95
Chicken Cutlets with Tomato Sauce and Cheese, 89
Cioppino, 203
cooking methods, 14
Eggplant Parmigiana, 162
Lazy Lasagna, 160
Lean and Light Lasagna, 67
Minestrone, 189
Pleasant Peasant Pasta, 158
Quick Curried Tomato Soup, 194
Ratatouille, 227
Saucy Eggplant Casserole, 148
Seafood Lasagna, 114–15
Simple Tomato Soup, 188
Spinach Lasagna Roll-Ups, 73
Super Salsa, 59
Swordfish with Tomatoes and Couscous, 130–31

Tomatoes (continued)
Tabbouleh-Stuffed Tomatoes, 236
Tangy Pork Chops with Rosy Tomato
Rice, 54
Tomato Cheese Quiche, 147
Turkey Cutlets with Couscous
Ratatouille, 98
Turkey Meat Loaf with Saucy Scal-
lion Noodles, 107
Vegetarian Macaroni Casserole, 171
Toppings
Blueberry Sauce, 29
Chunky Raisin Applesauce, 259
Honey-Apple Sauce, 29
Strawberry-Apple Sauce, 29
Tortillas
Bean Burritos Deluxe, 155
Garden-Style Burritos, 154
Low-Fat Tortilla Chips, 41
Stacked Enchiladas, 58
Tijuana Tortillas, 175
Tortilla Casserole, 89
Tostadas
Seafood Tostadas, 134
Turkey Tostadas, 109
Trout
Stuffed Brook Trout, 118
Tuna
Tuna Salad Supreme, 137
Tuna Steaks with Dijon Sauce, 116
Tuna Tabbouleh, 236
Turkey
California Avocado Turkey Melt,
105
Grilled Turkey Breast with Corn on
the Cob, 100
ground, 18
Italian-Style Turkey Rigatoni with
Mozzarella, 108
Mexican Turkey Scramble, 106
Taco Dip, 48
Turkey Bolognese Sauce and Linguine,
104
Turkey Cutlets with Couscous
Ratatouille, 98
Turkey Meat Loaf with Saucy Scal-
lion Noodles, 107
Turkey Picadillo, 104–5
Turkey Sausage with Home-Style
Potatoes, 30–31

Turkey-Stuffed Mushroom Caps,
46–47
Turkey Tostadas, 109

V

Vegetables, 209–36. See also specific
vegetables
Antipasto Salad, 234–35
Basil Gazpacho with Shrimp, 45
Chicken-Vegetable Soup, 181
Chicken and Vegetables with
Tarragon, 96
cooking methods, 210
Cream of Fresh Vegetable Soup, 184
for cream soup, 184–85
Curried Shrimp and Vegetable Salad,
137
Curried Vegetables with Rice, 151
frozen, 217
Garden-Style Burritos, 154
Garden-Style Pita Sandwiches, 154
Greek Vegetable Medley, 226
Halibut with Vegetables, 127
Herbed Vegetable and Brown Rice
Casserole, 164
Honey-Marinated Chicken with
Penne and Vegetables, 94
Pasta Primavera, 156
Pot Roast with Vegetables, 65
Rarebit Potatoes with Vegetables,
174
Ratatouille, 227
Rice Pilaf, 228–29
Roast Chicken with Vegetables, 103
Sweet-and-Sour Pork with Vegetables,
63
for thickening soup, 199
Tofu and Vegetables with Couscous,
145
Vegetable and Ground Beef Soup,
205
Vegetable Omelet, 32–33
Vegetable Pizza, 170
Wrapped Chicken and Vegetables,
85
Vegetarian dishes. See Main dishes,
vegetarian
Vichyssoise, 193
Vinegar, herb, 231

W

Waffles, 28–29
Walnuts
Date-Nut Bars, 262–63
Mixed Fruit Bars, 263
Rye, Wheat, and Walnut Bread, 243
Walnut Stuffing, 83
Zucchini-Nut Bread, 240
Wattage
testing for, 7
timing in microwave and, 8
Wax paper for covering foods, 11
Weight control, microwave cooking and, 5
Wheat, cracked. See also Bulgur
hot cereal, 21
Whole wheat
Whole Wheat Bread, 242–43
Whole Wheat Crêpes, 169
Whole Wheat Pie Shell, 266
Wild rice
Raspberry-Glazed Cornish Hens with
Pecan Wild Rice, 102
Winter squash
Acorn-Squash Pancakes, 224–25
cooking methods, 210, 225
New England Acorn-Squash Soup,
197
Winter-Squash Soup, 192
Wooden ware, microwave cooking and, 10

Y

Yeasted breads
Whole Wheat Bread, 242–43
Yogurt
Chive Yogurt Cheese, 51
Herbed Yogurt Cheese, 51
Minted Yogurt Cheese, 51
Pimento-Cheese Spread, 51

Z

Zucchini
cooking instructions, 185
Ratatouille, 227
Tijuana Tortillas, 175
Turkey Cutlets with Couscous
Ratatouille, 98
Zucchini-Cheese Casserole, 148–49
Zucchini-Nut Bread, 240